Heidegger and the Greeks

EDITED BY

DREW A. HYLAND

AND

JOHN PANTELEIMON MANOUSSAKIS

Heidegger and the Greeks

Interpretive Essays

INDIANA UNIVERSITY PRESS

Bloomington and Indianapolis

This book is a publication of

Indiana University Press
601 North Morton Street
Bloomington, IN 47404-3797 USA

http://iupress.indiana.edu

Telephone orders 800-842-6796
Fax orders 812-855-7931
Orders by e-mail iuporder@indiana.edu

© 2006 by Indiana University Press

The paper used in this publication meets the minimum requirements of American National Standard for Information Sciences—Permanence of Paper for Printed Library Materials, ANSI Z39.48-1984.

Manufactured in the United States of America

Library of Congress Cataloging-in-Publication Data

Heidegger and the Greeks : interpretive essays / edited by Drew A. Hyland and John Panteleimon Manoussakis.
    p. cm. — (Studies in Continental thought)
  Includes index.
  ISBN 0-253-34802-1 (cloth : alk. paper) — ISBN 0-253-21869-1 (pbk. : alk. paper)
  1. Heidegger, Martin, 1889–1976. 2. Plato. 3. Aristotle. 4. Philosophy, Ancient. I. Hyland, Drew A. II. Manoussakis, John Panteleimon. III. Series.
  B3279.H49H3422 2006
  193—dc22
                                            2006005555

1 2 3 4 5 11 10 09 08 07 06

For John S. Bailey, in gratitude

Contents

Preface

For some time now, Martin Heidegger's sustained reflections on Greek philosophical thought have been increasingly recognized as a decisive feature of his own philosophical development, and at the same time, have been the source of lively philosophical controversy, generating considerable disagreement concerning both their radical originality as interpretations of the Greeks and their place in his own development. It is especially appropriate and timely, therefore, that some of the major contributors to these controversies be brought together in a volume that, we hope, will at once shed light on the issues raised and at the same time stimulate further work in what is certain to be a continuing source of philosophical interest and controversy.

The idea for this volume arose originally out of a conference on the topic "Heidegger and the Greeks," held at the American College of Greece in Athens in the summer of 2003. Some, but not all, of the essays in the present volume were presented in earlier versions at that conference. We wish to thank our hosts at that conference, President John S. Bailey and Provost Theodore Lyras, for their gracious hospitality, and also for their support, in a fruitful conference that in part gave rise to this volume.

Martin Heidegger's writings on the Greeks have done much to stimulate new, original research, new ways of thinking about the Greeks. The contributors to this volume, even those who take a critical stance toward Heidegger's interpretation, have clearly learned much from him and are indebted to his groundbreaking thinking. We hope that together, the essays in this volume will continue the important new dialogue with Greek thinking begun and stimulated by Heidegger.

Drew A. Hyland

Acknowledgments

We would like to thank the Museum of Fine Arts, Boston, for allowing us to reproduce on the cover of this book one of the sketches that John Singer Sargent created as he was working on the murals that adorn the MFA's rotunda. The title of that work is "The Unveiling of Truth," and it can be seen, in its completed execution, above the entrance to the Museum's Library, flanked by the figures of Philosophy and Science. John Singer Sargent breaks new ground by deciding to represent "Truth" not as a static figure (a half-naked woman, for example), as was the artistic tradition of the past, but rather as a process ("the unveiling"). By capturing Truth in or as her unveiling—this, after all, is neither the unveiled Truth nor the Truth to be unveiled, but the precise moment of unveiling—Sargent leaves his work suspended, as it were, in undecidability. For, as we look in his sketch, we do not quite know whether the kneeling youth unveils the mysterious figure in the background (and thus the work confirms its title) or his actions have the opposite effect: that of veiling and covering. It is this ambiguity that resonates so deeply with what Heidegger found decisive in the Greek understanding of truth as *aletheia*.

We would also like to thank John Sallis, the general editor of this series, as well as Dee Mortensen, our sponsoring editor, for their unfailing support throughout the production of this volume.

Heidegger and the Greeks

Introduction: The Sojourn in the Light

John Panteleimon Manoussakis

[T]he more I find my way in my own work, the more certainly I am returned to the grand beginning which is to be found in the Greeks.

M. Heidegger, "Letter to Blochmann" (December 19, 1932)

"Heidegger *and* the Greeks": how is it that this joining "and" in the title
of this volume can bring together the German thinker, on the one hand,
and "the Greeks,"[1] on the other? How is this simple "and" to traverse a
span of two millennia and to stretch over—incompatible it would seem—
differences in geography, culture, and even philosophy? What does allow
this "and" between two so disparate contexts of thought to take place?
These questions are legitimate if we understand "and" as expressing merely
an element of addition or alongside-ness. However, far from simply joining two terms, the "and" in "Heidegger and the Greeks" wants to indicate all the ambiguity of a complex relation (of what Heidegger himself
calls *Auseinandersetzung*)[2] that has multiple layers and levels of reading:
"Heidegger *with* the Greeks"; "Heidegger *through* the Greeks" and "the
Greeks *through* Heidegger"; but also "Heidegger *against* the Greeks" and
even "the Greeks *against* Heidegger." All these possible variations are en-
tertained by the essays collected in the present volume.

There are, of course, more reasons that substantiate a collection that
exclusively discusses Heidegger's relation to Greek philosophy. For one
thing, Heidegger's own long-lasting engagement with "the Greeks"—an
engagement that dates back to Heidegger's first encounter with Bretano's
thesis "On the Manifold Sense of Being in Aristotle" and continues through
a number of Protean transformations in the subsequent years (the early
seminars on Aristotle, the *Destruktion* of Greek ontology heralded by *Being and Time,* finally a series of seminars and publications on Plato, Aris-

totle, and the Presocratics). Apart from this evident preoccupation with Greek philosophy, one could say that Heidegger, during all the years of his intellectual production, thought of nothing else but the Greeks (even when he read Nietzsche and Hölderlin, the most "Greek" of his compatriots). Heidegger, after all, was one of that rare breed of philosophical Cyclopes—all his life he had one single thought, Being, as it first appeared in the Greek beginning of philosophy.

Light—like thinking—is most difficult to be thought. And yet, it is the light that prevails as the distinctive quality of Greek landscape, but also of Greek thought. The bearing of light on thought—Giorgos Sepheris, the Nobel laureate poet, in his perplexity about the distinctiveness of Greek thinking, was bold enough to attribute to the light that which one perceives as essentially Greek.[3] Heidegger, in his own way, does the same. But the light for Heidegger is not the luminous splendor of visibility, intelligibility, and the ideas.[4] Light is not to be thought as a static quality. For Heidegger, light is light-*ing*, coming to light and withdrawing from it, in one word: *aletheia*. That is "the proper word of the Greek Dasein" (*das eigentliche Wort des griechischen Daseins*).[5] The Greek beginning (in relation to which Heidegger struggles to think the "other beginning" of thinking) is a beginning that his work has retrieved for us (one could say "rescued") out of centuries of canonical readings, and that he has brought in the light of *aletheia*. Thought as light. A metaphysics of light then? No. Rather, the (forgotten) light of metaphysics.

> Metaphysics thinks beings as beings. Wherever the question is asked what beings are, beings as such are in sight. Metaphysical representation owes this sight to the light of Being. The light itself, i.e., that which such thinking experiences as light, no longer comes within the range of metaphysical thinking; for metaphysics always represents beings only as beings. Within this perspective, metaphysical thinking does, of course, inquire about the being that is the source and originator of this light. But the light itself is considered sufficiently illuminated through its granting the transparency for every perspective upon beings.[6]

Metaphysics is blind to this light that is Being—metaphysics remains unable to think it as such. Heidegger's contribution, then, comes down to this single thought: light (read Being) as *aletheuein*, as emerging from darkness, a darkness that it presupposes and, in its emergence, it hides as its utmost secret: *mais render la lumière, suppose d'ombre une morne moitié.*[7]

* * *

As more and more of Martin Heidegger's work become available, and especially as it becomes translated into English, it is increasingly evident how important to his thinking was Heidegger's encounter with the Greeks—with the Presocratics, with Plato, with Aristotle. We have come to see that these encounters were not just occasional excursions into Greek Philosophy on Heidegger's part, but seminal moments in the development of his *Denkweg.*

We own it to Heidegger that the classic texts of the Greek masters have experienced a sort of a renaissance in contemporary continental philosophy, as they are read and re-read since Heidegger and, admittedly or not, through Heidegger's lenses by figures like Gadamer, Derrida, and Irigaray. The student of philosophy, therefore, as well as the informed classicist will discover in this volume a great deal of knowledge as to how this paradigm shift in reading classical philosophy was occasioned and how it has changed our reception of the Greeks.

It is high time, therefore, that some of the important interpretive work of scholars who have addressed this encounter in depth be brought together in a single volume that would enable readers to engage the fruits of their studies in a sustained way. The present volume attempts to do just that.

* * *

We begin at the beginning: that is with a reading of the opening lines of Hesiod's *Theogony* concerning the beginning of times. Drew Hyland offers a close textual but also philosophically innovative reading of Hesiod, challenging the traditional interpretation of the poem that see in it another yet mythological account of cosmic coning-to-be. Through such an examination, Hyland takes us to Plato and his famous triad of the *chora,* eros, and the Good—in some way, the successors of Hesiod's chaos. Hyland's thesis is that for the Presocratics, as well as for Plato, the between was never forgotten for the sake of beings, the becoming that first came-to-be was never abandoned altogether for a more metaphysical speculation of *ousia*. Difference, indeed ontological difference, was held in the foreground of Greek thought.

Claudia Baracchi offers a reflection on the inceptual thinking as this is thought in Heidegger's *Contributions,* namely, as the yet un-thought intertwining of the first beginning (with the Greeks) and the other beginning—still to come. Baracchi moves then on to identifying in the Greek beginning of thinking with Plato and Aristotle certain traits that would retrieve it from its canonization by the philosophical tradition and reveal it as intimately linked with what Heidegger attempts to think under the rubric of "other beginning." This is a task for thinking today, as it is through similar retrievals of the first beginning that the "other beginning" would realize itself as precisely the first beginning becoming conscious of itself and of its own history.

Things by nature can let themselves appear not as themselves—for Walter Brogan, it is this characteristic and not the opposing of *physis* to *techne* that exposes their complicity. Beings by *techne* "are," in some way, beings by *physis* that appear differently, that is, they relate to being otherwise than beings by *physis*. This difference, however, does not constitute two different kinds of being. Affectivity, *pathein*, the way that the *techne* beings come to be (by allowing themselves to be affected by the creative act of the technician) is a characteristic of *physis*. *Physis*, therefore, is always present in *techne*. This insight leads Brogan to an examination of the *physis/techne* relationship from the other side, that is from the point of *techne*. In order for the *poiein* of *techne* to take its effect, it needs the corresponding *pathein* of *physis*. *Pathos* (*erleiden*) is not necessarily passive—for its passivity is a *dynamis*.

The interrelation of the proper with the strange is what concerns Peter Warnek in his contribution on Heidegger's *Innigkeit*. Beginning with an exploration into the many paradoxes of translation, Warnek shows how one needs to acknowledge as strange what is one's own proper idiom in order to appropriate it as one's own. *Innigkeit*: "the belonging together of the strange" allows the strange—as beyond that which does not belong, the non-proper—to belong as strange, in strangeness. Heraclitus' "all one"—the unifying harmony of the polemical conflict—becomes a central insight for an interpretation of friendship in Greek philosophy.

How much indebted is Heidegger's hermeneutics of facticity to Aristotle's *logos apophantikos*? For Günter Figal, Heidegger remains an Aristotelian criticizing Aristotle. The *apophanesthai* (i.e., the assertive character of *logos*, to say something about something as something) is made possible, for Heidegger, thanks to a pre-given worldly (factical) relationship. That context or background of everydayness implied in the *apophansis* of *logos apophantikos* is revelatory of the Dasein. The multiplicity of life is brought in unity by the Dasein. The simple and the manifold of language do not contradict each other, but rather they stand in a complementary relationship. Out of such an examination a new understanding of *logos* emerges: "*dynamis meta logou*," language as the locus that possibilizes the different and the opposite. This new understanding of language, in turn, is largely indebted to the Aristotelian model of production (*episteme poetike*).

In a highly personal and testimonial account of his first visit to Greece, William Richardson connects the Marathon monument and the Vietnam War Memorial, by showing how both can serve as visual, concrete examples of the Lacanian knot of the symbolic, imaginary and real. Richardson's concern, however, is not solely Lacan, but how Lacan could relate to Heidegger and Heidegger to Lacan. Such a connection, Richardson suggests, would be found in the correlation of *aletheia*'s *lethe* with Lacan's real. In a section entitled "World as Revelation," Richardson tackles the *aletheia* from the alpha-privative perspective, that is, *a-letheia* not only in its literary sense of "unconcealment" but also as "revealment" of the world. The alpha-privative of *aletheia* would, thus, function as the equivalent of the symbolic and the imaginary in psychoanalytic discourse. Lacan's and Heidegger's projects are ultimately quite different: the first is an ontic endeavor, the second an ontological one. However, Richardson argues, the one stands in need of the other: Lacan's system would have been served by a concept of truth as *aletheia*, while Heidegger's ontological thinking could use the reminder (accentuate in Lacan's concept of the *parlêtre*) that all ontology is ultimately rooted in ontic experience.

How do dead bodies play such an important role in ancient Greece and why is it so difficult for us today to understand that significance? Dennis Schmidt's contribution shows how the understanding of what we owe the dead grounds our self-understanding of what it means to live with the living. How are the living best able to bear witness to the dead? Such is the guiding question that leads Schmidt's essay. His conclusions might come as a surprise to many a reader: for Schmidt, art is better equipped to deal with death than philosophy. This insight ultimately leads Schmidt to a second, even more shocking conclusion: philosophy is poorly equipped to take up the ethical life as its topic. En route of this discussion, Schmidt takes us through two distinct responses to death: mourning (Freud) and anxiety (Heidegger). A re-reading of seminal literary texts that address the topic of death and the dead body (the *Iliad, Antigone, Oedipus at Colonus*) is concluded with a treatment of those passages that discuss similar topics in Plato's corpus, namely, the *Republic* and the *Laws*. Once again, the literary is juxtaposed to (read "confronts") the philosophical. In the end, it is the body that emerges as the irreducible idiom of my identity. In death, after all, it is the body that is lost and it is this losing that feeds ethical consciousness.

Both Francisco Gonzalez's and Gregory Fried's essays offer a sound criticism of Heidegger. And both essays, in doing so, return to the Greek past (Gonzalez to Aristotle, Fried to Plato) in order to read the Greek masters as Heidegger taught us to read, turning, so to speak, Heidegger's weapons against himself. Gonzalez's contribution begins by assessing the implications of Heidegger's translation of the opening line of *Nichomachean Ethics*. Already at this point, it becomes evident, according to Gonzalez, that Heidegger—forcefully?—subordinates the *agathon* to *techne*. What might be the implications of such interpretive gesture? For Gonzalez, it signals the priority (and sovereignty) of existence over action, choice, and desire; the collapse of any distinction between ethics and ontology. The collapse of ethics into ontology is further indicated by Heidegger's moving from Aristotle's *Ethics* to *Metaphysics*—for ultimately, it is the latter that provides the hermeneutical key for the reading of the former. Virtue (*arete*) is rendered obsolete in Heidegger's account. The *telos* of human life is not a virtuous life (a life lived virtuously, that is, well) but rather life itself. Human existence (Dasein) is rendered autonomous and absolute. For Gonzalez, the violence that Heidegger's reading exercises on Aristotelian ethics results in "an ethics so distorted as to become the absolute negation of itself: an ethics that is an anti-ethics." Gonzalez's essay proceeds to examine a series of key terms of Aristotelian ethics (such as *hexis, hedone,* and *proairesis*) showing how Heidegger keeps the language (that is, the rhetoric) of ethics, emptying it, at the same time, of any determined content that would allow us to draw the distinction between virtue and vice. When it comes to ethics, Heidegger's language (truthfulness, courage, resoluteness, authenticity) remains little more than a series of formal indications.

Gregory Fried tries to show that there are two different "traditions" in the beginnings of Greek philosophy and subsequently two different readings of it: the *zetetic* (that seeks and questions knowledge) and the *echonic* (that has and holds it). The modern and postmodern criticisms of the Greeks, especially Plato—Heidegger's criticism included—emphasize too much the *echonic* reading and overlook the *zetetic*. Fried demonstrates how these two different understandings of Greek philosophy can approach anew such classical loci of Plato's work as the allegory of the cave. In the three major movements of the cave story (the breaking of the bonds, the ascent upward, and the return to the cave) Fried recognizes the equivalents of three hermeneutical attitudes toward the Platonic text (deconstruction, preconstruction, and finally reconstruction). For Fried all three movements are essential for the "full expression of human freedom." Plato's double discourse of *logos* and *mythos* is aligned with the *echonic* and *zetetic* readings respectively. In the *zetetic* tradition, Fried sees the awareness—painful as it might be sometimes—of our own limitation and the limitations of our thought. As he writes, the human condition is "suspended between finitude and transcendence." The *zetetic* tradition then, like the mythical element in Plato's work, calls always for a hermeneutics, and hermeneutics is, as Ricoeur has shown, an endless endeavor.

In ending, we return to the beginning. The beginning of Western tradition with the Greeks and one Greek in particular: Plato. Is the beginning of philosophy or metaphysics with Plato just *one* beginning? Or in that beginning something different also begins? John Sallis' essay begins with beginnings, in the arts as well as in philosophy. But most importantly, it begins with that beginning which Heidegger called "the first": the beginning of metaphysics with Plato. Then Sallis moves on to examine how that first beginning relates to what the *Contributions to Philosophy* envisions as "the other beginning." What gave rise to metaphysics in the first beginning was the determination of being as *idea*. For Heidegger, the other beginning can begin only once what is concealed by this determination is made manifest. This, according to Heidegger, can happen only insofar as one has left or overcome metaphysics, that is, only from the point of view of the "other beginning." Sallis' essay wishes to question precisely this assumption. By bringing Heidegger's insistence under question, Sallis argues that one is to find the "other beginning" already in the first, that is, already in Plato. Sallis takes under his hermeneutical scrutiny the same passage that Fried has chosen earlier, namely, the allegory of the cave. A close textual reading reveals that Plato inaugurates two beginnings at once: he provides the foundations for what is to become and be called "metaphysics" (first beginning) *and* he undermines these very foundations on which metaphysics rests (other beginning).

All of the essays presented here share a common trait, namely, the overcoming of those either/ors that the history of philosophy (or at least a certain dominant interpretation of it) has put in place. Such conceptual dichotomies are uniformly arranged into pairs of contraries (being and becoming, *physis* and *techne*, future and past, strange and familiar). Binary oppositions have been "successful," if one judges from their widespread presence in every philosophical discourse, simply because they make things easier. They themselves, after all, are a simple, unambiguous constellation that can cut through any complexities. Contrary to such facilitated thinking, the ten contributions collected in this volume wish to make things "difficult" again. They want to let thinking be confronted (*polemos, Auseinandersetzung*) with the subject matter in its full complexity and intricacy. The gain out of such a confrontation, we deem, cannot but be rewarding.

Notes

Epigraph: M. Heidegger, "Letter to Blochmann" (December 19, 1932), as quoted by Dennis J. Schmidt in *On Germans and Other Greeks: Tragedy and Ethical Life* (Bloomington: Indiana University Press, 2001), 231.

1. The singularity of "the Greeks" (who are the thinkers meant by this expression? what allows us to take them all together as a homogeneous group? etc.) has been questioned elsewhere (see D. J. Schmidt, "Heidegger and 'the' Greeks" in *Heidegger toward the Turn,* ed. James Risser [New York: SUNY Press, 1999], 75–91).

2. Heidegger refers to his discussion or confrontation (*Auseinandersetzung*) with ancient thinking in *Sojourns: The Journey to Greece* (SUNY, 2005), 11.

3. Giorgos Sepheris, *Dokimes,* vol. 2 (Athens: Ikaros, 1981), 14.

4. See, for example, Heidegger's comments in *Parmenides,* trans. A. Schuwer and R. Rojcewicz (Bloomington: Indiana University Press, 1992), 144–45.

5. *Sojourns,* 33.

6. Martin Heidegger, "Introduction to 'What Is Metaphysics?'" in *Pathmarks,* trans. Walter Kaufmann (Cambridge: Cambridge University Press, 1998), 277.

7. ". . . but in order to render the light, you need a somber moiety of shade." Paul Valéry, *Le Cimetière Marin,* 41–42.

1 First of All Came Chaos

Drew A. Hyland

Martin Heidegger's work on the Greeks has long been controversial. This very character has led some of us to write with a certain critical orientation toward his interpretations. Such is altogether appropriate in respect to one whose thinking is as groundbreaking as Heidegger's. Above all, however, the work of Martin Heidegger should teach us to think. By way, then, of trying to learn from Heidegger's ways of reading the Greeks:

> Tell me all of this, you Muses who have your homes on Olympus, from the beginning, tell who first of them (the gods) came-to-be.
>
> First of all Chaos came-to-be; but then afterwards Broad-breasted earth, a secure dwelling place forever for all [the immortals who hold the peaks of snowy Olympus], and misty Tartara in the depths under the wide-wayed ground, and Eros who, handsomest among the deathless gods, a looser of limbs, in all the gods and in all human beings overpowers in their breasts their intelligence and careful planning. And from Chaos came-to-be both Erebos and dark night, and from night, in turn, came-to-be both Aither and day, whom she conceived and bore after joining in love with Erebos. But earth first begat, as an equal to herself, starry sky, so that he might cover her on all sides, in order to be a secure dwelling place forever for all the blessed gods, and she begat the tall mountains, pleasing haunts of the goddess-nymphs who make their homes in the forested hills, and also she bore the barren main with its raging swell, the sea, all without any sweet act of love; but then next, having lain with sky, she bore deep-swirling ocean.[1]

An easy, even inviting interpretation of this Hesiodic beginning of all things presents itself if we take Hesiod's "chaos" in the modern English sense of the word. First of all there was an unintelligible, undifferentiated, unarticulable condition, perhaps a prefiguration of the now well-known "primal soup," chaos. Out of that primal mess, ever so gradually, developed the intelligible, identifiable cosmos. "From chaos to cosmos." Hesiodic chaos might then be read as a prefiguration of Anaximander's *to apeiron,* "the indefinite," as the *arche* of all. Or it might be read as akin to any number of accounts of the coming-to-be of things, in any number of cultures sharing this notion of a primordial, unintelligible confusion out of which an ordered cosmos arises. There is no doubt something attractive, perhaps even obvious, about such an account.

But in the case of Hesiod, this account is troubled by a number of considerations. Most of all it is troubled by the fact that Hesiod's Greek *chaos* does not mean the same as its modern English transliteration. Rather, it means something more like "gap," a "yawn," a separation.[2] Moreover, a second trouble, we are not told that the primordial chaos, understood as some sort of unarticulable confusion, *always was,* and out of it, gradually, a cosmos came to be. We are told that first of all *chaos itself* "came-to-be" (*genet'*).

So we must understand Hesiod as teaching that first of all a gap, a separation, came-to-be. This is altogether more puzzling and thought-provoking than the usual reading of a primordial chaos in the modern sense. First of all a gap came to be? One is tempted to ask almost immediately, a gap between what? Does not the very notion of a gap, a separation, require the prior presence, or at very least the co-presence, of the entities *separated* by the gap? Yet Hesiod does not say, "First of all came-to-be Chaos and earth and Tartara and eros . . ." He says, "First of all Chaos came-to-be; *but then, afterwards,* broad-breasted earth [*autar epeita Gai*]."

Nevertheless, almost from the time the original meaning of Hesiod's *chaos* as gap or separation was taken seriously, the question was asked, and answers ventured, as to what the entities were that *were separated* by Chaos. As early as Cornford's 1941 essay "A Ritual Basis for Hesiod's *Theogony,*"[3] what became the orthodox reading was established. Chaos is the gap or separation between earth and sky. Once this interpretation was reaffirmed in Kirk and Raven's *The Presocratic Philosophers: A Critical History with a Selection of Texts,*[4] it became virtually the standard reading. Chaos is the primordial separation between the two most primordial domains to be separated, earth and sky. After that initial separation, the rest of the cosmos can be gradually articulated. What could be more sensible?

But Mitchell Miller has shown definitively that this reading cannot be sustained. In a 1983 article, "The Implicit Logic of Hesiod's Cosmogony: An Examination of *Theogony* 116–133,"[5] and more recently and more fully in the 2001 article, "'First of all': On the Semantics and Ethics of Hesiod's Cosmogony,"[6] Miller has demonstrated the implausibility of the standard reading. I will not here go into the careful details of Miller's argument but only mention briefly the crucial problems with the standard view that Chaos is the gap separating earth and sky. First and perhaps most pointedly, it is only later, *after* Chaos, earth, Tartaros, and eros "come-to-be," that at line 125, Hesiod announces that "earth first begat starry sky." How could Chaos, which "first came-to-be," be the separation of earth and sky if sky only comes to be *after* the following deities: Chaos, earth, Tartaros, eros, Erebos, night, Aither, and day? Surely if Chaos were the separation of earth and sky, sky, along with earth, would have been part of the very first generation of beings that "came-to-be." But those, again, are Chaos, then earth, Tartaros, and eros. Even more, how could earth, *by herself* ("without any sweet act of love")[7] subsequently give birth to sky if Chaos, which again came-to-be first, was *already* the gap between earth and sky?

But if, as Miller demonstrates so conclusively, Chaos is not the gap separating earth and sky, the next plausible question might well seem, then what sort of a gap *is* Chaos if not the gap between earth and sky? Miller takes this question as the natural next issue, and in the rest of his article argues with great plausibility that by far the most likely candidate, indeed the one with overwhelming evidence in its support, is Tartaros. If Chaos is taken to be the gap between two primordial beings, and earth and sky are eliminated, the clear and plausible pair of candidates is earth and Tartaros. Again, Miller's argument for this is detailed and careful, and I will not rehearse those details here. He uses not only the opening cosmogonic passage of the *Theogony* (116–33), but a number of later passages that bear reference to Chaos and Tartaros (e.g., 726–28, 736–38, 693–94, 698–99, and 717–25) in his argument. The plausibility of the earth/Tartaros pairing is manifest if we simply remind ourselves again of the opening lines of the cosmogonic passage, where, after Chaos comes-to-be first, "then afterwards" come earth, Tartaros, and eros. Since eros is not a tangible and therefore local element (but itself, as we will later learn from Plato's *Symposium*, a certain "between" various binaries such as good/evil, beautiful/ugly, knowledge/ignorance, and divine/mortal), and if Chaos is taken to be necessarily the gap *between* two elemental loci, surely the most plausible candidates are these two that come-to-be in the same first generation, earth and Tartaros. As Miller puts it, "[W]e will take Hesiod to be declaring as the 'first of all' to come-into-being the *underworldly* 'gap' between earth and Tartaros," and he continues, "On this reading, the coming-into-being of Chaos is the originative separation of earth and Tartaros, and so their coming-into-being as well" (Miller, 257). And later, "We should therefore understand the coming-into-being of Chaos as the separation of earth not from sky but from Tartaros" (260). Miller works out the very important philosophical consequences of this difference in the balance of his article. Crucial among these consequences is that Tartaros, always described as "misty," or "gloomy," among other epithets, is the relatively (though not absolutely, as Miller is careful to observe) undifferentiated and unintegrated contrast to the differentiated and integrated "whole" of the "above-worldly" cosmos of earth, sky, and their inner articulations (271). The two are necessary and necessarily primordial because each is unintelligible without the other, and the gap between them, the very principle of differentiation, is Chaos.

Throughout my brief account of Miller's critique of the standard reading of Hesiod's cosmogony and his proposed alternative, I have reiterated the quiet assumption that both views share: If Chaos is the "between," the gap, then it must be a gap that separates and articulates a pre-existing field. Thus John Bussanich, writing on the same cosmogonic passage and in part in accord with Miller, says, "Relying on a literal reading of the text and on later conceptions of Chaos, many scholars have identified Chaos with the gap between heaven and earth. But it is unlikely that a gap between two cosmic masses could exist before the masses themselves."[8] Miller himself puts a similar point this way: "A gap can come-into-being only within some pre-existing 'field'; and for a gap to be the 'first of all' to 'come-to-be' implies that this pre-existing field did not itself come-to-be and suggests that before the gap arose within it, it was undifferentiated" (Miller, 260). Again somewhat later, "As we have observed, following Cornford, to interpret cosmogenesis as a process of division or differentiation implies a pre-existing undifferentiated field" (264). That is, both views assume that if Chaos is a gap or "between," it must be a gap in something that *precedes* (or is at least co-primordial with) Chaos, and that "something," Miller suggests, "implies a pre-existing undifferentiated field."

But does Hesiod's opening statement of the cosmogony support this? While I agree with Miller that *if we make the assumption that Chaos must articulate a pre-existing undifferentiated field,* it is much more plausible that Chaos separates and so differentiates earth and Tartaros, and in any case that *once earth and Tartaros come-to-be* it is most plausibly Chaos that separates them, I want to call into question this assumption that Miller shares with Cornford and others regarding the "pre-existing field."

I note first an initial difficulty with this assumption of a "pre-existing, undifferentiated field," before turning to an even more troubling difficulty.

If we assume such a pre-existing undifferentiated field as preceding the coming-to-be of Chaos, then the very modern conception of Chaos that we supposedly have left behind, the notion of some sort of original undifferentiated, unintelligible confusion, surreptitiously returns. On this view, Chaos *in the Greek sense* may have *come-to-be* first, but Chaos *in the modern sense was* first of all. But if this is so, Hesiod's opening account loses something of its stunning originality. It really is yet another account, like those of many other cultures, of a primal chaos in the modern sense.

But I want to ask again, do we need to make this assumption of such a "pre-existing undifferentiated field"? I do not think it is called for by Hesiod's words. The core of my argument focuses on the opening line (116) of Hesiod's cosmogony. Again, "First of all Chaos came-to-be; but then afterwards broad-breasted earth. . . . and Tartara . . . and eros" (*Etoi men protista Xaos genet'; autar epeita Gai eurusternos, . . . Tartara . . . Eros . . .*). Now it was open to Hesiod to say something like "First of all came-to-be Chaos and earth and Tartaros and Eros," or even more explicitly, "First of all Chaos came-to-be with earth and Tartaros and Eros." But he does not. Instead, emphatically, he says, "First of all Chaos came-to-be; *but then afterwards*" earth and Tartara and eros. With the *autar epeita*, Hesiod emphasizes the very separation from the subsequent comings-to-be of earth, Tartaros, and eros. *Autar*, according to Liddell and Scott, means "but, besides, moreover" and is employed "to introduce a contrast."[9] *Epeita*, in turn, means, again quoting Liddell and Scott, "when in strong opposition to the former act or state, with past tenses, 'thereafter, afterwards.'"[10] Since *autar* establishes precisely such a contrast with the preceding, I have altered Miller's translation slightly to try to bring out that contrast; hence my "but then afterwards . . ." rather than Miller's less strong "then next." My point, then, is that not only does Hesiod say "First of all Chaos came-to-be"; with the emphatic *autar epeita* he clearly distinguishes the coming-to-be of Chaos from what *comes afterwards*: earth, Tartaros, eros, and then gradually the rest of the articulated cosmos.

Difficult as it may be to understand, however counter to our intuitions that if Chaos is a gap or separation it must somehow *separate something*, I suggest we should take Hesiod's Greek in the passage under consideration to be indicating this truly remarkable thought: that Chaos, gap, separation, *comes before, is prior to, any pairings that it might subsequently separate. Difference precedes and is the condition for sameness or identity. The "between" somehow precedes the binaries that it distinguishes.* At work in Hesiod's words, I suggest, is a thought that goes deeper than the argument over which are the first two entities that in fact get separated and distinguished by Chaos—earth and sky, or earth and Tartaros. At work, in addition, is the crucial if very difficult ontological principle that *difference somehow precedes sameness or identity*. I am here taking seriously Bussanich's own acknowledgement that "Strictly speaking, mythical time is timeless, but its sequential flow can articulate qualitative relationships and ontological distinctions" (Bussanich, 213). It is, I propose, just the crucial ontological distinction between difference and sameness or identity that is at work in Hesiod's sentence.

To be sure, Mitchell Miller gestures in the direction of this point, though I believe he holds back from its full implications by keeping it tied to the argument about which two entities first get separated. Toward the end of his article, developing what he calls the "semantic conditions" for the order of comings-to-be that Hesiod employs, he says,

> Tartaros is not entitled to the status of the "first." On the contrary, it is at best third. The thought of "the un-differentiated and un-integrated" presupposes the thought of "the differentiated and integrated"; it is only as *not* differentiated and *not* integrated, hence as the contradictory to the differentiated whole of earth and sky and ocean, that Tartara can be brought to mind. Hence earth, in her implicit partnership with sky and ocean, is semantically prior to Tartara. And prior to the earth-centered upper world and Tartara alike, in turn, is the very contrast or difference between them; the pairing in thought of the differentiated whole, on the one hand, and the undifferentiated and unintegrated, on the other, is possible only by virtue of the thought of the difference, as such, between them. Hence Chaos, the "gap" or "yawning space" that, as the differentiation of each from the other, first lets earth and Tartara *be*, precedes them. Seeing this, Hesiod chooses to give Chaos the status of "first" (*protista*, 116), then, even as he pairs them (cf. *T[e]*, 119), to mention earth second and Tartara third. (Miller, 271)

It may indeed be that, as Miller says, "the thought of '*the* un-differentiated and un-integrated' presupposes the thought of '*the* differentiated and integrated.'" But that will be so *only after* there even *is* an identifiable, nameable "differentiated" (earth/sky/ocean) and "undifferentiated" (Tartara), something that we can call "the." But *that very distinction* requires *difference itself*, and that is why Chaos must come first.

Did Hesiod self-consciously intend to indicate this priority of difference to identity? *Could* he have done so at this early stage of mythical thinking?

I suggest that we have no idea and we do not need to know. I am only trying to indicate that such a stunning and fateful thought was *at work* in Hesiod's words. Surely among the things Heidegger has taught us is to listen for what he sometimes calls the *unsaid* in what is said, the unthought in a thinker's thinking. Here I would not even go so far as to claim that this thought is *un*-said in Hesiod. Whether thought by Hesiod or unthought, I suggest, it is *at work* in his work, or perhaps better, in *play* in the play of this thinking. Indeed, coming here in this first decisive cosmogonic sentence, one could hardly even call it marginal.

If so, let us consider further some of its implications. First, consider Chaos as the principle of "difference." "Difference" precedes and is the condition for "identity" or "the same," and thus precedes and is the condition for any "beings." Right from the beginning, it seems, *ontological difference comes first*. At play in Hesiod, that is, is the thought that entities, *any* entities, whether earth, Tartaros, or sky, cannot come-to-be first. *There is something prior to beings. Difference, Chaos, comes-to-be first*.

But second, difference, Chaos first *comes-to-be* (*genet'*). Not one but two "events" "happen" before there are (one might venture, with a gesture to Heidegger, "*Es gibt*") beings. Difference, Chaos, happens, and *coming-to-be* (*genet'*) "happens." Or, the first "happening," the first "coming-to-be," is Chaos, difference. Or yet again, happening, coming-to-be (dare we say "*Ereignis*") *happens first and happens as difference, as Chaos*.

Mitchell Miller insightfully recognizes at least one aspect of the extraordinary character of this first "event" of coming-to-be. It is extraordinary, he acknowledges, because coming-to-be (*genet[o]*) has "the inescapable connotation of birth" (Miller, 271), yet Hesiod does *not* characterize the coming-to-be of Chaos in terms of mythical parentage, but only and simply as "coming-to-be" (*genet'*). Instead, Miller suggests, Hesiod, while remaining confined to mythical/genealogical thinking, here comes up against the limits of that thinking, or as Miller puts it, "But because Hesiod has only genealogy and anthropomorphic narrative to work with, he cannot himself explicitly articulate the distinctions that his vision involves. The best he can do, working from within these modes of discourse, is to think *against* them at crucial moments, selectively defying the expectations they generate" (272). Consequently, "what is remarkable is not that Hesiod says of Chaos that it *genet[o]*, 'came-to-be' or connotatively, 'was born'; he has little choice. Rather, what is remarkable is that, in face of the assumption that what 'comes-to-be' must have a parent, he holds back from naming one and instead declares Chaos to have come-to-be 'first'" (272–73).

But need we impose this judgment on Hesiod's confrontation with the limitations of mythical discourse? Why, then, does Hesiod, after saying that first of all Chaos came-to-be, add that "but then afterwards" not just earth and Tartaros came to be, but also *eros*? Why does eros join with earth and Tartaros in this second generation after Chaos? Does it not suggest Hesiod's recognition that *before there could be anything like genealogical parenting, there must be eros*? That is, does not this subsequent (though still very early) coming-to-be of eros along with earth and Tartaros indicate Hesiod's full recognition that there is a coming-to-be that is non-erotic or perhaps better, pre-erotic, non-genealogical, non-parental, and that this coming-to-be, this sheer happening, is first?

Hesiod, I venture, *says* this; what his word says is that coming-to-be *happens* and *happens first* as difference. The ontological difference, the *difference* between beings and the *coming-to-be* of things is hardly "forgotten" in Hesiod; it is at play in his thinking and at play precisely where Heidegger has taught us it belongs: first of all.

A second striking implication of Hesiod's thought, another provocation, emerges if we think of Chaos in terms of its meaning as "between." Then Hesiod's stunning word might be formulated as "First of all the between came-to-be." This suggests several remarkable points. First, it indicates that already at work in Hesiod is the recognition that in the end there is no such thing as a simple pair of binaries, of the sort that what later came to be called "metaphysics" supposedly espouses again and again. How often have we been told that the pre-Socratics thought in terms of "opposites" (hot-cold, dark-light, up-down, good-evil, etc.), and that this thinking of oppositions determines later metaphysics? Yet what Hesiod seems to tell us is that every apparent pair of opposites is *always already* at least a triad, for every pair of opposites can only *be* opposites in terms of and thanks to the "between" that allows them to be distinguishable. Moreover, second, the "between," this gap, is *heterogeneous* to the binaries, whichever they are. Hot and cold, dark and light, or earth and Tartaros for that matter, are each as a pair homogeneous on a certain intelligible continuum. The between of them is not of the same order. Still further, third and perhaps most strikingly, Hesiod suggests that the between is *prior* to the binaries that it establishes. Once more, *"First of all Chaos came to be."* If the between comes first, prior to any binaries, can Hesiod or his successors be said to become fixated on the binaries, on opposites, on beings (*seiendes*), and to begin the forgetting of the ontological difference?

Do I mention Hesiod's "successors" too quickly and easily? Heidegger himself, particularly in his "earlier" studies of the pre-Socratics, attributes to them, to Anaximander, to Heraclitus, even in a qualified way to Parmenides, what we can call the "non-forgetting" of the question of Being, as opposed to its more abject falling into oblivion with Plato and Aristotle. Michael Nass, in his "Keeping Homer's Word: Heidegger and the Epic of Truth," clarifies this account, as well as the apparent withdrawal from it in Heidegger's later work on the pre-Socratics.[11] Walter Brogan has shown that in Heraclitus, some of the same thinking is at work as I have tried to draw out of Hesiod.[12] For Heraclitus, according to Brogan, change, becoming (recall Hesiod's *protista genet'*) is somehow *prior to* any of the beings that come to be and pass away. As he puts it, "He is the philosopher for whom the all is *metabole*, change, in the sense of exchange and immediate transition, an exchange that is *more primordial* than the polarities that undergo change" (Brogan, 269, my emphasis). Indeed, Brogan *distinguishes* Heraclitus from Hesiod on precisely these grounds. Responding to what he says might be conceived as a certain kinship of Hesiod and Heraclitus, Brogan says, "But then perhaps Heraclitus would respond that we have misunderstood him. *Polemos* is an originary strife, a difference that comes before the splitting apart of things into different beings" (Brogan, 272–73), whereas for Hesiod, "In the genealogy of the gods, Hesiod does not think the difference as original" (Brogan, 273). I want to suggest that in the opening line of his cosmogony Hesiod *does* think the difference as original, that on this point at least Heraclitus and Hesiod are very much akin.

But what about Hesiod's later Greek successors, and in particular, what about Plato? As is well known, in his earlier work Heidegger locates in Plato, and in particular in the famous cave analogy of the *Republic,* the moment when the "forgetting" of being fully begins in the transformation of *aletheia,* truth, from unhiddenness to correctness.[13] Even when, in his later work, he retracts this account of philosophical development, he does so not only by taking back his account of Plato as participating in, if not inaugurating, the "forgetting of Being," but also by rethinking his earlier view that in pre-Socratic thinking *aletheia* meant not correctness of statements but unhiddenness. Thus when he famously says in "The End of Philosophy and the Task of Thinking," "In the scope of this question, we must acknowledge the fact that *aletheia,* unconcealment in the sense of the opening of presence, was originally only experienced as *orthotes,* as the correctness of representations and statements. But then the assertion about the essential transformation of truth, that is, from unconcealment to correctness, is untenable,"[14] it is clear that he is *not* retracting his earlier view that in Plato the forgetting has taken place; it is clearly his earlier view that the pre-Socratics *had* preserved the distinction that is now "untenable."

But again, what about Plato? Is Heidegger right that in Plato, with his affirmation of Ideas, the forgetting of Being, of the ontological difference, reaches a decisive turning point? With excessive brevity, I want to cite just three moments in the thinking of the dialogues that I think point in a very different direction. They point, I want to suggest, to the view that in the dialogues, *as* with Hesiod or Heraclitus, the thinking of difference, the thinking of the between, the thinking beyond beings, is very much at work: those moments are *chora,* Eros, and the Good.

First, the *chora:* here my brevity is warranted because the point has been made with great detail and power by John Sallis.[15] The *chora,* as it is introduced by Timaeus in the dialogue named after him, clearly has an ontological status utterly different from any of the "beings," from any of the physical beings, from soul, even from the Forms. It is spoken of, can be spoken of, only in metaphors: the mother, the nurse, the receptacle, of all becoming. Even our mode of intellectual comprehension of it is unique; it is accessible to us, we are told, only by a certain "bastard reasoning."[16] Perhaps most decisive for the point I am making, the *chora* decisively interrupts, indeed forces a reformulation of, any sort of "dualism" of Forms and their instantiations, that is, of that concentration on beings of one sort or another for which we eventually formulate the word "Platonism." Timaeus, in his first attempted formulation of the structure of the cosmos (to 47e ff.), indeed attempts to save the phenomena by just such a dualistic account in terms of Forms and instantiations. He fails, and must make another beginning, one that undercuts any dualism by the introduction of the *chora,* the *chora* that, as "mother" of all that comes-to-be, must have, however obscurely, a certain priority. The *chora* means, if it means nothing else, that beings, whether intellectual beings called Forms or physical beings, cannot explain themselves and are not "the whole." "Saving" their appearance requires the introduction of an altogether different, of an "other" to beings, an other somehow, however obscurely, decisive *to* the very being of beings.

Second, eros. Has there been in the history of philosophy a more sustained account of the priority and primacy of "the between" than in Plato's account of eros? In the *Symposium,* we are told by Diotima of only some of the many ways in which eros has a peculiar ontological status, that of being *in the middle* (*metaxy*), *between,* any of a number of sets of binaries. Eros is between beauty and ugliness, between good and evil, between knowledge and ignorance, crucially, between the mortal and the divine.

This last interruption of a standard binary enables Diotima to give a descriptive name to eros's status as between: it is *daimonic*. Moreover, its daimonic status means that it has a different *function* from any of the beings, whether mortal or divine. For in a remarkable formulation, Diotima tells us that eros the daimon not only conveys "messages" back and forth and thus is the intermediary between the binaries, but "binds the two together into a whole" (*hoste to pan auto hauto xundedesthai: Symposium*, 202e). *Without the mediating power of eros, its unique status as metaxy, there would be no whole.* Such is Diotima's remarkable teaching. There are various binaries, various oppositions: divine/mortal, good/evil, beautiful/ugly, knowledge/ignorance; and there is the daimonic eros, through which, and only through with, the binaries become an intelligible whole.

The unique ontological status of eros is brought out subtly in another way, by the peculiar mode of knowing by which we might come to "know" of eros. Almost uniquely, two Platonic dialogues are devoted to a meditation on eros, the *Symposium* and *Phaedrus*. Both dialogues make at least significant reference to what comes to be called Platonic Ideas or Forms. Why, then, if according to "Platonism" the way we come to know anything is via an insight, however partial, into its "Idea," why are we never, in any dialogue, introduced to the thought of an "Idea of Eros," through an insight into which, like good "Platonists," we should come to know "Eros itself," the Form Eros? The *Symposium* is perhaps the most dramatic problematic in this regard. For there, the dramatic force of the dialogue clearly builds to Diotima's speech, related by Socrates, as the highest revelation on eros, and Diotima's speech itself gradually builds to its height at the introduction of a divine Idea, through which we understand certain phenomena. Is it the Idea of Eros? No: we are introduced instead, in this great dialogue that truly does shed so much light on eros, not to the Idea of Eros but to "Beauty Itself" (210a ff). Why Beauty Itself, or more pointedly, why *not* Eros Itself? The dialogue itself gives us the answer. The Ideas are "divine"; they have the usual characteristics of the divine in the dialogues: they are changeless, eternal, neither coming to be nor passing away, and so on. *But we were explicitly told that eros is not divine.* Eros, Eros itself, as *between* the mortal and the divine, cannot be divine and cannot therefore be an Idea. We are thus not introduced to an Idea of Eros as the culmination of the *Symposium* or any other dialogue because there is not and cannot be an Idea of Eros. But, and this is decisive, we *do* learn about eros, we do understand something of eros, but not via insight into a Platonic Idea. How can we have knowledge of eros if not in the standard "Platonic" way, via insight into a putative Idea of Eros? Yet another conviction of that metaphysics called Platonism is thereby undercut. There is not *one* mode of knowledge, via insight into a relevant Idea. Knowledge is not homogeneous but heterogeneous. In particular, we know what we know of eros' through an other knowledge than "formal" knowledge. How do we know and what sort of knowledge is it? Altogether appropriately, we are not told, but shown. For it is, to borrow Diotima's remarkable words, "*oude tis logos oude tis episteme,*" "neither some logos, nor some epistemic knowledge" (*Symposium* 211a). Yet another knowledge through a "bastard reasoning."[17]

Finally—and it is indeed final in the dialogues—there is the Idea of the Good, or simply "The Good," as it is more usually called. For our purposes here, we need not ask after the abyssal question of just what the Good means, but only gesture toward the question of the ontological status of the Good. For this only one text is necessary, the famous passage in Book VI of the *Republic,* at 509b–c, where we are told of the Good this: "Therefore say that not only being known is present in the things known[18] as a consequence of the good, but also existence and being [*alla kai to einai te kai ten ousian*] are in them as a result of it, although the good is not being [*ouk ousias ontos tou agathou*] but is still beyond being [*eti epekeina tes ousias*], exceeding it in dignity and power." Here I venture only a cautious remark about this altogether incautious remark of Socrates. If the Ideas (at least, the other Ideas) are being, and the things that are in the light of the Ideas, those that come to be and pass away, are "becoming," what is the being-status of the Good as *not being (ouk ousias) but beyond being*? We need not answer that question here in any further detail than to say, *different.* Perhaps even difference itself, so long as we understand that it is a difference characterized by, heeding Socrates' last quoted word, excessive power (*dynamis*). The very least we can say here is this; there can be no question of finding in this text "Platonism," this time in its classic form as the dualism of being and becoming. There is (*es gibt*) being, there is becoming. And there is the Good, *beyond being,* which indeed and almost literally *gives* both being and becoming. The Good, like *chora,* like eros, undercuts "Platonism" from the beginning.

My reflection on the first line of Hesiod's cosmogony was meant to support the "early" Heidegger's view that in pre-Socratic thinking, there was very much at play a recognition of the ontological difference, that there is not just being and beings, but presencing as well, difference, the between. Not only, my reflections were meant to suggest, was it at play, it was at the forefront of this thinking, in Hesiod's case, first of all. My brief consideration of Plato was meant only to suggest that the central—not marginal—role of *chora,* eros, and the Good, their *said—not unsaid*—significance in the thought of the dialogues, means that in the dialogues too the ontological difference in its own way is very much still at the forefront, not at all "forgotten," not at all marginal, not at all fallen into "oblivion."

But if these concerns are also still at work in Plato, perhaps we should rethink Heidegger's own apparent judgment that his "early" view about the presence of this recognition in the pre-Socratics but not in Plato was "untenable." Perhaps the issue should not be that of the "early" Heidegger's affirmation of the pre-Socratics against the "forgetting of Being" in Plato and Aristotle *versus* the "later" Heidegger's apparent decision that for the pre-Socratics the forgetting of Being was already at work. Perhaps we should think in the opposite direction; that for the pre-Socratics and yes, for Plato as well, the thinking of beings was still and always also a thinking of the between, of difference, of that which is not and cannot be "a being."

If so, what is perhaps called for after Heidegger is an appropriate and appropriating rethinking of Heidegger's own critical reading of Plato. Fortunately, that is already being done. If it is determined, as I have only suggested here, that the ontological difference in its various moments is still at work in the dialogues, then can we give in easily to the temptation to say that the full forgetting of being really begins with Aristotle? Or will we not rather have to rethink Aristotle's work in a more open way? Does not the questioning power of Heidegger's thought, more than his particular assertions, then call us to rethink all of Greek philosophy, openly, ever and again?

Notes

1. Hesiod, *Theogony,* lines 115–33. I use, with slight alterations, the translation of Mitchell Miller in his seminal article, "'First of all': On the Semantics and Ethics of Hesiod's Cosmogony," *Ancient Philosophy* 21 (2001): 251–76, 252. Hereafter "Miller."

2. See Miller, 254, for an excellent discussion of the etymology of this word.

3. It appeared in his *The Unwritten Philosophy and Other Essays* (Cambridge: Cambridge University Press, 1950), and was reformulated in his later *Principium Sapientiae: The Origins of Greek Philosophic Thought* (Gloucester, Mass.: Peter Smith, 1971).

4. G. S. Kirk and J. E. Raven, *The Presocratic Philosophers: A Critical History with a Selection of Texts* (Cambridge: Cambridge University Press, 1957). Restated and reaffirmed in Kirk, Raven, and Schofield, *The Presocratic Philosophers: A Critical History with a Selection of Texts,* 2nd ed. (Cambridge: Cambridge University Press, 1983).

5. Mitchell Miller, "The Implicit Logic of Hesiod's Cosmogony: An Examination of *Theogony* 116–133," *Independent Journal of Philosophy* 4 (1983): 131–42.

6. Mitchell Miller, "'First of all': On the Semantics and Ethics of Hesiod's Cosmogony," *Ancient Philosophy* 21 (2001): 251–76.

7. Hesiod, *Theogony*, 132.

8. John Bussanich, "A Theoretical Interpretation of Hesiod's Chaos," *Classical Philology* 78, no. 3 (July 1983): 212–19, 216. In a footnote, Bussanich notes that "This salient criticism is made by G. Vlastos in his review of Cornford's *Principium Sapientiae* (*Gnomon* 27, 1955; 75)."

9. H. Liddell and R. Scott, *A Greek English Lexicon* (Oxford: Clarendon Press, 1961), 278.

10. Ibid., 615.

11. Michael Nass, "Keeping Homer's Word: Heidegger and the Epic of Truth," in *The Presocratics after Heidegger*, ed. David Jacobs (Albany: SUNY Press, 1999), 73–100. Nass concentrates on Heidegger's reading of Homer to illustrate this transition.

12. Walter Brogan, "Heraclitus, Philosopher of the Sign," in *The Presocratics after Heidegger*, ed. David Jacobs (Albany: SUNY Press, 1999), 263–276.

13. Heidegger, "Plato's Doctrine of Truth, With a Letter on Humanism," in *Pathmarks*, ed. William McNeill (Cambridge: Cambridge University Press, 1998), 155–82. Martin Heidegger, *Platons Lehre von der Wahrheit (mit einem Brief uber den Humanismus)* (Bern: Franke Verlag, 1947). This critical reading of Plato begins with Heidegger's earlier (1924–25) lecture course on the *Sophist*. For my critical evaluation of this reading, see my *Finitude and Transcendence in the Platonic Dialogues* (Albany: SUNY Press, 1995) and *Questioning Platonism: Continental Interpretations of Plato* (Albany: SUNY Press, 2004).

14. Heidegger, "The End of Philosophy and the Task of Thinking," in *On Time and Being*, trans. Joan Stambaugh (New York: Harper and Row, 1972), 70.

15. In John Sallis, *Chorology: On Beginning in Plato's Timaeus* (Bloomington: Indiana University Press, 1999).

16. Plato, *Timaeus*, 52b.

17. This manifestly opens an enormously broad topic. One might mention, as a second decisive example of a non-epistemic, non-formal knowledge in the dialogues, Socrates' own famous self-knowledge as "knowing what I know and what I don't know." Does he have this knowledge by virtue of his insight into the "form" of self-knowledge?

18. It is thought-provoking that the Greek here is *"tois gignoskomenois. . . . to gignoskesthai"* rather than forms of *epistasthai*. This in itself points to a different sense of any "knowledge" we would have of the Good.

2 Contributions to the Coming-to-Be of Greek Beginnings: Heidegger's Inceptive Thinking

Claudia Baracchi

Contributions to the occurring of the past: from the outset, I am speaking of the past. I am not for the moment concerning myself with the appropriateness of this determinate and singular mention of the past, as if it obviously were *the* past and *one*. I am speaking as though the past would require a supplement (contributions, indeed), so that it will have been what it was to be. Note, I am not saying: so that it (the past) may be what it is, for this is never a prerogative or possibility for (the) past as such. Nor am I saying, without qualification: so that it (the past) may have been as it will have been—as though the past, in its determination, were a matter of arbitrary retrospective projections, a future invention.

In order to avoid viewing the past merely as a matter of later constructions, the articulation illuminating the past as coming from the future must be qualified. The past would be dispensed, dictated by the future. Yet, the intimation here is that the past out of the future, the past that will have been, *arrives* or will have arrived as what it was to be, that is, "as itself." This needs to be emphasized because what is at stake is not, or not simply, allowing the proliferation of possible projections of the past according to a multiplicity of manners of retention, interpretation, or reconstruction—re-creations of the past that, in their relative plausibility, would lie alongside one another, as it were. Often the desire to counteract one-sided or totalizing accounts of the past leads to this kind of response. But, precisely in its reactive character, this response is itself one-sided, for it leaves unscrutinized one of its apparent corollaries, namely, that the past might be the mere aftereffect of optional interpretive strategies or, literally, the creation (an optional creation) of historical revision. To the extent that it neglects the investigation of the disquieting problems thereby implied, such a response seems indeed superficial, even irresponsible.

Thus, I am speaking as though the past would require supplementary contributions, so that it will have been what it was to be, so that it will have arrived, reached itself—become itself. Quite decisively, this way of speaking is oriented toward a disclosure of the past in essential terms. And yet, in the same movement, it points beyond essence. For it appeals to essence and, at once, reveals it as a matter of temporal unfolding, as what-it-was-to-be. And not even the teleological structure clearly announced here may give unity to the temporalizing movement of essence and cast essence in terms of unqualified cohesiveness and completion. For the determination of the what-it-was-to-be, that is, the identity of what-it-was-to-be and what-will-have-been, remains a task (*ergon*). (Quite self-consciously, my language evokes Aristotle here.) In this sense, essence bespeaks the unbound, as-yet-undecided openness of the movement of temporality.

These considerations, then, cast light on the past *both* in its necessity *and* in its unexhausted possibility, on the past in its becoming (therefore as yet unfulfilled) necessity. On the one hand, then, the past is exposed as shining through the necessity and necessitating force of those narratives that will have become dominant. On the other hand, and simultaneously, the past is exposed in its no less necessary irreducibility to necessity, in its necessarily overflowing its own necessity (or in its self-overflowing necessity). Thus, the "itself" and "necessity" of the past come to be understood in terms of superabundance, non-self-coincidence, and temporal dispersion. The past is illuminated as that which still remains in play, moving, yet to be decided—to be supplemented, indeed. The essence of the past will not possibly have been collected into one whole, let alone recollected—for it comes out of the future, as the *yet-to-come* (*zukünftig*) or arriving still.

It is in light of these remarks, then, that I am venturing to speak as though the past would rest on a future both possible and necessary—in order not so much to have come to pass at all, but to have come to pass otherwise, irreducibly. As though the past would call out to its heirs and successors—in order not so much to occur, but to be freed from the narrative incrustations of its occurrence and keep occurring, indeed recurring, flowing into itself from the future. In this way, the future may be disclosed as the past to come. The past may reenact itself in a repetition whose prerogative is uniqueness (*Weiterwinken eines Winken*). At stake is glimpsing and, at once, showing and undergoing, at the heart of the Greek beginning, the rift of thinking—letting the rift that thinking is, in its tension and self-differing, keep enacting itself. Repetition would, thus, bespeak enacting the beginning in its rift: enacting thinking, sustaining the effort of its restlessness and intensity.

Hence the call for contributions, for the decisive supplementation. But contributions from whom, whence? Who or what is it that stands exposed to such an assignment?

*   *   *

In the *Beiträge zur Philosophie* Heidegger speaks of a "hidden history" (*verborgene Geschichte*) of which, in the nineteenth century, the figures of Hölderlin, Kierkegaard, and Nietzsche would have been symptomatic. Such a history would by no means be secret in the sense of unknown, yet remains unreleased in its essential implications, latent, as if beneath the threshold of ordinary experience. In the course of such considerations, Heidegger asks: "does this history as the ground of Dasein continue to be inaccessible to us, not because it is past, but because it is still too futural [*zukünftig*] for us?" (143/204).[1] It is in light of this question that a renewed understanding, in fact, experience of "our" history imposes itself in its urgency—a crossing over into that which remains unacknowledged in our dominant discourses "about" ourselves. Indeed, the task of "[t]hinking in the crossing," as Heidegger envisions it, entails bringing "into dialogue [*Zwiesprache*] that which has first been [*das erste Gewesene*] of the being [*Seyns*] of truth and that which is futural in the extreme of the truth of being [*Seyns*]" (*Beitr.* 5/5–6), that is, what was first constructed (secured) out of the experience of being and what remains yet to come in the arriving of being.

Thus, at the heart of the *Beiträge* is the attempt at coming to terms with the "originary positioning [*Setzung*] of the first beginning" (*Beitr.* 119/170), that is, the Greek inception.[2] Out of this positioning an *other* (or, in fact, *the* other)[3] beginning is to "play forth," as the *Zuspiel* of "inceptual thinking" grounded in the yet to come. However asymmetrical and incommensurable, the two modes of inception are indissolubly intertwined. Indeed, for the other beginning to unfold, "a more originary retrieval [*Wiederholung*] of the first beginning" and "the mindfulness [*Besinnung*] of its history" must be pursued (40/57). Such a retrieval, then, at once signals the inception of the other beginning and the restitution of the first beginning to itself. Crucial to this endeavor is cultivating an unprecedented intimacy with the first beginning, such that the first beginning may show itself anew and a deeper insight into it may be seized. For this, a mode of thinking attuned to beginnings and itself incipient is called for. As Heidegger says, "*inceptual* thinking is necessary as an encounter [*Auseinandersetzung*] between the first beginning, first to be won back, and the other beginning to be unfolded" (40/58). In a certain sense, let it be noticed in an anticipatory fashion, "winning back" the first beginning and "unfolding" the other beginning are to be comprehended in their sameness.

Not unlike his analyses in previous works, Heidegger's approach to the Greeks in the *Beiträge* is dynamically twofold. It presents a distinctive oscillation, or tension. On the one hand, it calls for a de-sedimenting reading of the Greek texts, which would show them as irreducible to later systematizations and encounter them more primordially. On the other hand, however, the Greeks, most notably Plato and Aristotle, are decisively inscribed within the comprehensive framework of the "history of being," or of metaphysics; the Greek inception is seen as already entailing an orientation, impressing a direction, prescribing the history of thinking leading to "us"—quite decisively, it is seen as finding its fulfillment in that history.

Thus, the first beginning (*der erste Anfang*) is understood as metaphysics, or Platonism.[4] Concomitantly, Plato is recognized as the threshold, the *locus* in which the question of the truth of being is both raised and deflected, obscured. For here a turning would have taken place from the primordial insight into truth as disclosure to the understanding of truth as correctness already anticipating the doctrine of *adæquatio*.

The first beginning, thus, would have begun with a lapse, or as a lapse—primarily because of the faintness (literally, an *asthenia*) characterizing the way in which the question of being was posed. The question of being (*Seyn*) was formulated in terms of beingness (*ousia, Seiendheit*) and accessed by reference (by turning) to beings. In this perspective being is approached as itself a being. In other words, the question was raised concerning the truth of beings, the being of beings, without, however, broaching the question concerning truth:

> *The first beginning* experiences and posits [*erfährt und setzt*] the *truth of beings*, without questioning toward truth as such, because what is unhidden in it, a being as a being, necessarily overpowers everything and uses up even the nothing, taking it in or annihilating it completely as the "not" and the "against."
>
> *The other beginning* experiences [*erfährt*] the truth of being [*Seyns*]

and questions toward the being [*Seyn*] of *truth* in order first to ground the essencing [*Wesung*] of being [*Seyns*] and to let beings as the true of that originary truth spring forth. (*Beitr.* 125–26/179)

The "leading question" concerning being as *ousia* (the question asking "what is . . . ?") overshadows the "grounding question" of *Seyn*, that is, the question "toward" the being of truth (I maintain the awkward translation above in order to emphasize questioning as a matter of orientation, of aiming). It is the prevalence of the former and the simultaneous occultation of the latter that constitute metaphysics as such. Folded within such a movement is the reduction of privation to denial and negation.

In the first beginning, Heidegger suggests, human Da-sein would undergo and be overwhelmed by beings in their peremptory upsurge. In virtue of this "inceptual experience [*Erfahrung*]" Da-sein would come to understand itself as *animal rationale* (*Beitr.* 126/180). Out of the emergence of beings (of nature) and of the protective self-distancing of Da-sein, there arises Da-sein's self-understanding in terms of *ratio.* The question of the truth of being is as such covered over and, concomitantly, the experience of beings is lost as well, for beings are retained only as conceptually made present, as secured to presence, re-presented, objectified by the "knowing animal." The contraposition subject/object, and hence the priority of the knowing subject, of knowledge as mastery, is already inscribed here. Being becomes a matter of knowing; truth (distanced and mastered in its arising) turns into certainty:

> Why, in the open of *physis*, did *logos* as well as *nous* already have to be named early on as the grounding sites of "being" [*des* "*Seins*"] and why was all knowing arranged accordingly?
>
> . . .
>
> *physis* is so overpowering that *noein* and *logos* are experienced as belonging to it, even belonging to *beings* in their beingness (not yet grasped "generally" in terms of ideas). But as soon as experience, as originary knowing of beings themselves, unfolds *unto* questioning *towards* beings, questioning itself, retreating before [*vor*] beings, grasped as differentiated and in a certain sense independent with respect to beings, as such setting itself *before* [vor *dieses . . . sich stellend*] beings, must set them *forth* [her-*stellen*]. (*Beitr.* 133/190)

The fading of the question of being occurs precisely in thinking being on the basis of beings. But, again, in such thinking the sense of beings is also obscured. In the final analysis, beings will have been apprehended by reference to being as the supreme, most encompassing being (onto-theology).

I should, in passing, underscore Heidegger's sweeping gesture (especially in §§95–114), allowing him to gather into a relatively seamless narrative (the one history of Western metaphysics) the Greek beginning and its developments through medieval scholasticism, modernity, and German idealism, all the way to Nietzsche—as though the translation of *zoon logon echon* into *animal rationale,* of *logos* into *ratio,* were an unproblematic matter; as though the conflation of *logos* and *nous,* and the understanding of both in terms of *ratio* or *intellectus,* were equally obvious; as though the Greeks should essentially be comprehended as proto-Cartesian in their thrust, or even as laying out the task that Hegelian teleology will have accomplished; as though the Greek inception were to be reduced to that which became possible or thinkable in its wake, without considering how it also indeterminately exceeds that which it enabled and made possible. In fact, without considering how the enabling may have been predicated precisely on the forgetfulness, on part of the enabled, of the enabling source as excessive; without considering how the oblivion of excess may precisely have allowed for the arising of the "history of the West" as distinctively forgetful. (Here the challenge would be to think the creativity of oblivion, oblivion as generative force.) In other words, it may be that, far from seamless, continuous, or causally calculable, the "history of metaphysics" developed in a fragmented fashion, through radical discontinuities and fissures of forgetfulness, following unexpected, far-from-rectilinear turns. It may be that the Greek beginning, neither the first nor the last, lies more hidden and inaccessible than ever precisely in its alleged epigones, in the schools bearing the names of its key figures. I signal these issues here as eminently worthy of being examined further.

However, in the tense unfolding of his meditation, Heidegger also highlights the degree to which the other beginning would inceptively occur out of the first and belong in it. In this sense, the *Übergang* (passage, crossing) from the first to the other beginning can be understood as a retaining that overcomes, a destruction that remembers, a freedom that at once recognizes and is owned. "Retaining bespeaks: questioning towards the *being* of *beings.* But the overcoming bespeaks: questioning beforehand towards the *truth* of being [*Seyns*], towards that which in metaphysics *never* became a question and never could" (*Beitr.* 128/182). The overcoming occurs as a sustained engagement with and insight into that which is to be overcome. This, Heidegger points out, was undertaken already in *Sein und Zeit:* "This double character in the crossing, which grasps metaphysics more originarily and thus at the same time overcomes it, is through and through the mark of 'fundamental ontology,' i.e., of *Being and Time*" (ibid.). Indeed, as Heidegger will repeatedly emphasize,

> [m]indfulness of "ontology" is necessary in the crossing to this [other beginning] from that [first beginning], so much so that the thought of "fundamental ontology" must be thought through. For in fundamental ontology the leading question is first grasped, unfolded and made manifest . . . as a question. (*Beitr.* 143/205)

In fundamental ontology the guiding question of Platonism is made to appear, revealed as such. It is grasped as what it is, as itself—grasped, that is, in a manner that is attuned to it, truer to it than even its own self-understanding. Addressing the "remarkably shallow 'critique' of 'ontology'" undertaken, for example, by Jaspers, Heidegger continues:

> A bare rejection of "ontology" without an overcoming of it from its origin accomplishes nothing at all; at most it endangers every will to thinking. . . . Conversely, an overcoming of ontology first requires therefore precisely the unfolding of ontology from its beginning. (ibid.)

Again, this is precisely what was at stake in *Sein und Zeit*. For "the thinking willing . . . in *Being and Time* seeks a way of crossing from the leading question to the grounding question" (ibid.).

Thus, again in the *Beiträge* it is a matter both of destroying the sediment *and* of recollecting the forgotten, bringing it back to life and light, seizing it in the inceptive unfolding of its essence. Destruction and overcoming occur only as radical understanding, as taking up anew, as if for the first time. This is why, among other things, history (*Geschichte*) is not an addendum to an autonomous systematic development, is neither historiography (*Historie*) nor historicism (*Historismus*), but rather constitutes the very possibility of an other inception:

> Playing forth is of historical essence and a first thrusting [*Brücken-schlagen*] of the crossing, a bridge [*Brücke*] that swings out to a shore first to be decided.
>
> But the playing forth of the history of the first inceptual thinking is not a historical [*historische*] addendum to and portending of a "new" "system" but rather is in itself the essential transformation-promoting preparation of the other beginning. Therefore, in a manner more incon-

spicuous and more decisive, we must perhaps direct the historical mind-fulness only toward the thinkers of [belonging in] the history of the first beginning and, through a questioning dialogue with their question-ing posture, suddenly plant a questioning that one day finds itself ex-pressly as rooted in an other beginning. (*Beitr.* 119/169)[5]

In the *"task"* (*Aufgabe*) here outlined it is neither a matter of opposing metaphysics nor of leaving it behind:

> But even for this very reason, thinking in the crossing dare not succumb to the temptation of simply leaving behind [*hinter sich zu lassen*] that which it has grasped as the end and in the end, instead of *accomplishing* [*hinter sich zu* bringen] this end, i.e., apprehending this end now for the first time in its essence and letting this be transformed and played into the truth of being [*Seyns*]. The talk of the end of metaphysics dare not mislead one to the opinion that philosophy is finished with "metaphys-ics." On the contrary: in its essential impossibility metaphysics must now first be played forth into philosophy and philosophy itself must be played over into its other beginning. (*Beitr.* 122/173)

The task entails that we become mindful, aware of what it means to in-herit, that we experience such inheriting as nothing automatically befall-ing those who come afterward. It demands that we *thoughtfully become heirs*, for "[o]ne is never an heir merely by the accident of being *one who comes later* [Späterer]" (*Beitr.* 138/198).[6]

But Heidegger's intimation may be understood in an even more radical fashion, for ultimately adumbrated here is the other beginning as nothing other than the first beginning more primordially understood, taken be-yond its own self-understanding or self-representation. To be sure, the first beginning, while remaining "decisively as *first*," must also be "overcome as beginning" (*Beitr.* 5/6). Indeed, in the thinking that announces the other beginning, "reverence before the first beginning . . . must coincide with the relentlessness of the turn away [*Abkehr*] of an other questioning and saying" (*Beitr.* 5/6). And yet, Heidegger also emphatically recalls that "[t]he style of thoughtful mindfulness in the crossing [from one begin-ning to the other], too, is already determined by this allotment [*Zugewie-senheit*] of the one and the other beginning to each other" (*Beitr.* 4/5). Again, and even more decisively, the beginning as such "reaches ahead and thus otherwise reaches beyond that which is begun through it and deter-mines accordingly its own retrieval [*Wieder-holung*]" (*Beitr.* 39/55). It is in and as the insight into that which, however essential, remained concealed in the first beginning that the other beginning finds its inception. It is in glimpsing that which the first beginning never consciously saw but only blindly enacted, that which the first beginning could not remember but only obliviously thrived on, that the other beginning becomes possible and (perhaps) necessary. In beginning to experience that which the first beginning, in its very unfolding, could not experience, the other beginning begins. It begins, that is, as the inceptive responsiveness to that which necessitated the unfolding of the first beginning, to that whose obscuration was precisely the function of the first beginning in its unfolding glow. In a way, then, the other beginning indicates the first beginning in the movement of becoming aware of itself (*Selbstbesinnung*), of what prompted it—the first beginning gaining "*historical* mindfulness" over and beyond its crystallized historical self-account (*Beitr.* 4/5). The other beginning points to the inceptual manifestation of the heretofore necessarily, essentially non-manifest. It could be said that implied here is a certain liberation, a certain transpiring of the first beginning beyond its own constraints.

Yet, if the "crossing" from the first to the other beginning may be understood in these terms, this strand of Heidegger's thinking, in its power and radicality, exposes the radically problematic character of another strand of his efforts to read the Greek beginning as the promise that finds its genuine fulfillment first in modernity (in modern as well as premodern, scientific as well as theological, dualisms), then in Hegel, and finally in Nietzsche (the one who would have inverted Platonism). At the heart of Heidegger's meditation one finds this deep disquietude or rift. On the one hand, a thread of his thinking pursues the richness, the as-yet-unfathomed, hence irreducible, fecundity of the first beginning, and emphasizes the grounding function of the first beginning with respect to the other beginning. On the other hand, his narrative of a unitary and homogeneous "history of metaphysics" formulaically reduces the Greek beginning, makes the first beginning simple, reifies such an origin. It could even be surmised that this discourse sets such a beginning up in order to tear it down: "This erecting of the towering [*Ragenden*] of the first beginning is the sense of the 'destruction' in the crossing to the other beginning" (125/179). The difficulty I am here bringing to the fore is that this narrative may forget the Greek beginning in its uniqueness as well as complexity, and do so in a twofold way: (1) in the first place, by obliterating the forgetfulness of the Greek beginning which is *necessary* for a phenomenon, say, such as Cartesian scientism to arise at all (again, the creativity of oblivion); (2) secondly, and at the same time, by obliterating the obliteration, by forgetting the forgetfulness it enacts, making such forgetfulness even more elusive, even more arduous to catch. In this dimension of Heidegger's thinking one may find a potent gesture of occultation, which gains its rhetorical force precisely in virtue of its repeated appeals to the task of manifestation.

Even as one considers what lies at the heart of Heidegger's meditation toward the other beginning, one wonders whether there may not be reasons to discern deep (if barely audible at this point) resonances between the movement of this thinking and certain dimensions of the ancient Greek experience. Heidegger is seeking an emancipation from subjective, psychologistic, or "personalistic" manners of investigation, stretching out to a mode of thinking that in more than one crucial sense does not say "I":

> Said in the preparatory exercise is a questioning that is neither the goal-oriented doing of an individual nor the limited calculation of a community. Rather, it is above all the further hinting [*Weiterwinken*] of a hint [*Winkes*] that comes from that which is most question-worthy and remains allotted [*zugewiesen*] to it.
>
> Disengaging from any "personal" fabrication succeeds only from the intimacy [*Innigkeit*] with the earliest belonging [*Zugehörens*]. (*Beitr.* 4/4)

In the other beginning, Heidegger is striving inceptively to say, to announce "the *great turning around* [*die* große Umkehrung] . . . which is beyond all 'revaluation of all values,' that turning around in which beings are not grounded in terms of human being, but rather being-human is grounded from being [*Seyn*]" (*Beitr.* 129/184). He warns that "[i]t is no longer a case of talking 'about' something and presenting something objective [*ein Gegenständliches darzustellen*], but rather of being owned over to [appropriated by] that which owns [*sondern dem Er-eignis übereignet zu werden*], which amounts to an essential transformation of the human from 'rational animal' (*animal rationale*) to Da-sein" (3/3). In this turning "Dasein's *allotment* [Zuweisung] to being [*Seyn*] comes into its own" (4/4). Crucially, then, what is announced concerns us (again, *Selbstbesinnung*)— the way in which we do not find our measure in ourselves but dwell, belong in mystery. Indeed, the way in which we are "used" by being, which, owning us, takes place and eventuates in and through, over and beyond us, in glowing affirmation as well as in the even more originary "no" or withdrawal (125/178).[7] Heidegger continues:

[I]s not the yes and no an essential possession of *being* [*Seins*] itself—
and the no even more originarily than the yes?

But how? Must not the "no" (and the yes) have its essential form in
the Da-sein that is used by being [*in dem vom Seyn gebrauchten Dasein*]? The no is the great leap-*off* [*Ab-sprung*], in which the *Da-* in Da-
sein is leaped open [*ersprungen*]. The leap-off, which both "affirms" that
from which it leaps off, but which also has itself as leap no nothing
[*nichts Nichtiges hat*]. The leap-off itself first undertakes to leap-open
the leap, and so here the no surpasses the yes. Therefore, however, seen
externally, this no is the setting-apart [*Ab-setzung*] of the other beginning against the first beginning—never "negating" in the usual sense of
rejecting or even degrading. Rather, this originary negating is of the
kind of that not-granting that refuses a still-going-along-with out of
knowing and recognizing the uniqueness of that which in its end calls
for the other beginning. (*Beitr.* 125/178)

The "no," the privation not to be understood in merely privative terms,
points to that which, in and as Dasein, eludes (*lanthanein*) Dasein. It
points to latency as "essential" and "constitutive" of being-there, as inti-
mating the "structure" (here words are lacking, or must signify anew) of
coming to pass. The "no" indicates being-there as dispossessed, as not cog-
nitively mastering, let alone owning itself in its becoming, but rather as
belonging—belonging in that which can hardly be a ground.

What is foreshadowed is the truth of being as *Ereignis,* as the coming to
pass of being-there: "Being [*Seyn*], however, up to now the most general
and most current in the shape of beingness, becomes as *Ereignis* the most
unique and most wondrous [or most estranging, *Befremdlichste*]" (*Beitr.*
124/177). *Ereignis* names being as being-harbored in the coming to pass of
beings, for beings are made manifest as "sheltering [*Bergung*] of the truth
of *Ereignis*" (*Beitr.* 144/207).[8] In turn, being-there, "used" by being, is said
to be that through and as which being eventuates, properly comes into its
own, appropriates, that is, comes to pass, takes place (*ereignet*). The transition from truth as correctness of judgment to truth as the turning of
Ereignis (*Beitr.* 130/185) is made perspicuous through the recognition of
"time" as "the naming of the 'truth' of being [*Seins*], and all this as a task,
as '*on-the-way*' ['*unterwegs*']; not as 'doctrine' and dogmatics" (*Beitr.*
128/183).

If, however, these are crucial lineaments of Heidegger's work in the *Bei-*

träge, one must wonder whether similar concerns may not be heard in the inaugural articulations of Greek thinking. Is the Greek beginning, precisely in its irreducibility to dominant historiography, altogether other with respect to these insights in the inceptive work Heidegger announces? Is the Greek beginning, in its exceeding the scribes' narratives and canonizations, other than the other beginning? Even the briefest re-turn to the Greeks raises doubts concerning, first of all, whether the thinking that says "I," be it in a psychologistic or transcendental mode, can be ascribed to them; whether they truly inaugurate the thinking of the priority and centrality of the human being, most notably as *animal rationale* (which heralds the priority and centrality of *ratio tout court,* hence of omni-intelligibility); whether, in its culmination, their thinking does in fact obscure the truth of *aletheia* as disclosure, thus laying down the conditions for the possibility of truth as certainty, of representation, of dualism in its various forms; and lastly, whether, blinded by the overwhelming luminosity of what is, overly filled with the arriving of phenomena, they exhibit a desensitization to the crevices and interruptions pervading being-there—a desensitization or "blindness to the 'no'" that would only allow them to affirm, to say "yes."

Indeed, how would the "I," let alone "personality," or even the priority of reason without any further qualification, be thinkable on Plato's terms (and I am not here speaking of Platonism and its many souls)? Isn't Plato, to mention but one of the fathomless difficulties inscribed in his body, the thinker of *eros,* of desirous rapture and loss of self, of love as that which, alone, would allow for recollection, and hence for knowledge as the contemplation of what is? Isn't knowledge, thus understood, groundless and belonging in a movement that is neither autarchic, nor autonomous, nor yet subjective? And, if knowledge articulates itself in the lack of ground, or if its "ground" is love (for love endows one with different eyes, allows one to see what would otherwise remain shrouded), does this not suggest that, *prior* to all knowing in the strict sense, one is always already in the world, belonging there, exposed and involved in all manners of action? After all, isn't Plato the thinker of—not just any ultimate principle, but a principle he calls the good, in light of which, he indicates, all knowing gains its sense and worth, but which remains itself unknown, impervious to dialectical/eidetic grasp, beyond being as beingness (*epekeina tes ousias*)? Does this not compromise any idealistic or dualistic program?

Furthermore, isn't much of Plato's work, just as is the case with Aristotle's, a sustained response to the anthropocentric claims of the sophists?

Finally, what about the shivering of Plato's *logos*, restlessly oscillating between demonstrative and mythical elocution, for reasons that are neither extrinsically "stylistic" nor the result of authorial strategy, but rather have to do with the intractable limits of language and reason?

Again, concerning the centrality of the *anthropos* and the all-encompassing work of rationality, one asks: Did Plato as well as Aristotle not recognize *physis* above all as that which, in its orientation and scope, exceeds the human, marks the limits of human grasp, indeed encompassing the human as that which the human cannot bring back to itself, that which remains opaque, illegible (vs., e.g., §97)? Is this not symptomatic of a nascent insight into being-there as being-owned, appropriated, belonging in that which is neither mastered nor reducible to the human? In this connection, one thinks of *Timaeus* as well as of various Aristotelian observations disseminated throughout the corpus (e.g., *EN* book Z, where we find a reflection on the *anthropos* as relatively unremarkable vis-à-vis the splendor of other phenomena in the cosmos). Suffice it here to mention the following crucial moment of *Metaphysics* Λ, in which Aristotle, through an unusual (for him) and all-the-more-remarkable appeal to myth, articulates the nexus of divinity and *physis* and barely hides a smile in mentioning the anthropomorphizing stratagems of humans:

> The ancients of very early times bequeathed to posterity in the form of a myth a tradition that the heavenly bodies are gods and that the divinity encompasses the whole of nature. The rest of the tradition has been added later as a means of persuading the many and as something useful for the laws and for matters of expediency; for they say that these gods are like human beings in form and like some of the other animals, and also other things which follow from or are similar to those stated. But if one were to separate from the later additions the first point and attend to this alone (namely, that they thought the first substances to be gods), he might realize that this was divinely spoken and that, while probably every art and every philosophy has often reached a stage of development as far as it could and then again has perished, these opinions about the gods were saved like relics up to now. Anyway, the opinion of our forefathers is evident to us to just this extent. (1074b 1 ff.)

This takes place at an utterly crucial point in *Metaphysics*, when Aristotle must cogently argue for the oneness of the sky in kind and in number. One is struck here by the vigorous indications of a philosophy of history sustaining itself in the face of the irretrievability of origin and impenetrability of its mystery; by the suggestion of the fluctuating life (and death) of ways of thinking; and by the thought of human finitude, not understood as diminishment but instead revealing the unique luminosity of human debris, of the traces left across the expanses of time. Coming to Aristotle in this manner makes it arduous, if at all feasible, to consider his thought as the mere, and for that matter unfinished (imperfect), projection of Thomism, or even of the Hegelian longing for the system.

Again, concerning the crucial issue of being as beingness, *ousia:* is this a *doctrine*? Aristotle is conspicuously the thinker articulating being in terms of *physis* (*Physics, Met. Γ*), as Heidegger himself acknowledges in the "*Physis*" essay.[9] The *Metaphysics* constitutes a sustained and unresolved elucidation of the difficulties inherent in the language of *ousia* as well as, more broadly, in the polysemy of being. It is, after all, Aristotle who announces that understanding being in terms of *ousia*, far from constituting an answer, let alone a doctrine, was and remains a question concerning which "in early times, and now, and always" one experiences *aporia* (*Met.* Z, 1028b 3 f.). Aristotle is, moreover, the thinker of the human as integrally involved in the self-reproducing workings of life, which the human serves without owning or even grasping it, as if the human were an *organon* of *physis*, "used" by it. For *physis*, albeit assumed in its teleological orientation, remains ultimately inscrutable, hidden, its purposefulness operating according to causes not always determinate or determinable, mysterious. Aristotle articulates the *that*, not the *what*, of teleology. The task of thinking is yet to be accomplished.

In the final analysis, *nous* itself, just as all first principles, remains excessive vis-à-vis the demonstrative procedures of knowledge, calling attention to the excess of intellection or intuition with respect to knowledge and, in fact, the radical alterity of *nous* with respect to *logos*. This latter point may also account for the convergence of *nous* and *aisthesis* suggested in *EN* book Z. Quite consistently, Aristotle is the thinker of unexhausted *aporia* and enduring wonder.

One concluding specification: Is Aristotle not, as Heidegger also remarks in *Sein und Zeit*, the thinker of truth as phenomenon? Does Aristotle not, in the opening of *Metaphysics*, use the terms *pragma, aletheia,* and *phainomenon* synonymously, suggesting that it is truth, understood as "fact" or what shines forth, that motivates inquiry and orients it with necessitating force (*Met.* A, 984a 18, 984b 10, 986b 31)? Aristotle will never simply have discussed truth as the mere property of statements. On the contrary, he will relentlessly have underscored the problem of the dissociation of *logos* from the sensible/intuitive stratum of experience (most notably in *Met.* Γ and *EN* VIII, where incontinence is treated not as a vice, but as the dissociation of *logos* from desire or experience), warning against it precisely as a problem. And this understanding of truth as phenomenal disclosure could not be more remote from a conception of phenomenon as opposed to purely intelligible form, of appearance as opposed to essence, and hence sensation to cognition. The phenomenon of truth discloses the primordiality of truth with respect to the scientific pronouncement and points to the pre-epistemic dimension of experience, indeed, the non-demonstrative ground or un-grounding condition of demonstration. Aristotle further develops what in Plato is the object of sensibility, apprehended in and by trust (*pistis*), in terms of the nonscientific, in fact ethical, prerequisites of science. For the taking in of truth in its necessitating self-evidence is a matter of comportment, of posture, of being "healthily disposed with regard to the truth." (*Met.* Γ, on the so-called law of non-contradiction, signals the import of ethics for ontology. Aristotle is far from simplistic or rationalistic in his ethical discussion.)

Thus, let it be recalled parenthetically, the privileging of affirmation and concomitant oblivion of the primordiality of the "no" is not articulated, even at the zenith of Greek thinking, in an epistemological/cognitive vein. It appears indeed that the privilege the Greeks accord to the radiance of phenomena, to being, to the affirmation and positivity of what is there, far from revealing and addressing a need for conceptual control, has a root in a certain priority of the ethical.[10] In this sense, Heidegger's emphasis on and prioritization of the "no" (withdrawal, privation) is revealed in its problematic character or qualified cogency. For only in light of the priority of the pursuit of knowledge does the emphasis on affirmation and positing engender the problems Heidegger appropriately underlines. But, in light of the intertwined dimensions of *ethos*, sensibility, and experience, how would one deny that affirmation is originary, in fact radically so, precisely because lying beyond the claims, values, and authority of knowledge *stricto sensu*?

The mention of these vital moments in the Greek inauguration can here only be contracted, abbreviated in the extreme. To be sure, such aspects of the meditations of Plato and Aristotle, while by no means secondary or marginal, are for the most part obscured in the traditional canonization of these thinkers, that is, in the assimilation and transformation of them into "the tradition"—an assimilation and a transformation through and as which "the tradition," in the singular, is itself as such formed.

Yet, precisely to the extent that Heidegger undertakes to encounter the first beginning in a more primordial way, it seems that the acknowledgment of these traditionally repressed aspects of the Greek inception would most properly belong here. Otherwise the forgetfulness, indeed, the forgetfulness of the forgetting or unconscious blindness that may remain at work in Heidegger's readings of the Greeks could end up in complicity with, even reinforcing, the "history of metaphysics" that Heidegger is seeking thoughtfully to traverse. Or is the impoverished schematization of the first beginning necessary in order to set into relief more starkly and cogently the articulation of the other beginning as unprecedented? Is the patricidal logic of the new truly inescapable?

But Heidegger says: "From a new originariness the other beginning assists the first beginning towards the truth of its history, and thus towards its inalienable and ownmost otherness [*Andersartigkeit*], which becomes fruitful solely in the historical dialogue [*Zwiesprache*] of thinkers" (*Beitr.* 131/187). As was suggested above, the other beginning may announce itself as the first beginning becoming aware of itself, inceptively remembering itself, allowing its own oblivion to surface as such—above all, illuminating itself in its self-difference. The other may announce itself *in and as* the first beginning recovering its irreducibility, always already, to what it may relate or may have related "about" itself—that is, *in and as* the first beginning making itself manifest as other than itself, as neither self-identical nor self-contained, and hence as a problem. And just as, in their dynamic interplay, mindlessness and mindfulness or forgetfulness and remembrance do not simply succeed each other in terms of linear temporality, but interpenetrate in a movement of unfolding and withdrawal, manifestation and latency, so the interplay of first and other beginning may not be understood merely in terms of succession or supplanting but in terms of the self-differing of the same—in terms of the movement, neither internal nor external, holding together in their difference *and* inseparability that which comes to shine and that which is overshadowed in the shining, the unfolding and that which it enfolds in its unfolding, the emergent and that which remains hidden, buried, precisely through the emerging. The transition from the first to the other would indicate the becoming manifest of the "hidden history," of the history of the first beginning, hidden *in* as well as hidden *to* the first beginning.

The first and the other beginning would, thus, be thought as the same—which does not mean as identical. This would call for a retrieval of the first beginning as the other beginning—for a retrieval of the otherness, strangeness, and estrangement in those texts that have been made mindlessly familiar but may not be so. The traces and symptoms of an agitation haunting these discourses, destabilizing them, consistently qualifying even the most central systematic outcomes, are pervasive and cannot be relegated to the order of the subliminal or the accidental.

*   *   *

A brief reflection, to conclude, on the luminous insightfulness and simultaneous blindness or unresponsiveness characterizing Heidegger's *Wiederholung*. An insight lights up and for an instant starkly illumines, in the nocturnal expanse, the contours of what-is. However, for the organs used to the dark, what follows is not clarity, but rather disorientation and, for a time, even dimmer perception. What was momentarily wrested from obscurity is swallowed back into latency, forgotten. Insight undergoes deflection and dissipation in the course of time (*Met.* Λ). Not only does it tend to fade, but also it comes to be deformed, even at odds with itself, an aberration of its own originary disclosure, in the literal sense of an erring or straying-from itself. One begins in a beginning that commands a certain turning, a certain trajectory. Yet, in the wake of beginning, apparently one cannot maintain that orientation, diverges, even turns against oneself, betrays oneself, proceeds in a contrary direction—all the while believing one is proceeding along the same path. It is the latter aspect of this phenomenon that demands attention—not so much the sliding or straying from originary insight, the loss and obscuration of it, but the forgetfulness or the unapparent element of this, the belief that the straying has not happened.

This phenomenon lies at the heart of the problem of memory, transmission, history. It is as though one cannot *live* in the understanding that occasionally releases itself into manifestation. Errancy bespeaks the continuity of the movement away from itself, without the awareness thereof: it does not take place as the conscious, explicit interruption of a course, but as the claim to a seamless unfolding of it. Thus, in the name of one's beginning or initial opening, one may comport oneself, whether in the deed of thinking or in other endeavors, according to ways that counter that beginning. What is at stake is a certain rift between the letter and its temporal enactment—or, rather, its lack of enactment, for it tends to die away, to remain only as citation when one has long before lost track of it and of oneself. The root of "political" problems, in general of problems of action, and of all manners of folly, even collective folly, lies here. Consider, for example, the *wars* waged in the name of *Christianity,* that is, the rift between the words Christ is said to have uttered and the reception and retention thereof. But this dynamic may be discerned even in the context of the work of one individuated *psyche,* of one single thinker. One forgets oneself, in spite of oneself, is carried away from one's own vision. . . . A structure of oblivion, self-alienation, and drifting may be operative at the heart of the unfolding of thinking. And it may have to do with positing, with a positing that posits itself in an unqualified, unmoving way. It is as though the *energy* of beginning(s) could not be sustained, endured. It seems to grow dimmer, becomes unreadable.

But is this necessary? Inevitable, ineluctable? What kind of awareness would it take, if not to avoid this altogether, then minimally to remain conscious of this phenomenon, to remain vigilant, questioning, and not become oblivious of the curvatures, of the fateful tropisms, that seem to inhere in all positing and project?[11] It might take, among other things, a certain lightness with words—a certain necessarily qualified trust in them. For alone, out of context, even if carefully analyzed in their etymology, they may not carry and reveal much. What seems crucial is: how do they live? How do they play with one another, indeed, *each time* receive their signification in virtue of their interplay? Above all: how are they embodied, how are they themselves deeds, incarnated, at work? How are they necessitated by the upsurge of disclosure? An unqualified love of words for their own sake, which abstracts them from the element in which they *live,* from their unique context, may be dangerous indeed: potentially desensitizing, dis-integrating, forgetful. A historical narrative such as that of the "history of Western metaphysics" or of being, aiming, in its homogenizing strategy, at drawing continuities based on the systematic stability of signification, may entail a certain oblivion of oblivion. It may display a tendency to downplay oblivion, not taking it seriously enough, that is, not taking seriously a certain indeterminacy marking the past, the past as yet to come. The leap of an other beginning, the leap that an other beginning would be, instead, would indicate: staying with the same, illuminating it otherwise.[12]

Notes

1. Here and throughout the essay, the parenthetical references to the English translation (*Contributions to Philosophy (From Enowning),* trans. P. Emad and K. Maly

[Bloomington: Indiana University Press, 1999]) are followed by those to the German text (*Beiträge zur Philosophie (Vom Ereignis), Gesamtausgabe* 65 [Frankfurt am Main: Klostermann, 1989]). However, my own rendition of the German passages here quoted significantly diverges from the available translation.

2. I will, in this context, forgo questioning Heidegger's retrieval of ancient Greek thinking according to the logic of beginning, indeed, *the* first and only beginning of what will have been called the tradition of Western philosophy. Heidegger's equation of Greek (Western) philosophy with philosophy *tout court* is a systemic feature of his work that, however remarkable, mostly goes unremarked precisely (1) because of the apparent obviousness of this identity and (2) because in it a fundamental assumption of the dominant historiographic narrative is at once harbored, echoed, protected, and preserved as unconscious and unexamined.

3. *Beitr.* 4/5.

4. Regarding the incidence of the language of beginnings, see, among others, the exemplary moments in *Plato's Sophist* (trans. R. Rojcewicz and A. Schuwer [Bloomington: Indiana University Press, 1997]), 154, and "On the Essence and Concept of *Physis* in Aristotle's *Physics* B, 1," in *Pathmarks,* trans. W. McNeill (Cambridge: Cambridge University Press, 1998), 204 and 229.

5. As Heidegger will insist in the "Letter on 'Humanism'" (*Basic Writings,* ed. by D. F. Krell [New York: HarperCollins, 1993], 217–65), "the thinking that thinks into the truth of being is, as thinking, historical. There is not a 'systematic' thinking and next to it an illustrative history of past opinions" (238). This text returns time and again to the question of history, in which the eventuation of thinking properly belongs or inheres: "Thought in a more primordial way, there is the history of being to which thinking belongs as a recollection of this history, propriated by it. Such recollective thought differs essentially from the subsequent presentation of history in the sense of an evanescent past" (239). The past emerges as anything but evanescent. It is also noteworthy that in the "Letter" the language of experience pervasively structures the ar-·ticulation of the question of history: "Assuming that in the future the human being will be able to think the truth of being, he will think from ek-sistence. The human being stands ek-sistingly in the destiny of being. The ek-sistence of the human being is historical as such, but not only or primarily because so much happens to the human being and to things human in the course of time. Because it must think the ek-sistence of Da-sein, the thinking of *Being and Time* is essentially concerned that the historicity of Dasein be experienced" (ibid.). The language of history, experience (*erfahren*), and *Seinsverlassenheit* is variously intertwined in the *Beiträge* (e.g., §§87, 91, 100, 110).

6. Concomitantly with these remarks regarding history, we may recall certain reflections by Husserl in *The Crisis of European Sciences and Transcendental Phenomenology,* trans. D. Carr (Evanston: Northwestern University Press, 1970). In the *Beilage* "Denial of Scientific Philosophy" (1935), Husserl broaches the question of philosophy as the practice of becoming other, of becoming "a different philosopher" (393), and observes: "There is no doubt, then, that we must engross ourselves in historical considerations if we are to be able to understand ourselves as philosophers and understand what philosophy is to become through us" (391). And again, in the *Beilage* "The Origin of Geometry" (1936): "The ruling dogma of the separation in principle between epis-

temological elucidation and historical, even humanistic-psychological explanation, between epistemological and genetic origin, is fundamentally mistaken. . . . Or, rather, what is fundamentally mistaken is the limitation through which precisely the deepest and most genuine problems of history are concealed" (370).

7. On the language of "usage," see "The Question Concerning Technology," in *Basic Writings*, 337, and "The Anaximander Fragment," in *Early Greek Thinking*, trans. D. F. Krell and F. A. Capuzzi (San Francisco: Harper and Row, 1984), esp. 50–58. The eventuation of being through and as us and our belonging in the mystery of such a "use" are related to the problem of the self-concealment of *physis*, discussed in "On the Essence and Concept of *Physis* in Aristotle's *Physics* B, 1."

8. *Eigen:* of one's own, proper. *Eignen:* to be appropriate, fit, suitable, inherent, to belong. In "On the Essence and Concept of *Physis* in Aristotle's *Physics* B, 1," Heidegger turns to related terms to think through the language of *dynamis.* In the course of his discussion of *hyle* as *to dynamei,* he translates *dynamis* as *Eignung, Geeignetheit* (appropriation, appropriateness, suitability) and *to dynamei* as *das Geeignete* (the appropriated, the appropriate) (214). A gesture toward a thoughtful evocation, if not proper translation, of the word *Ereignis* may be found in the term "propriation" or in phrases such as "propriative event," "that which owns, appropriates," "gaining itself back," all of which point to the intersecting orders of propriety and property.

9. Heidegger, "On the Essence and Concept of *Physis* in Aristotle's *Physics* B, 1."

10. Consider other authors emphasizing affirmation, as diverse as Nietzsche, Derrida, and Levinas.

11. Aristotle's words in *Metaphysics* α may be poignantly appropriate to the problem posed by this particular phenomenon: "Perhaps the cause of this difficulty, which may exist in two ways, is in us and not in the facts. For as the eyes of bats are to the light of day, so is the intellect of our soul to the objects which in their nature are most apparent of all (*phanerotata*)."

12. In a possible continuation of this essay, I would propose a reading of the *Sophist* lectures as exemplary of the Heideggerian ambivalent approach to Greek philosophy here discussed. This discussion would (1) lay out Heidegger's reading of Aristotle, especially of the *Ethics;* (2) emphasize the luminosity of Heidegger's insight regarding the continuity of *phronesis* and *sophia,* both considered in terms of gazing, but differing in their overall orientation; both remaining essentially of/in the order of the phenomenal; (3) observe how, nevertheless, the analysis ends up reasserting the inveterate and conventional polarity of practical vs. theoretical thought; however construed in unusual terms (in relation to *techne,* etc.), *sophia* ends up being opposed to and detached from what concerns action.

3 The Intractable Interrelationship of *Physis* and *Techne*

Walter A. Brogan

In a rather remarkable passage in Heidegger's *Beiträge zur Philosophie,* Heidegger asks:

> What happens to nature in technicity, when nature is separated out from beings by the natural sciences? The growing—or better, the simple rolling unto its end—destruction of "nature." What was it once? The site for the moment of the arrival and the dwelling of gods, when the site—still *physis*—rested in the essence of be-ing. Since then, *physis* quickly became a "being" and then even the counterpart to "grace"— and, after this demoting, was ultimately reduced to the full force of calculating machination and economy.... Why does earth keep silent in this destruction? Because earth is not allowed the strife with a world, because earth is not allowed the truth of be-ing. Why not? Because, the more gigantic that giant-thing called man becomes, the smaller he also becomes? Must nature be surrendered and abandoned to machination? Are we still capable of seeking earth anew? Who enkindles that strife in which the earth finds its open, in which the earth encloses itself and is earth?[1]

In this paper, I will claim that at the time of the writing of this manuscript, which is so preoccupied with the problem of *Machenschaft,* in the late 1930s, and even later in the 1950s, when Heidegger wrote his essay on "The Question Concerning Technology," Heidegger's thought is centered around the recovery of the question of the intractable interrelationship of *physis* and *techne.* For Heidegger, it is never a question of thinking *physis* apart from *techne.* Not even in his analysis of our time, which Heidegger calls the age of *Machenschaft,* does Heidegger claim that something like *techne,* transformed into technicity, truly operates outside of its relationship to *physis. Machenschaft* relies upon what Heidegger calls the disempowerment of *physis,* the failure to acknowledge the *dynamis* that belongs to *physis* and makes human undertakings possible.[2] This disempowering is not the result of human activity. It is rather, in fact, the opposite. Human activity and human making are themselves dependent upon *Machenschaft.* Beings give themselves over machinationally, not because of the force of human intervention, but because of the abandonment of beings by being. At the summit of the reign of technicity, calculative thinking, and measureless repetition, *physis* still reigns in its abandonment. There can be no *techne,* not even the absolute reign of *techne* without nature, outside of the relationship of *techne* to *physis.* But for Heidegger, it seems to me, the opposite is equally true. That is, there can be no revealing of *physis* without *techne.* The distortion of the meaning of nature, its virtual disappearance in the technological age, occurs in part as a result of the severance of this interrelationality. What Heidegger calls for is not the turn away from *techne,* back to *physis,* but a return to the mutual favoring that inclines one to the other.

In the opening remarks to his *Physics B 1* essay, Heidegger speaks of the many different interpretations of nature that have been offered in history. He points out that these interpretations were always offered in dichotomies on the basis of which, under the guidance of an underlying understanding of nature, beings from nature were differentiated from another way of being.[3] He calls this originary event an *Ent-scheidung,* a de-cision, recalling (to me) the power of Zeus in Hesiod's account of the genealogy of the gods, when Zeus distributed the territory belonging to each of the gods. Increasingly in later decades, Heidegger became convinced that the **decisive** incision, on the basis of which being as *physis* is partitioned into regional ontologies, is the division between the natural and the artificial. What I would like to suggest is that this originary parting of being that gives rise to history is not in itself the decline into metaphysics and the forgetting of being, which culminates, on Heidegger's reading, in the reign of the gigantic and machination in our times. This parting belongs to *physis.* Rather, it is the failure to think from out of this division of being and beings that Heidegger's philosophy calls us to question.

Both beings from *techne* and those from *physis* have being, but they have their being in different ways. In other words, it is not a question of two different senses of being, but of two different ways in which beings belong to being. In both cases, movement and being produced or brought forth into being characterizes the way of being. But in each case the *poiesis,* the movement of production, occurs in a different way. No doubt Heidegger's interest in Aristotle's tendency to think of *physis* in the context of this *Ab-hebung*, or divisive character, is in order to retrieve an originary insight into nature that contrasts to Hegel's dialectical movement or *Aufhebung*. For Heidegger, the being-together and being-as-a-whole of beings does not imply a notion of a totality of beings, nor does he seek to arrive at a sense of an originary *physis* that overcomes this fundamental discord. Similarly, Heidegger's claim that the ancient Greeks knew nothing of modern subjectivity no doubt is an implicit critique of Hegel's philosophy of spirit, or of a theory that would posit an overarching, guiding, external force that would determine the meaning of and movement of being. But it is also a philosophical commitment on his part to allow *physis* to take the lead in the bringing forth and disclosure of all beings, and to rethink the meaning of human knowledge, and the relationship of *physis* and *logos* on this basis. In the middle of his discussion of art and the artist in "The Origin of the Work of Art," Heidegger suddenly reminds us: "Yet all this happens in the midst of the being that surges upward, growing of its own accord, *physis*."[4] This retrieval of a nonsubjective sense of a *techne* that belongs to *physis*, a kind of human knowing that is for Heidegger more utterly human than subjective knowledge, is at the heart of Heidegger's project in reading Aristotle, as is evident in his essay on Aristotle's *Physics B 1*, as well as his treatment in *Platon: Sophistes* of the relationship of *techne* to *sophia* in the *Nicomachean Ethics*.[5]

Aristotle's distinction between natural beings and produced beings serves to articulate the way in which *kinesis* is the being of natural beings. Produced beings come into being and are through *techne*. In contrast, natural beings emerge out of themselves and stand forth in their being of themselves. In the emergence and appearance of both kinds of beings, the human being's openness to truth plays a role, but this role is different. To grasp the natural being in its being requires *aisthesis*, perception, and what Aristotle calls *nous*, the immediate view of the givenness of the being as such. In contrast, the power of *techne* as a way of knowing and revealing lies in its ability to heed and draw upon the hiddenness of *physis*, the capacity of natural beings to not-be, and to stand ontologically in relationship to what they are not, a capacity that also belongs to natural beings by virtue of their coming to be. This relationship to truth and disclosure of what is that characterizes both *physis* and *techne* has been lost sight of in contemporary technology. For this reason, technology, which attempts to turn away from the project of revealing what is, needs to be distinguished from Aristotle's notion of *techne*, which Heidegger sees as still operative within the framework of *poiesis,* the bringing forth into appearance of what is and can be, rather than the non-attentive making on its own that characterizes technology.

What is the Greek meaning of *techne?* Heidegger traces the origin of this word in his essay "Building Dwelling Thinking":

> The Greek for "to bring forth or to produce" is *tikto.* The word *techne,* technique, belongs to the verb's root tec. To the Greeks, *techne* means neither art nor handicraft but rather: to make something appear, within what is present, as this or that, in this way or that way. The Greeks conceive of *techne,* producing, in terms of letting appear.[6]

Heidegger further depicts the Greek sense of *techne* as originally the same as *episteme:*

> The word *techne* denotes a mode of knowing. To know means to have seen, in the widest sense of seeing, which means to apprehend what is present as such. For Greek thought, the essence of knowing consists in *aletheia,* that is, in the revealing of beings. It supports and guides all comportment toward beings. *Techne,* as knowledge, experienced in the Greek manner, is a bringing-forth of beings in that it brings forth what is present as such out of concealedness and specifically into the unconcealedness of their appearance; *techne* never signifies the action of making.[7]

The need for involving *techne* in any discussion of the truth of natural beings, I believe, lies in this capacity to relate to the concealedness that belongs to the being of natural beings. *Techne* is a mode of knowing governed by *aletheia,* and for Heidegger, to stand in the truth involves a relationship to both concealedness and unconcealment. The realm of *techne* comes to be associated with the artist, the carpenter—not because he engages in the action of making and producing, but because the artist and carpenter have a certain relation to being and beings that forms the basis for these actions. In "The Origin of the Work of Art," Heidegger makes the bold statement: "Beings are never of our making, or even merely our representations."[8]

Heidegger translates *techne* as *Sichauskennen*—a knowing one's way around, a being-familiar with the presencing of beings among which one lives so as to know how to let beings appear in one's world. *Techne* opens up the world in which beings are disclosed.

The *arche* of natural beings is that which originates and governs the being-moved of these beings. *Kinesis* is their way of being. Change is always from something to something, and therefore presupposes a relationship between beings that are placed and therefore determined in their being. The relationship of beings to each other is not founded in Aristotle on the totality of beings, but on the being-together and being-as-a-whole of beings and on the *metabole* that governs this way of being. Beings are disclosed in their truth when they appear in their worldly character, and Heidegger attributes to *techne* in a special sense an opening to the world in which beings appear.

The most significant way in which natural beings and produced beings are the same is given to us in Aristotle's text—they both have *kinesis* as their way of being. This is also the source of their difference. The *arche* of the being-moved of produced beings is different from that of natural beings. As Heidegger says in the *Beiträge, physis* is not *techne*.[9] But it is precisely this **not** that interests Heidegger. The difference between *physis* and *techne* indicates a fundamental complicity. Aristotle needs the discussion of *techne* in order to accomplish the authentic disclosure of the being of *physis*, because this ability to be taken over, this being-able to be other than it is, belongs to the nature of beings from *physis*. *Techne* is possible precisely because it attends to this negativity at the heart of natural beings, and brings forth beings by allowing this force of negativity to be revealed.

The Dependency of *Techne* on *Physis*

Techne is the kind of knowing that one carries along in one's everyday dealings and that makes it possible for one to be situated in one's encounters with beings. *Techne* is not first of all a specific knowledge of some particular individual, but a *hexis*, a disposition or comportment that provides the foundation (*arche*) for such knowledge. Thus *techne* is not primarily the process of manufacturing or the manipulation of goods in such a way as to produce a product. Knowing in the sense of understanding and being at home with beings in the world of one's preoccupation is the prerequisite for all producing. It is this knowledge that governs all bringing-forth and from this that a produced being emerges. Heidegger says: "With produced things, the *arche* of their movement and of the rest of being completed and finished is not in themselves, but in another, in the *architekton*, the one who governs over the *techne* as *arche*.[10] Aristotle says as much in the *Ethics:* "All *techne* is concerned with the realm of coming-to-be, i.e., with planning and meditating on how something which is capable both of being and not being may come into being, a thing whose *arche* is in the producer and not in the thing produced" (*NE* 1040a 11–13).

In the *Metaphysics*, Aristotle says that the architect is not wiser because he can do things but because he holds himself in relation to *logos* (dwells in *logos*) and knows the causes (*Met.* 981b 6–7). Like *episteme*, then, *techne* is founded on knowledge of the causes and of the whole and is concerned with the application of this knowledge. Aristotle says that it is this kind of knowing that differentiates *techne* from sense perception: "Sense experience is a knowledge in relation to the individual, *techne* in relation to the whole" (*Met.* 981a 16–17). Both *techne* and *episteme* are guided by *nous*, the seeing of being as such, as a whole. *Techne* concerns itself not so much with its capacity to know as such, that is, with the opening that grants to it knowledge of the whole, but with its way of revealing beings on the basis of that knowledge. Nevertheless, it is important in order to understand what Aristotle means by *techne*, and how it is distinguished from *physis*, that we not forget that *techne* presupposes this capacity to stand among beings in such a way that they are open in their being. Aristotle places *techne* alongside *episteme*, *phronesis*, *sophia*, and *nous* as ways in which the soul through *logos* is in the truth. *Techne*, then, is far from the disinterestedness in worldly disclosedness that characterizes technology. *Techne* is not world-poor. Nor is *techne* a form of subjective domination that creates beings after its own image in a milieu of infinite repetition without regard to the task of knowing as attentiveness to what is coming to be.

Techne is rather a *hexis*, a being-disposed toward, adopting a stance toward. In that sense, *hexis* involves *prohairesis*, the already having a view of (*skopos*), which guides one's encounters and actions. It is this having-in-advance a view of the being that guides *poiesis*. It is not just *hexis* and *proairesis* that are required for *techne*. It is *hexis meta logou*, a holding oneself in relation to *logos*. And, in *techne*, this means adopting in advance a position toward beings that is governed by *logos*. When this happens, Aristotle tells us, the soul is in the truth. That is, *techne* is a mode of *aletheuein*. But what is this kind of *logos* for Aristotle and what is *aletheia*? *Techne* is only one of five ways *aletheia* is in the soul. How is *techne* as a mode of *aletheuein* differentiated from *nous* and from the *aisthesis* of experience?

Aristotle differentiates *techne* from experience in that experience is a being-among and encountering of beings but without *hexis*—without that prior understanding of world that allows the human being to see beings in their unity and relation. But *techne* requires *aisthesis* in order to discover what can be brought forth. And this is why Aristotle says that experience precedes *techne* and, in this respect, *techne* is founded on experience. But ontologically speaking, *techne* is prior to experience since it is what at all makes experience possible. How is, according to Aristotle, *techne* different from *aisthesis*? The one who has *techne* knows the whole—that is, he knows the *eidos*, he knows what the being is. He also knows how the being is—the causes that are responsible for its being what it is. *Logos*, then, becomes the gathering together of what is responsible for a being's being. In *techne*, this means the bringing of the *hyle*, that out of which the being is constituted (which is discovered in experience) into the *eidos* that is the *telos*—that which fulfills it in its being.

But what is the *hyle* from which *techne* can bring forth its product? The one who has *techne* finds this already there for him in his dealings. It is there from *physis*. Thus *physis* is always present in *techne*, but it does not show itself forth as itself. This means that produced beings are not natural beings. And yet the *not* is not such as to completely deny the relation to nature that is present in such a being. For, it is precisely this capacity to not be itself that defines natural beings. Here the question emerges: what is the being of beings from *physis*, such that they can show themselves as they are not?

Aristotle tells us in the *Ethics* that *techne* is concerned with *genesis* and with bringing about of something and viewing how this something comes into being which can both be and not be, and whose *arche* lies in the one who brings forth, however not in that which is brought forth. Like produced beings, natural beings are not *always* there but are rather governed by coming into being and going out of being. These are the beings with which *techne* is concerned. Natural beings are only differentiated from produced beings in that their *arche*, the emerging and governing of their beings, is not in another, but in themselves. But this way of coming into being is therefore much different from that of *techne*. This can be made clear by showing how it is that *poiesis* works. Beings from *physis* tend by nature toward their fulfillment. However they do not come to be necessarily. If nothing gets in the way, their *kinesis* will be toward their being themselves. But natural beings are related to other beings in such a way that they can be affected by them. *Techne* is possible because it is an awareness of this fundamental relationality that belongs to beings. Moreover, this being-able-to-be-affected-by, this *pathein*, cannot be something extrinsic to their being. It is the *physis* of natural beings. *Techne* needs *physis*, and the primary way in which the revealing of this relationality that belongs to *physis* occurs is through *techne*. I think this is why Heidegger analyzes equipmentality in *Sein und Zeit*, that is, not in order to ignore *physis* and establish his ontology on the basis of *techne*, but in order to uncover this relationality, and the reciprocity between *physis* and *techne* that it implies.

How does *techne* bring-forth? Through *logos*, that is through the gathering together of the causes with a view of the *telos*. The *telos* is there in advance in the mind of the architect. It is a pre-view, a viewing in advance, a seeing (*theoria*) of that which the being is (its *Wesen*, its *eidos*) that governs, as *arche*, the orderings of what is to be brought forth. This preview is a *prohairesis;* that is, a foresight that is reaching out toward beings and sees in advance, and yet is resolute in holding itself out toward being, on the basis of which it determines its relation to what is to be brought forth. There is a circle involved here. As previous pre-view, it comes first. But as a holding of something in view it is always coming from and directed from what is to be determined by it. Thus experience precedes *techne* and yet *techne* governs experiences. While *noein* is the pre-view of the being of a being (its *eidos*), and *aisthesis* is a view of beings as not in their being, the *logos* of *techne* holds both in relation to one another. *Techne* is the site where the correlation and inextricable interrelationship of *aisthesis* and *nous/eidos* can be revealed. It is in this relation that they arise into their sameness and maintain themselves in difference. The *prohairesis* has always to do with the *pragmata*, and it arises on the basis of its constant already-there relation to the beings it encounters. *Poiesis* involves deliberation, that is, a step-by-step disclosing of what is necessary in order to bring about that which the producer determines as to be brought about. Since this is always particular to the situation, such disclosing cannot be founded entirely on knowledge of the *eidos* of what is there. *Techne* approaches and relates to natural beings by also seeing them as they are coming to be, and thus not in their being. That such things can be taken and perceived in ways that they are not, in and of themselves, means that such beings must have this "not" as a characteristic of their way of being. Also, if natural beings can be taken over and made into other beings, that is, incorporated in a way that they no longer have a being of their own but only appear in another being, then such beings must already be related to other beings in such a way that they can be radically affected by them.

The Dependency of *Physis* on *Techne*

In Heidegger's course on *Metaphysics* Θ 1–3, he discusses the relationship of *physis* to *techne* in terms of what he sees as the fundamental question in Aristotle's treatment of *physis,* which is the way in which *kinesis* or *metabole* ontologically defines natural beings. In contrast to natural beings, the defining characteristic of beings from *techne* is that the origin of the movement and coming to be is from outside, in another. Were we to understand *arche metaboles en allo,* change as exchange, as meaning the *arche* of change in the being that changes, so that the change does not belong intrinsically to the being but is imposed upon it, then a typical example for us might be the potter who changes the lump of clay into a mug. Change in this case would appear to be the alteration that incidentally happens to a thing. But Heidegger insists that *metabole* here also has an active sense, and does not simply mean that something is done to something else. That which undergoes change is in some way itself a force in that it enables the change. The force of *techne* in relationship to *physis* then gets understood not so much in terms of imposition as in terms of exchange. Change in this sense is both active and passive and the issue is not how things that *are* get affected and changed, but about the capacity for change that belongs to the being as such. It is not about what one thing does to another but about *dynamis* and *metabole* as the being of beings. Heidegger's analysis also requires a rethinking of *symbebekos,* what belongs to natural beings but only incidentally. The accidental is what can be taken over and taken away from the being because it is other than the being itself as such. But the *symbebekos,* the otherness that belongs to natural beings, and gives itself over to *techne,* is for Aristotle one of the many senses of being. It is because of the nature of natural beings that they can let themselves be brought forth in such a way as to be produced through *techne.* In this insight, Heidegger restores the power to *physis* in the relationship between *physis* and *techne.* This yielding power belongs to the essence of *physis,* and makes possible the power of *techne* for the artist who attends to this *dynamis.* In *techne,* this yielding power and this capacity to resist that belongs to *physei on* become manifest.

Similarly, Aristotle also speaks of the *dynamis* that co-constitutes the being of natural beings as *aitia,* as cause. But Heidegger cautions us not to understand causality according to the modern notion of cause-effect that is prevalent in the technological approach to beings. We tend to view cause in terms of a mechanistic transfer of force onto an object. Instead Heidegger says cause and effect need to be seen as mutually and reciprocally binding each other. The discussion of causality provides a frame for similarly interpreting the *poiein-pathein* structure in Aristotle's understanding of *physis.* By *poiein,* Aristotle means the capacity to cause something to be brought forth, and by *pathein*—the capacity of that which is brought forth to be affected. Noteworthy for Heidegger is the fact that both *poiein* and *pathein* are understood as *dynameis*, as causes and capacities. There is a mutuality and reciprocity involved here in the interrelationality of the change that occurs. Aristotle says that all force is also *paschein*, a being affected, a suffering (*Met.* 1046a 11–16). This is usually understood as opposite to a doing (*poiein*) or effecting. But Heidegger translates it as *Erleiden*, to tolerate, in the sense of not holding back, not resisting. Force as *pathein*, as letting happen, presupposes a lack, a not-having and not-being, a not-standing-against. Aristotle also speaks conversely of a *pathos* in natural beings that does not let itself be affected (an *a-pathein*), namely the power of *physis* to resist. In fact, Heidegger points out, often we first become aware of the phenomenon of force when something blocks the fulfillment of an occurrence. Resistance (*Widerständigkeit*) involves the being's holding itself there as being-against, as opposing the *dynamis* of change. The being resists that with which it interacts. Thus the being remains. Both coming to be and remaining in this active-passive sense of resisting are governed by *dynamis*. The fragile force of bearing and resisting is just as decisive as the force of doing, of producing. Human *techne* is the exchange of this twofold. The power of *techne* lies precisely in this relation and reference of *poiein* and *pathein* to each other. *Poiein* always implicates *pathein* and vice versa. *Dynamis* is this implication (*Einbezug*).[11] The primary way in which we experience force is opposition. What awakens us to *dynamis* is the *not coming through*, the not-being-able. Resistance invades power both among natural beings and in relationship to human *techne*. All coming to be occurs in relationship to that which one is not. In *Sein und Zeit*, the structure of equipmentality and the analysis of significance and involvement (*Bewandtnis*) parallel what Heidegger here discovers in Aristotle. The human interaction with *physis* in *techne* discloses in particular the *steresis*, the capacity to be deprived of being that belongs to the being, the *physis* of natural beings.

Heidegger's analysis of the *dynamis* that belongs to human being, which Aristotle calls *dynamis meta logou*, is also driven by his aim to rethink the relationship of *physis* and human knowing or *techne*. To have *logos* in a human way is to be empowered with and by *logos*. If we translate *logos* for a moment as language, then what we are discussing here is Aristotle's definition of the human being as the one who has the command of language, what Heidegger calls poetry, *poiesis*—the power to bring forth. Why is this *dynamis,* why is the poetic saying and gathering, fundamentally distinguished by Aristotle from those beings whose power or force is without *logos*? Is the *dynamis* of the rose not also a bringing forth? Yes, but in a different sense. The rose is not conversant (*Kundschaft*). It does not deliberate and choose and direct its power. It is not worldly. What particularly distinguishes human *dynamis* from force that is without *logos*, according to Aristotle, in that it is open to opposites, to contraries. So what makes *poiesis,* poetic saying, possible is that human being has the power that sees and relates to opposites, that is empowered to hold itself open to the opposition at the heart of being. To bring forth in a human way requires an awareness of what one is not—an awareness of what one needs to bring something about, an awareness of what is available, what is not suitable, what is contrary to and resists our working with it, and so on. It is awareness of contraries, and thereby of otherness, that opens up the neighborhood and world of involvements. This openness to contraries means that there is an inner division, a discordance and finitude that belongs to this force; finitude in the sense that it is awareness of the not, of what does not belong, of what is revealed as other than itself in its dealings. Heidegger says: "*Wo Kraft und Macht, da Endlichkeit.*"[12] It is mostly through our dealings with things, through *techne,* that we become aware of *dynamis logou,* of the *dynamis* that belongs to non-human beings. And we encounter these *dynameis* primarily in terms of a certain resistance, a not being able to bear the forces that encroach upon them. For Heidegger, art has the power to engage and rekindle the strife and divisiveness that belongs to *physis.*

In Heideggger's discussion in his chapter on *Metaphysics* Θ 3 of the Megarian argument against Aristotle's understanding of *physis*, it becomes clear that the failure to understand properly the relationship of *physis* and *techne* was already prevalent at the time of Aristotle and led to a metaphysics of presence and the disempowering of *physis.* The Megarians, as Eleatics, are unable to think of privation (*steresis*) and incapability as intrinsically and essentially belonging to the actuality of beings. What disturbs the Megarians is that cessation of activity, holding back and remaining in one's being, is a not-doing, a not-being actualized, which implies that the *not* can also be present. Moreover, when *dynamis* is present only in the process of an actualization of a *work,* then no separation of human power and the work that is being produced is possible. The *pragma,* the work as work, can be only to the extent that it is being worked on; its being belongs to the one who is working. The power to set beings to work, the power to engage *physis* in effect gets reduced to appropriation and the power of domination. The independence and self-reliance of beings is denied.

According to Heidegger, Aristotle offers this counterargument to the Megarians: "The actuality of the *dynamis* as such remains completely independent of the actuality of that of which it is capable, whether it has actually been produced, or is only half-finished, or even not yet begun."[13] Here, in my opinion, Heidegger has worked out the difference between the Aristotelian view of *techne* and the version of power as domination that is prevalent in modern technology. This philosophical moment of insight rescues the *dynamis meta logou*, human conversance, from its mere confinement to *techne* in the restricted sense of technicity. It also frees *techne* for a thoughtful relationship to *physis*.

Heidegger shows in his discussion of Aristotle's confrontation with the Megarians that *techne* is not primarily a transferring of itself onto something else, but a recoiling power in which what is set forth as a work is empowered to be on its own. But then *dynamis* is a double movement, a going forth that makes possible the production of things, and at the same time withdraws, letting the otherness of the things it produces come forth.

The Reciprocity of *Physis* and *Techne*

I would like to conclude with a brief reference to "The Origin of the Work of Art" where Heidegger takes up the question of the intractable interrelationship of *physis* and *techne* on a new level by shifting the ground of the discussion away from *techne* as a human activity and toward a discussion of the work that is produced. I will simply quote two passages. The first:

> If the work is indeed to bring thingness cogently into the open region, must it not then itself—and indeed before its own creation and for the sake of its creation—have been brought into relation with the things of earth, with nature? Someone who must have known all about this, Albrecht Dürer, did after all make the well-known remark: "For in the truth, art lies hidden within nature; he who can wrest it from her, has it." Wrest here means to draw out the rift and to draw the design of the rift. . . . But we at once raise the counterquestion: how can the rift be drawn out by the pen of the artist on the drawing board if it is not brought into the open by the creative projection as a rift, which is to say,

brought out beforehand as strife of measure and unmeasured? True, there lies hidden in nature a rift-design, a measure and a boundary, and tied to it, a capacity for bringing forth—that is, art. But it is equally certain that this art in nature becomes manifest only through the work, because it lies originally in the work.[14]

The work of art is the site for the disclosure of the strife between earth and world. What this means is made evident in the final passage with which I would like to close, namely Heidegger's discussion of the Greek temple:

> A building, a Greek temple, portrays nothing. It simply stands there in the middle of the rock-cleft valley. The building encloses the figure of the god, and in this concealment lets it stand out into the holy precinct through the open portico. By means of the temple, the god is present in the temple. This presence of the god is in itself the extension and delimitation of the precinct as a holy precinct. The temple and its precinct, however, do not fade away into the indefinite. It is the temple-work that first fits together and at the same time gathers around itself the unity of those paths and relations in which birth and death, disaster and blessing, victory and disgrace, endurance and decline acquire the shape of destiny for human being. The all-governing expanse of this open relational context is the world of this historical people. Only from and in this expanse does the nation first return to itself for the fulfillment of its vocation.
>
> Standing there, the building rests on the rocky ground. This resting of the work draws up out of the rock the obscurity of that rock's bulky yet spontaneous support. Standing there, the building holds its ground against the storm raging above it and so first makes the storm itself manifest in its violence. The luster and gleam of the stone, though itself apparently glowing only by the grace of the sun, first brings to radiance the light of the day, the breadth of the sky, the darkness of the night. The temple's firm towering makes visible the invisible space of air. The steadfastness of the work contrasts with the surge of the surf, and its own repose brings out the raging of the sea. Tree and grass, eagle and bull, snake and cricket first enter into their distinctive shapes and thus come to appear as what they are. The Greeks early called this emerging and rising in itself and in all things *physis*. It illuminates also that on which and in which man bases his dwelling. We call this ground the *earth*. What this word says is not to be associated with the idea of a

mass of matter deposited somewhere, or with the merely astronomical idea of a planet. Earth is that whence the arising brings back and shelters everything that arises as such. In the things that arise, earth occurs essentially as the sheltering agent.

The temple-work, standing there, opens up a world and at the same time sets this world back again on earth, which itself only thus emerges as native ground. But men and animals, plants and things, are never present and familiar as unchangeable objects, only to represent incidentally also a fitting environment for the temple, which one fine day is added to what is already there. We shall get closer to what *is*, rather, if we think of all this in reverse order, assuming of course that we have, to begin with, an eye for how differently everything then faces us. Mere reversing, done for its own sake, reveals nothing.[15]

Notes

1. Martin Heidegger, *Beiträge zur Philosophie (Vom Ereignis),* ed. Friedrich von Hermann (Frankfurt am Main: V. Klostermann, 1989), 277–78.

2. Martin Heidegger, *Beiträge zur Philosophie,* 115.

3. Martin Heidegger, "Vom Wesen und Begriff der *Physis,*" in *Wegmarken* (Frankfurt am Main: V. Klostermann, 1967), 309.

4. Martin Heidegger, "Der Ursprung des Kunstwerkes," in *Holzwege* (Frankfurt am Main: V. Klostermann, 1972), 48; "The Origin of the Work of Art," in *Basic Writings,* ed. D. Krell (New York: Harper and Row, 1993), 184.

5. Martin Heidegger, *Gesamtausgabe 19, Platon: Sophistes* (Frankfurt am Main: V. Klostermann, 1992).

6. Martin Heidegger, "Bauen Wohnen Denken," in *Vorträge und Aufsätze* (Tübingen: Neske Verlag, 1954), 154; "Building Dwelling Thinking," in *Basic Writings,* 361.

7. Heidegger, "Der Ursprung des Kunstwerkes," 48; "The Origin of the Work of Art," 184.

8. Heidegger, "Der Ursprung des Kunstwerkes," 41; "The Origin of the Work of Art," 178.

9. Heidegger, *Beiträge zur Philosophie,* 190.

10. Heidegger, "Vom Wesen und Begriff der *Physis,*" 322.

11. Martin Heidegger, *Gesamtausgabe 33, Aristoteles,* Metaphysik Θ *1–3: Von Wesen und Wirklichkeit der Kraft* (Frankfurt am Main: V. Klostermann, 1981), 89.

12. Martin Heidegger, *Aristoteles,* Metaphysik Θ *1–3,* 158.

13. Ibid., 187.

14. Heidegger, "Der Ursprung des Kunstwerkes," 58.

15. Ibid., 30–31.

4   Translating *Innigkeit:* The Belonging Together of the Strange

Peter Warnek

The concept of politics rarely announces itself without some sort of adherence of the State to the family, without what we will call a *schematic* of filiation: stock, genus or species, sex (*Geschlecht*), blood, birth, nature, nation—autochthonal or not, tellurian or not. This is once again the abyssal question of the physis, the question of being, the question of what appears in birth, in opening up, in nurturing or growing, in producing by being produced. Is that not life? That is how life is thought to reach recognition.

Jacques Derrida

Greece will have been, for Hölderlin, this inimitable. Not from an excess of grandeur—but from a lack of proper being. It will have been, therefore, this vertiginous threat: a people, a culture, constantly showing itself as inaccessible to itself. The tragic as such, if it is true that the tragic begins with the ruin of the imitable and the disappearance of models.

Philippe Lacoue-Labarthe

A genuine repetition and retrieval erupts only from an originary transformation.

Martin Heidegger

In the short text that is included as an appendix to the *Gesamtausgabe* printing of his *Erläuterungen zu Hölderlins Dichtung* and that bears the title "Prologue to a Reading of Hölderlin's Poems,"[1] Heidegger speaks of Hölderlin's poetry as a destiny which awaits the response of mortals, which awaits its *Entsprechung*, a correspondence or a reception that is also a responsive speaking. The possibility of such a receptive speaking by mortals in response to Hölderlin's poetic word, a possible speaking that has yet to come, would arise only in the experience of the flight or departure of the gods, the flight or departure that Hölderlin's poetry both announces and suffers. But Hölderlin's poetic word, according to Heidegger, says that the absent gods still protect the mortals while they are not yet able to dwell in the nearness of the gods. And this not being able to dwell in the nearness of the gods means that these mortals still lack a home. As an awakening to the absence of gods, Hölderlin's poetry is thus also an awakening to the lack of the home, to *the lack of proper being for mortal human life,* an insistence upon a *tragic* estrangement or alienation at the heart of that life. And although Heidegger suggests that coming to dwell in the nearness of the gods would bring about "a turning in the present world condition [*eine Wende des gegenwärtigen Weltzustandes*]" (GA4, 195), his reading presents itself as neither programmatic nor productive. It does not promise to bring about such a transformation, does not even depict or describe the transformation, but seeks only to take the first step toward the correspondence, as a receptive responsive speaking. Here Heidegger presents the task of a reading of Hölderlin only as a *preparation* for something that has yet to come, an opening to the future, a world transformation that remains unimaginable, unforeseeable. But at first what is at issue is simply becoming receptive to the poetic word in a way that is appropriate to it. Such reception would already have to *repeat* the poetic word, but to repeat it in a way that is also responsive to it. Accordingly, Heidegger asks us to listen to several guiding words taken from Hölderlin's poems. The first of such guiding words, which Heidegger offers here in this way, reads: "*Alles ist innig.*"[2]

This chapter can be understood simply as an attempt at the translation of this *Leitwort,* or guiding word. It is dedicated to revealing such a translation as a task of repetition, to opening up to what is at stake in this task. This requires in one sense only being able to hear the word itself, to listen to what it says in its own singular way—so that, as Heidegger proclaims more than once, we might be translated in the translation, *transposed* to another shore, transferred to another place.

In the *Ister* lectures (1942), Heidegger speaks of translation as nothing other than interpretation itself. Not only is every translation already an interpretation, but interpretation itself is always already caught up in an originary translation, even when it only moves within one and the same language (GA54, 75/62). And although Heidegger wants to assert precisely that translation does not consist first of all in the movement from one language to another—from the *Fremdsprache* to the *Muttersprache,* for example—he nevertheless makes this assertion in the context of addressing what are taken to be controversial translations into German of Greek words, such as *aletheia* or *to deinon.* What is at issue in such translations is not simply the experiences these words should convey, but rather the world itself for which these words and the experiences opened up by them play a constituting role. When *aletheia* is rendered as *Unverborgenheit* or *to deinon* as *das Unheimliche,* by no means can it be said that this does not already effect an interpretive transformation, that such translation does not already amount to an interpretation. But it is also the case that nothing in itself has been made clear simply in this operation, which simply connects one word to another, through a form of transcription. What appears as the words of one's native tongue, here as *Unverborgenheit* and as *das Unheimliche*—but also perhaps as "unconcealment" and as "the uncanny"—are themselves words that for their part still call for translation or interpretation. And yet, it is also the case that the encounter with the foreign word can in a new way put into question what is to be said with the words of one's own language.

Heidegger thus says provocatively that translation "concerns the relation of human beings to the essence of the word and the worthiness of language. Tell me what you think of translation and I will tell you who you are" (GA53, 76/63). Who we are, in other words, can be discovered or discerned in our way of translating, in our interpretation of translation, even, therefore, in our translation of translation, since in translation our very relation to language comes to be determined; we are who we are by virtue of how we relate to what is opened up in the word, but such an opening is also always originally the movement of translation. In the lectures on Parmenides (1942–43), in the semester that follows the *Ister* lectures, Heidegger speaks of translating as the movement of one's native language into its own proper word, the translation, then, of the word into itself. Translation becomes in an original sense simply how one comes to one's words, the very movement of the word, speaking as such. "To speak and to say is in itself a translation [*Sprechen und Sagen ist in sich ein Übersetzen*]. . . . In every conversation and in every conversation with oneself an original translation prevails [*In jedem Gespräch und Selbstgespräch waltet ein ursprüngliches Übersetzen*]" (GA54, 17/12). In this context one might recall how Plato's Socrates in the *Theaetetus* tells us that thinking must also be thought as a movement caught up in difference, must be thought namely as a way of dialogue, returned to a *dialogical* movement: *dianoeisthai* is said to be nothing other than a kind of *dialegesthai,* a *logos* that life (or soul) goes through by itself before itself.[3] Socrates in this Platonic dialogue thus *translates* thinking into a twofold movement, returns it to dialogue, by exposing it as already dialogical, still as a self-relation but one that is bound to the *logos,* and thus protracted, already ahead of itself in its movement. Thinking, taken in this Socratic way, as dialogue, is an ecstatic movement, a dispossession that must rupture the simple identity of the self, the self as merely self-same. And thus the task of self-knowledge, as it is imposed upon human life by the inscriptions at Delphi, would also be a task of dialogue, bound to the necessity of the *deuteros plous* as Socrates speaks of that necessity in the *Phaedo.* The task of self-knowledge, imposed by the god, already exposes one's self-relation to a *having become other* in the movement that follows and attends to the disclosive *logos.* And yet, what is decisive is that Heidegger returns this sense of *Gespräch* or *Selbstgespräch* to a *translating* movement: the movement of thinking would be not only dialogical but already a matter of translation, but—one must add—only if translation is also then thought as the dialogical movement of thinking's own expropriation, the movement that transforms what is taken as already proper, as already one's own. Thus, translation can be said to be the originary movement of language only if translation first allows itself to encounter the translating power of the word, where the translation becomes the way in which the word is able to appropriate us to itself as something still strange and foreign.

In this context, Heidegger raises the paradox of translation as an originary repetition, as the possibility of the word being received *once more and yet as if for the first time.* Still in the lectures on Parmenides, he says:

> The poetry of the poet, the treatise of the thinker stand within their own proper, unique and singular word [*in ihrem eigenen, einmaligen, einzigen Wort*]. They compel us again and again [*immer wieder*] to take this word in such a way that we hear it for the first time [*als hörten wir es zum ersten Mal*]. These first words, these beginnings of the word [*diese Erstlinge des Wortes*] transpose us each time to a new shore. The so-called translation [*Übersetzen*] and transcription always only follows the transposing [*Übersetzen*] of our whole essence into the realm of a transformed truth. Only when we are already appropriated over into this transposing, are we in the care of the word. (GA54, 18/12)

Heidegger can insist, precisely on the basis of this strange sense of repetition—repetition as original speaking, speaking as if for the first time—that the more insidious difficulty arises when it comes to the translation of one's own language into itself, when it comes to letting the word say what it already has to say. What is difficult here has to do with the fact that one has *already* appropriated one's own language and thus believes that one *already* understands what is being said:

> But the more difficult task is always the translation of one's own language into its ownmost word. That is why, for example, the translation of the German thinker into the German language is especially difficult—because there reigns here the tenacious prejudice to the effect that we who speak German would understand the German word without further ado, since it belongs, after all, to our own language, whereas, on the contrary, to translate a Greek word we must in the first place learn that foreign tongue. (GA54, 18/13)

According to this account, German would remain the most difficult language of all precisely and first of all for the Germans themselves. Heidegger is saying—in a way that repeats a decisive statement made by Hölderlin—that what is one's own must be *learned* no less than the foreign, since what is one's own in this sense still calls for its translation. The sense of the proper is exposed in this way to a temporality, as it becomes only a kind of promise. The proper as such has *no presence* except by virtue of its future and absence, as it continually calls for its translation into itself, and as it remains withheld therefore in such a call. But learning in this sense can no longer be regarded then simply as the act of appropriation, as the acquisition of the meaning of the word that would then be available for deployment by the acting subject. Instead, learning in this sense must be thought as the ecstatic movement through which one allows oneself to be appropriated by the word, even the word of one's own language, as still strange or foreign. Encountering this need for translation, therefore, as Heidegger speaks of it, already transforms the possible sense of the proper, already must alter the way in which it is possible to think one's ownmost being, since encountering what is properly one's own now demands the movement into what is most strange, the strange as it is somehow still bound to the proper.

What is *most difficult* is precisely this decisive reversal in which the proper as such finds itself displaced, expropriated *into itself* as strange. This, however, should not be mistaken for the utter abandonment of the proper, should not be confused with the simple privileging of the strange, whereby, through a mere inversion, the strange would now be given a priority over the proper. Instead, through this decisive reversal, the proper as such appears itself as the most strange, as if, therefore, it lacked propriety. One might be tempted to say that translation only releases both the strange and the proper to themselves or to each other, but this would then be to speak as if the strange as strange can have a proper being; it would be therefore to refuse the strange as such, to refuse the estranging movement of translation, the very difference enacted by translation. How, then, to speak of the strange *as such*, when the strange has to be thought as the rupturing of the very sense of the "as such," and thus of the strange *as proper*?

It is in this sense that I wish to insist that the difficulty of thinking and saying *Innigkeit* poses a task of translation; it is this very difficulty of translation that is at issue in the word itself. In the short text with which I began, found at the end of the *Erläuterungen* as an appendix, Heidegger already offers a translation of the word, already translates it into itself with a little phrase that for its part also calls for translation: *das Zusammengehören des Fremden*. After reading the guiding word, "*Alles ist innig*," Heidegger then states:

> This wants to say: one thing is appropriated into the other, assimilated by the other, owned over to it, but in such a way that the one remains in what is its own, even thereby first finds itself, first becomes itself: gods and humans, earth and sky. The *Innigkeit* means no fusion and extinguishing of differences. *Innigkeit* names *das Zusammengehören des Fremden* the belonging together of the strange, the holding sway of the estranging, the claim or address of diffidence. (GA4, 196)[4]

Innigkeit names precisely the belonging together of the strange. We could say: the being together in such a strange belonging, the rightful or proper being together of what does not *belong*, does not belong *together*, the belonging together, then, of what does *not* belong together.

The word *Innigkeit*, which Heidegger translates into itself with the little phrase *das Zusammengehören des Fremden*, the belonging together of the strange, is thus itself already a stranger to itself, inaccessible to itself in this very translation, as if it lacked all propriety. Precisely for this reason, the word *Innigkeit* continues to call for translation. It thus cannot be said that the goal of the translation of this word consists simply in rendering the word familiar or comprehensible. The goal of the translation cannot consist in rendering clear the meaning of the word because the saying power of the word has to do with the way in which obscurity can become manifest, precisely *as obscure*. The word says or reveals a necessary concealment in the becoming manifest of things. The translation has as its task, then, only to translate the word into such concealment, into its ownmost strangeness, into the strangeness most proper to it, so as to let that strangeness be said in the word, to let the word say what it already has to say.

In his first lecture course on Hölderlin, Heidegger speaks of *Innigkeit* precisely as *Geheimnis*. *Innigkeit*, he says,

> is the *Geheimnis* belonging to being. What emerges purely is never only inexplicable from a certain point of view, as some one mode of being, but remains enigmatic through and through. *Innigkeit* does not have the property of a *Geheimnis*, because it remains impervious and inaccessible; but rather it is in itself present as *Geheimnis*. There is *Geheimnis* only where *Innigkeit* prevails. If, however, this *Geheimnis* is named and said in this way, then thereby the *Geheimnis* does become manifest. The unmasking of its manifestness is precisely the not wanting to make clear; even more, it is the understanding of the manifestness as the self-concealing concealment. Making *Geheimnis* understandable is indeed an uncovering, but this may be carried out only in song, in poetizing. (GA39, 250)[5]

Innigkeit, as it names this strange belonging together of all things in a concealment, also has to be heard as the tragic poetizing of human life, as a way of belonging in the loss or lack of the home, belonging in estrangement. What is uncanny or *unheimlich* about human life can be said to be that its way of belonging remains concealed from it, that it belongs only in such concealment. Such concealment can become manifest only in and through the poetic word. Heidegger calls it the not being at home within the home.[6] What Heidegger calls here the *Geheimnis* is, therefore, not simply the "mystery" of being, but has to be thought also as the way in which human dwelling is *grounded* in a hiddenness, or, said otherwise, the way in which the human world belongs to the earth. *Geheimnis* is thus the concealing that also grounds the home, the concealing as a sheltering. The poetizing of *Innigkeit* as the hiddenness that belongs to being brings to word the way in which the human world belongs to the earth precisely in a concealing. The earth thus can be called the *place* of the home, if place can be taken in the sense of what is first of all *receptive* to something, allowing it to be, but withdrawing in such allowing, in the way that Timaeus's *Khora* can be said to be an utterly receptive place. Reading Hölderlin, Heidegger says that the home is the "power of the earth." "In such a home, the human first experiences itself as belonging to the earth" (GA39, 88). The home in this sense, as such a belonging, enables, to an extent, a human mastery over things. And such mastery and familiarity can be thought as the very constituting of the world. But the enabling sheltering of the earth can also mean the destruction of a world, the demise or undoing of all human mastery. The poetizing of the *Innigkeit* of human life as *unheimlich* thus reveals what can be called the tragic relation between earth and world. In the essay "Hölderlin and the Essence of Poetry," Heidegger speaks of *Innigkeit* as the way of the belonging itself that holds world and earth together, the belonging itself between the human world and the earth, to which that world belongs but which it does not master.

> To what does the human attest? Its belonging to the earth. This belonging consists in the fact that the human is the inheritor, the one who learns all things. All things, however, stand in conflict. What holds things apart in conflict and thereby at the same time keeps them together Hölderlin names "*Innigkeit*." The attestation of the belonging to this *Innigkeit* transpires through the making of a world, through both its upsurge and its destruction and downfall. (GA4, 36)

My strategy here is to begin by reading and repeating, no doubt selectively, those passages where Heidegger undertakes to interpret this Hölderlinian word, a word that Derrida, without any sign of hesitation, wants to think as "intimacy" or "interiority."[7] Heidegger would have to insist that it matters little whether the word, which I am leaving here to resound in the German, is heard as the word of a foreign tongue, because the word—which can be heard already to speak of the foreign or strange—preserves its own strangeness simply in its being said, in its being allowed to say what it has to say. Thus, before any single or definitive translation could be insisted upon—in German, in Greek, in English, or in any other language—it would first be necessary to attend to the diverse and multiple ways in which this word, which Heidegger says is one of Hölderlin's "central words" or "basic words" (GA39, 117, 249), comes into play in both Heidegger's and Hölderlin's texts. Yet it cannot be said that the Derridian translation is simply *wrong*. But by being correct or proper it also passes by precisely the difficulty at issue in the word. In making use of the word, Derrida does not make explicit how this word, *which names translation*, still calls for translation. Heidegger states explicitly that *Innigkeit* is not to be taken to mean "interiority" (*Innerlichkeit*) (GA39, 117). *Innigkeit* names nothing romantic or sentimental, but rather the "fundamental tone" or mood, the

Grundstimmung of the poetizing. The word itself, even for one who never hears it as the word of a foreign tongue, thus still calls for the translation that would only preserve the power of the word itself to say the strange, to let the strange become manifest as such. But the translation, therefore, only has to open up and to preserve the translating power of the word itself, its power both to name and to enact the movement into the strange, the movement through the strange or foreign.

The task of translating *Innigkeit* thus demands the translation of the movement of translation itself, the thought of the *difference* that joins all things together. The translation that Heidegger offers with this phrase, "the belonging together of the strange," already recoils on itself, in a certain doubling, as what is said in it cannot be divorced from the saying itself, from its way of being said. The word and the phrase that here is offered as its translation both speak of the strange in a way that is strange, in a way appropriate to the strange. The translation thus has to be regarded as both word and deed, as it enacts or performs what it says, bringing together in a strangeness what belongs together but what also, precisely by virtue of being strange, does not belong. In this most simple but difficult sense, the translation of *Innigkeit* as the belonging together of the strange already says the difficulty of thinking and saying this word, the difficulty of thinking and saying the belonging together of the strange. The strange, therefore, has to be thought neither as what belongs nor simply as what does not belong; the strange is rather strange precisely in the belonging together that would preserve the strange, the strange as strange. Or, said otherwise, what is most strange *is* simply the belonging together itself, because here it is a matter of the belonging together of the strange as such. *Innigkeit* would only say this belonging together of the strange, would only say the translation into the strange as what is most proper, as the way in which the proper first appears or finds itself.

Innigkeit, according to Heidegger, does not simply name all things, but names the granting of things in their discrete difference and oppositional relation, the difference as it holds all things together. This sense of the conflicted unity of the all also indicates, therefore, what is dangerous about *naming. Innigkeit* is a name for unity because it is also a name for the unifying character of poetic naming. This is especially apparent in the first lecture course from 1934–35. "The originally unitary holding together of the greatest oppositional conflict is what Hölderlin names especially in his later period with one of his own words: *Innigkeit*" (GA39, 117). "What unifies originally and thereby singularly is that ruling unity, which Hölderlin, if he speaks of it, names with the word *Innigkeit*" (GA39, 249). "What Hölderlin names with this newly said word is named in a poetic naming: better, it is given the name that it is. The *Innigkeit* is that originary unity of the polemical powers of what emerges in itself" (GA39, 250). As the name for the difference or movement of translation, the movement into the strange, *Innigkeit* also names unity.

The first word that is supposed to guide us in our reading and hearing of Hölderlin, "*Alles ist innig,*" thus can be heard as a repetition or translation of the violent *hen* of Heraclitus, the *one* that already says *panta,* but also therefore of the *logos* that, if we listen to it, says with us, *hen panta.*[8] Heidegger will state that *Innigkeit* needs to be thought as the *harmony* that remains hidden in the *polemos* of Heraclitean thought, the war or conflict that steers all and yet, at the same time, holds all together in the tension of violent opposition. *Innigkeit,* says Heidegger, first allows us to encounter such Heraclitean *polemos.*

> The poet thinks and poetizes oriented toward this *harmonie organou* when he says the word *Innigkeit* and *innig.* . . . The opening of the proper oppositional conflict opens the harmony, which means: places the conflicting powers each within their limits. . . . From here we first grasp that word . . . a singular word of Heraclitus: conflict (*polemos*) is the father of all things. (GA39, 124–25)

If *Innigkeit* names the difference that grants the unity of all things, the difference that grants what is, in the way that the sky and earth belong together, or in the way that the very sense of the human already presupposes a monstrous coupling with the divine, however obscurely, such poetic naming also only occurs in a being claimed by this difference that grants all things. Such being claimed, which can be heard as a translation of *thaumazein* of the Greek experience of wonder, Heidegger calls *die Scheu* or *der Anspruch der Scheu,* the address, claim or appeal of diffidence, timidity, and hesitation. Thus, the community or kinship of all things, as the *Innigkeit* that preserves the strange, which is the holding sway of estranging, holds things both apart and together. In the essay "Language," Heidegger speaks of the *Innigkeit* of world and things, as the jointure of things that allows neither separation nor confusion: "The *Innigkeit* of world and thing is no conglomeration. *Innigkeit* prevails only where what is *innig,* world and thing, purely split themselves apart and remain sundered" (*Unterwegs zur Sprache* [*US*], 24). But then also: "The *Innigkeit* of the difference is the unifying of *diaphora,* the pervasive accord which grants" (*US*, 25). A similar statement is found in the essay "On the Origin of the Work of Art": "Conflict (*Streit*) is no tearing as the tearing apart in a mere cleaving, rather conflict is the *Innigkeit* of the belonging to themselves of what is in conflict."[9]

At this point it is now possible to make explicit a more general concern, which has to do first of all with the way in which the saying power of words can be thought and experienced as the possibility of transformation in human life, as the transformation of that life. How does a receptive responsive speaking of the poetic word, as Heidegger introduces it, as *Entsprechung*, as it would repeat and listen to what the word says, expose us to an occurrence that lies beyond the powers of human agency, of our own calculation and making (*menschliches Rechnen und Machen*) (GA4, 195)? How does such a receptive responsive speaking promise, then, to interrupt the machination or *Machenschaft* of contemporary life, the technological imperative that is mobilizing the earth, transforming it into a planetary resource solely for the discharge of power? But this concern, which I am raising through the voice of Heidegger, can also be formulated through another and perhaps more ancient idiom: what limits the way in which words or *logoi* are able (or not able) to bring about, for better or worse, a change in our ethos, understood as our way of dwelling on the earth, our way of dwelling between earth and sky?

Now while I take up this question through Heidegger's reading of Hölderlin and *Innigkeit*, I believe it is also necessary to bring these reflections into the context of Greek philosophy and poetry, or to expose, rather, how it is that they already unfold within such a context. It should be possible for the thinking and saying of *Innigkeit*, as it occurs in Heidegger's engagement with Hölderlin, to be brought to bear upon an interpretation of friendship and community in the texts of Greek philosophy. Here I can make only the most preliminary of beginnings by gesturing toward an interpretation of the place of friendship in the tradition of Greek philosophy and the way in which this interpretation might be further developed so as to help with this task of translating *Innigkeit*. At the same time, it should be recognized that the task of this translation already invites us to think once again about the role of the mythic or poetic word in the formation of human community, as it also invites us to think more originally about the relation between philosophy and poetry.

The question of *Innigkeit*, as a task of translation, thus already returns us in a new way to one of the most basic matters at issue in Greek philosophy and poetry.[10] The difficulty of thinking and saying the belonging together of the strange, as it names the being together of gods and mortals and of earth and sky, can also be heard as an encounter, or perhaps even as a conversation between thinking and poetizing, between *Denken* and *Dichten*, because what is at issue here is simply the possibility of opening up the transformative power of a word. *Innigkeit* can thus be heard to name also "a certain ancient difference," spoken of by Socrates near the end of the *Republic*, that prevails between philosophy and poetry, the *palaia men tis diaphora philosophias te kai poietikes* (*Rep.* 607b). It can be said that this ancient difference shows itself to be sustained in a certain *Innigkeit*, the *diaphora* itself as the strange belonging together of thinking and saying, but also, perhaps, of *logos* and *mythos*. Let me say, however, from the very beginning, that by attending to what might be called the old *Innigkeit* between philosophy and poetry, what also becomes manifest is precisely the *tragic* character of human life, its way of belonging to nature in its own estrangement from nature, being but without a proper place, being most out of place, *atopotatos* or even *to deinon* as *das Unheimliche*, being without home. It cannot be disputed that the question of the possible natural good of human life, its way of belonging or not belonging, is at the center of every Platonic dialogue, especially the *Republic*. The so-called Platonic critique of the poetic tradition in fact, if one can speak of such a thing, has to be understood precisely as it arises out of the concern with the way in which the poetic tradition has failed to respond to this question of the human good as it is grounded in a certain cryptic relation to nature or the divine. But one should not overlook how one also finds in the Platonic dialogues the question posed, in a variety of ways, that concerns the difficulty that Heidegger calls *Entsprechung*. At issue in this question is the way in which words—things said or written—continue to call for an original repetition. The dangers of such an original repetition are made thematic in the concern over the limits of a philosophical writing (as it is addressed in the *Phaedrus*, for example), but also in the way in which Plato's Socrates again and again repeats and engages the speeches and stories of the "wise," including those of the poets. At issue here, in other words, is the question concerning how it is possible to speak for the dead, or of how the dead continue to speak through us, the question concerning what we owe the dead, the question even, therefore, of the *Innigkeit* between life and death.

If *Innigkeit* speaks of a kind of community or kinship, such kinship no doubt also remains irreducible to the political as such. What is at issue here can be said to be rather the kinship of nature as it exceeds or precedes every political boundary. Such *Innigkeit*, as much as it speaks of the harmonious but polemical nature of Empedocles and Heraclitus, also repeats the kinship of nature of which Socrates speaks in the Meno (81d), the kinship that would ground the movement of the *logos* as a recollection, a movement that is always oriented toward things as they are *already* manifest, as they already belong together. But let me propose further, no doubt with certain risks, that the poetic word that speaks of all things in a certain *Innigkeit* has to do with such kinship precisely as it would also ground human community, and in a way that would open that community, not merely to the "more than human," but to itself as more than human. What is at issue, therefore, in the *Innigkeit* proper to human life is the way in which that life belongs ecstatically to the nature both that it is and that exceeds it.

Here we are given to think *ta panta,* or *the all* that, according to the Platonic text, is what friends are said to have in common, the sense of the common, therefore, that would give rise to the very possibility of the friend, the shared having in terms of which the friend might first become a friend.[11] Above all, in the *Republic,* the enigmatic saying that "friends have all things in common" comes to be thematically addressed as the most basic difficulty to be resolved in the making of the best city, the city to be produced in the *logos.* The possibility of community in human life presents, in other words, something that cannot be produced or contained through human strategy and design. There is no *techne* that would have mastery over this sense of what we have in common, of what binds us together, and gives us our proper place, just as there is no craft of justice, no *production* that leads to the good. It should be recalled how this difficulty of what is common, of what grounds community, as it calls for a new beginning, launches the three waves that lead finally to the greatest paradox and scandal of the entire dialogue, namely the assertion that the philosophers should rule, that there must be a reconciliation between the political and the philosophical. The attempt is thus made in the *Republic*—no doubt with questionable success—to demonstrate how such a philosophical rule over human affairs would be not only what is best for human life, but also something possible, even if exceedingly difficult, standing at the very limits of the possible, verging even on impossibility. And yet, what is decisive here is that such a rule by philosophy can be distinguished only by the way in which it promises to open up the community of human life to what exceeds it, to open such life to the ecstatic nature that it both is and yet never masters. A reconciliation between the political and the philosophical would amount to nothing less than a reconciliation between the human and the natural, because only the philosopher can promise to fulfill the excessive friendship that would be grounded in the community of all things, in the *Innigkeit* of all things. One might thus venture to say that the philosophical task of Socrates, as it arises in response to the Delphic inscriptions, thus proves to be a sustained engagement with the tragic insight that is announced in the wisdom of Silenus and that arguably comes to be repeated in some form in every Greek story. The political problem at the center of the *Republic* would thus be bound to the estrangement of human life from nature—nature within nature at odds with nature—an estrangement that must be regarded therefore no less as a form of monstrosity or self-estrangement than as a decisive manifestation of the task of self-knowledge. If the possibility of justice can be reformulated in this way, as a possibility of friendship—even if such friendship is first of all only a possible friendship with oneself—this possibility of justice is no less a matter of one's relation to the nature that one is. The question of such friendship thus opens onto the question of the place of human life within the whole or all that exceeds the walls of the city. From this perspective, the question posed in the Socratic task of self-knowledge is not simply a regional question that can be confined to matters of ethics and politics, but is also a more radical posing of the original philosophical question concerning *physis*. The enigmatic possibility of friendship, then, would have to be grounded in the most cryptic of all friendships, the friendship of all things. To follow Heraclitus, where it is wise to agree, one many, we must also say that all of nature is in kinship, even if, at the same time, nature *loves* to hide.

When Heidegger first comes to take up the question of poetizing he does so in a certain turn away from what can be called the scientific (and therefore non-mythical and non-poetic) determination of the *logos*. But this does not lead him to oppose the philosophical *logos* to poetry, does not lead him to oppose philosophy and poetry. Rather, beginning in 1931 at least,[12] the *logos* itself will be returned to and grounded in an interpretation of poetizing as the most original moment of language. In the lecture course on Aristotle's *Metaphysics*, which is delivered three years before the beginning of his most overt engagement with the question of the artwork and poetry, Heidegger already articulates the sense of poetizing, or *Dichtung*, that will become decisive for him. Aristotle's basic determination of the human being, as the *zoon logon echon*, is thought in terms of speech, *Rede*, but, remarkably, "taken in the original sense of speaking and expressing oneself about the world and to the world in poetizing [*Sichaus-*

sprechen über die Welt und zu der Welt in der Dichtung]" (GA33, 129). Language in this sense is not primarily a means of expression and communication, and emphatically not simply what the human "has" in its possession. The sense of the *logos*, as it is in play in both Plato and Aristotle, must, according to Heidegger, be thought as:

> Being in the power of language. . . . Language as that within which the manifestness and conversance of the world can break open at all and be. Hence language is original and proper in *Dichtung*, *Dichtung* not taken as the occupation of writers but as the calling up of the world in the calling forth of the god in *Dichtung*. (GA33, 128)

Poetizing, prior to the poetic work of the poet, prior to the activity of writing, is thought here as the originary *logos*, as the language within which the world emerges, breaks open. The quote is remarkable in the way in which it anticipates the later engagement with Hölderlin, and not simply because of the reference to the divine. What is most remarkable here is the way in which the philosophical determination of the *logos* is thought to be grounded in poetizing.

In the first lecture Heidegger delivers on Hölderlin (1934–35), for example, the dialogical discourse of Hölderlin's *Hyperion* will be cited in order to develop a similar determination of poetizing or *Dichtung*. Again the *logos* of philosophy is returned to a more original moment found in poetry. The Greeks "would never have been a philosophical people without poetizing." Speaking in a way that repeats Schelling's sense of the origin and destination of philosophy, Heidegger says: "Poetizing . . . is the beginning and end of this science [i.e., philosophy]" (GA39, 21). For both Schelling and Heidegger, philosophy is to return to the ocean of poetry from which it came.[13]

And yet, if poetizing is offered here as a translation of *Dichtung*, it should be remembered how Heidegger repeatedly seeks to distinguish rigorously what is said in and with this word from what is said otherwise with the word *Poesie*. *Dichtung*, Heidegger tells us in "On the Origin of the Work of Art," names what is distinctive about art as such; all art has its "essence" in poetizing, which is to say that poetizing as such pertains to "the setting into work of the truth" (*das ins Werk setzen der Wahrheit*). Heidegger's displacement of the metaphysical determination of the truth, a displacement that he thinks and experiences in the move from the essence of truth to the truth of essence, allows him to reconfigure the traditional opposition between truth and poetizing: truth arises not as a moment of correspondence or correctness with what is, but instead in an originary conflict and opposition of world and earth, an originary conflict that Heidegger thinks as and in *Innigkeit.* In this sense, the truth of Hölderlin's poetry stands outside not simply metaphysics, but also outside the essential realm of Western art, insofar as art and metaphysics hang together, insofar as both are determined by Platonism and the opposition between the sensible and the intelligible. Poetizing, as *Dichtung,* thus remains irreducible to a making within the sensible through a mimetic relation to a transcendent ideal.

And yet, whereas *Poesie* in this regard ought therefore to be reserved for only one way in which the work of art happens, as such a movement of truth, Heidegger will nevertheless also find it necessary to grant to language, and therefore to the work that is language (*das Sprachwerk*), an exceptional and privileged position within art as a whole. Such a claim, Heidegger tells us, is grounded in the way in which language first of all brings beings into the open. Language, far from being reducible to mere "communication" (*Mitteilung*), is the original movement of being becoming manifest.[14] Thus, in the essay "Hölderlin and the Essence of Poetry," Heidegger will state that the essence of language is to be understood from out of the essence of poetizing; poetizing first makes language possible (GA4, 43). But this means nevertheless that such an original poetizing of language is also encountered in a privileged way in the work of poetry.

How, then, according to Heidegger, is philosophy (or thinking) to encounter the poetizing work of the poet, to gain access to that work, to experience it? What is to happen in the encounter with the work? How might that encounter open up the poetizing from out of itself, in a way proper to the poetizing, being responsive to it, being responsive precisely to what is opened up in the poetizing? And why does poetizing present just this difficulty, such that it does call for the response of those who encounter it, insisting thereby that the question of an interpretive responsibility be taken up and addressed in an explicit way? Does the poetizing need such response? How is the strangeness of the poetizing, what is peculiar or proper to it, to be granted and preserved in its own right in this way, allowed to be itself, but in such a manner that it still might speak to us, and precisely in its own way, namely from out of its strangeness and foreignness?

In the foreword to the fourth edition of his *Erläuterungen,* Heidegger tells us that these "explications" belong to the "historically singular" conversation or dialogue of a thinking with a poetizing (*das Gespräch eines Denkens mit einem Dichten*). Perhaps a certain priority is given here precisely to the *thinking* character of this singular conversation. Its historical singularity (*geschichtliche Einzigkeit*) cannot be demonstrated through any historiography of literature, but can only be made evident in the movement of the thinking encounter itself, through the thinking conversation (*durch das denkende Gespräch*).[15] As a thinking conversation, however, it remains both a thinking and a speaking, thinking as a dialogical saying, *dianoeisthai* as *dialegesthai*.

Heidegger will leave open at this point what such explications might be able to accomplish, whether in the end they, like all such commentary, must be regarded as only snowfall on a bell, which silently puts the bell out of tune. But all such commentary, along with what is attempted in that commentary, must each time confront its own destruction, must shatter (*sich zerbrechen*), so that what is purely poetized in the poem might come forth a bit more clearly (*damit das im Gedicht rein Gedichtete um einiges klarer dastehe*). Precisely for the sake of what is poetized, the commentary must allow itself to become superfluous. The last but most difficult step to be taken by every interpretation (*Auslegung*) is to disappear with its commentary before the pure presencing (*Dastehen*) of the poem, so that the poem comes to stand under its own proper law (*das dann im eigenen Gesetz stehende Gedicht*) (GA4, 8). This suggests, however, not at all that the commentary is a hindrance or an obstacle to accessing the poetry, but rather something much more subtle, that such commentary, precisely in and through its own destruction, is the indispensable way to the poetry and what it poetizes. The interpretation must be overcome, and this has to be achieved through the thinking conversation itself.

The 1934–35 lecture begins likewise with the worry over the dangers and difficulties of the encounter with Hölderlin's work. What could it mean to undertake to speak about poetizing, about *Dichtung*, when whatever a poem might have to say will be said best by the poem itself? Will the poetizing not be destroyed through the crude blathering (*Zerreden*) of the lecturer? Still more dubious and dangerous is the prospect that philosophy, in the attempt to "explain" the poetizing, to make it clear, will seek to bring that poetizing under the frigid audacity (*kalte Kühnheit*) of its conceptual language, thereby violently transposing the poetic work into doctrines and propositions, attempting to assemble a philosophical system from out of the poetizing (GA39, 5–6). Here, again, Heidegger will respond to this difficulty by developing his encounter with Hölderlin in terms of the relation between thinking and poetizing. Precisely because Hölderlin's poetizing is itself already a thinking, Hölderlin, more so than any poet, demands that his poetizing be subdued thinkingly, that it undergo its overcoming through thinking, that it be submitted to what Heidegger calls here a thoughtful overcoming (*denkerische Eroberung*). Such "overcoming" is not to be imposed upon Hölderlin externally, but is to be taken up in a way that Heidegger again interprets in terms of law, only "under the singular law" of Hölderlin's work itself, *unter dem einmaligen Gesetz des Hölderlinschen Werkes*. The overcoming, as such a coming to stand under the law, demands that Hölderlin, the singular poet, be released as the thinker that he is.

What is necessary is the movement from the poem as mere text, as a piece merely read (*Lesestück*), to the poetizing itself, the movement from *Gedicht* to *Dichtung*. This movement can happen only *thinkingly*, thoughtfully, *denkerisch*. But in this way the poem must *transform itself* (*sich verwandeln*) into this poetizing, must make *itself* manifest precisely as the poetizing it is. And this may happen only if it is released into the *thinking* that it already is (GA39, 19). Thus Hölderlin is the singular poet because in his poetizing he poetizes and thinks nothing other than poetizing and thinking itself, even what Heidegger calls the *belonging together* of poetizing and thinking. Hölderlin's poetizing, as a thinking, is a matter of *knowing* and a *wanting* to know, even a will to knowledge, but one that bears precisely on thinking and the thinker. Heidegger says: "Hölderlin is then the *poet of poets*, as well as the thinker most closely related to the poet [*der dem Dichter zuinnerst verwandte Denker*], who at the peak of his creative power wants to think and to know, and indeed even *must* want to know, what thinking is, and who the thinker is" (GA39, 30).

Once the poem will have achieved this self-transformation, or will have been allowed to effect such self-transformation, only then would the thoughtful encounter with the poem find itself in what Heidegger calls the realm of the poetizing power (*Machtbereich der Dichtung*). The entrance into this realm of power means that "the poetizing reigns over us, such that our Dasein becomes the bearer of life [*Lebensträger*] of the power of the poetizing" (GA39, 19).

It is just at this point that I would like to return now to what I take to be the most decisive Heideggerian provocation concerning the sense of community and friendship, the way in which what is to be said and thought in *Innigkeit* must also return that community more originally to the estranging movement of translation, the translation into the strange, the journey into the foreign. Such a movement would require suspending the prevailing determinations of community and nature, and the way these two are typically linked together in a certain complicity, determinations that appeal to the native or the national in more predictable and recognizable ways, as grounded in an inviolable sense of the proper, of property and ownership, the home to which we take ourselves to belong in advance and from which we are thought to emerge, but also therefore the home over which we suppose ourselves to have ownership and which we take to belong to us. I want to open up this provocation without yet attempting to decide what possibilities there are for thinking community after Heidegger, assuming for the moment that Heidegger can be spoken of in this way, as someone we have left behind. I also recognize that I must at this time leave unaddressed those important passages where Heidegger finds it necessary to draw what appear to be the most *bewildering*—if not *idiotic*—conclusions, for example, that America's entrance into the war is the final act of ahistorical aggression against the West and its history. And yet, there is no question that the interpretations Heidegger brings in this way to the contemporary events witnessed by him are not simply derivative; they are neither tangential nor incidental to the way in which Heidegger wants to think the possibility of community through Hölderlin's poetizing of *Innigkeit*. This becomes unmistakably evident as Heidegger's sense of the foreign—as it would arise from within the proper—is given more precise determination. The translation into the foreign that would open up a possible authentic German community must begin in no other way than as *the translation into what is Greek*. If history demands the singular encounter with the strange or foreign, Heidegger is careful to make clear that the foreign is not at all something arbitrary and indeterminate, simply what is other than the proper: "the Greek world is what is foreign with respect to the historical humanity of the Germans" (GA53, 67/54). The foreign is not simply what is other and, most emphatically, is not the *foreignness* of "America" in its complete "ahistoricality." It is not at all a matter of indifference, for example, whether Germans learn English or Greek in the *Gymnasium* (GA53, 81/66). Such a decision is bound to the historical decision concerning the German people as a people or nation. The movement into the strange, through which the Germans might find what is their own, demands learning Greek. In a remarkable passage, Heidegger states:

> We learn the Greek language so that the concealed essence of our own historical commencement can find for us its way into the clarity of our word. Yet it belongs to such a task that we recognize the singular essence of the Greek world and acknowledge it in its singularity. We may learn

the Greek language only when we must learn it out of an essential historical necessity for the sake of our own German language. For we must also first learn our own German language; and because we think that this happens of its own accord, we shall learn it with greatest difficulty and thus endanger it most readily through mere neglect. To learn language means to learn to hear, not only to hear pronunciation [*Aussprache*], but rather to hear what is pronounced [*Ausgesprochene*]. Hearkening [*Horchen*] and being able to hearken are the fundamental condition for any genuine reading of the genuine word. (GA53, 81/66)

It cannot be disputed that Heidegger's conversation with Hölderlin maintains itself only within its own emphatic historical singularity, as if it could be a distinctly German conversation, or German-Greek conversation, between only Germans . . . and Greeks, or, as Dennis Schmidt might say, between "Germans and other Greeks,"[16] restricted, then, to the context of a certain time and place. In this sense, it is the case that my reading has already violated that conversation. I am an intruder, listening in but not belonging; and, of course, I am not the only one. But it is also the case that this conversation seeks thereby to preserve for itself an impossible privacy, one that also prevents it from becoming the conversation that the German people would have in common, that could be foundational for their community. And this fact, the more it is insisted upon, only heightens the demand that this conversation, as a singular movement of thinking, still be translated, which is to say, repeated and retraced, heard and said as if for the first time, expropriated into itself. In other words, Heidegger's own thought of *Innigkeit* must rupture any possibility that his discourse, his conversation with Hölderlin, be put to work for the sake of a merely proper and exclusive German community. And this is the case whether Heidegger would admit it or not.

The thinking character of Hölderlin's poetic word is bound to his singularity and his futurity, according to Heidegger. His greatness as a poet thus lies no less in his greatness as a thinker. Heidegger insists most emphatically, however, upon the distinctively *German* character of this singular greatness and futurity of the thinking poet. The thinking encounter with Hölderlin in its singularity thus cannot be dissociated from the question of the German nation and people, and the historical *decision* (*Entscheidung*) that Heidegger sees facing that nation and people. "The hour of our [i.e., German] history has struck" (GA39, 294). This decision is nothing other than the decision that will in fact decide the people as such, a moment that would mark the very emergence of a people into its history, first allowing the German people to become the people they are or can be. Hölderlin is "the poet of poets" because he is "the poet of the Germans," "the poet who first poetizes the Germans" (*der Dichter, der die Deutschen erst dichtet*). But he is this Germanic poet only as the poet of the *future:* he is the "founder of German being [*Stifter des deutschen Seyns*] because he has projected this being the furthest, thrown it out and ahead into the most distant future" (GA39, 220). "As the poet of poets Hölderlin is the poet of the future Germans and as such he is singular [*als dieser einzig*]" (GA39, 221).

Hölderlin becomes the unsurpassable boundary of the future of thinking who at the same time is the poet who would first give to the Germans the possibility of becoming German. Yet one must also be careful to acknowledge that the Germans who are poetized by Hölderlin *do not exist*—or rather, if they exist, they do so only *futurally.* The poetizing, the originary language of a people, its *Ursprache* (GA4, 43), even as "the voice of the people" (GA4, 46), is a language not yet spoken by that people, a language, therefore, without a people, still awaiting a people. But the Germans to whom Heidegger lectures, and all those who would already call themselves German, do not yet hear their own language, do not know who they are, do not dwell on the earth (poetically) *as Germans.* While they might *speak* "German," says Heidegger, in fact they are *talking* like Americans (GA53, 81/65). When Heidegger repeats Hölderlin and says, "We are a conversation and are able to hear one another" (*Wir sind ein Gespräch und hören können von einander*), what is also asserted is that such a poetic conversation falls on deaf ears. Heidegger says: "We are strangers to our own proper historical time. The world-hour of our people remains concealed from us" (GA39, 50).[17]

How does Heidegger speak of this community and how is the role of the thinking poetizing to be thought in such community? Heidegger lectures in 1934–35:

> Poetizing—it is no play, and the relation to it is not the playful relaxation which induces self-forgetting; it is rather the awakening and the pulling together of the most proper essence of the individual, through which the individual reaches back into the ground of his Dasein [*in den Grund seines Daseins zurückreicht*]. If every individual comes from such a place, then the true gathering of the individuals into an originary community [*die wahrhafte Sammlung der Einzelnen in eine ursprüng-*

liche Gemeinschaft] has already taken place in advance. The crude sticking together of the all too many in a so-called organization is merely a preemptive amelioration, not the essence. (GA39, 8)

It is a serious question for serious individuals to ask: who is being addressed here? When Heidegger speaks of Hölderlin as belonging already to the German people, he already seems to claim the community in question. The language that is invoked here, of what can be *for us,* already enacts the promise of Hölderlin's poetry, its great future: "In an exceptional sense Hölderlin is *for us* the poet of poets" (GA4, 34). And again: "Hölderlin is one of *our* greatest thinkers, and this means most futural thinkers, because he is *our* greatest poet. Poetically attending to his poetizing is only possible as a thoughtful encounter [*denkerische Auseinandersetzung*] with the becoming manifest of being [*Offenbarung des Seyns*] accomplished in this poetizing" (GA39, 6; my emphasis). This community of individuals, called together in the awakening that is Hölderlin's poetry, is only thinkable in and through the experience of a transformed way of the *Offenbarung des Seyns,* a transformation of being's manifestation in the experience of *Innigkeit.* It thus has nothing to do with any kind of privileging of *egos.* It is barely a human community, and it is most certainly not at all a community of subjects. In the *Ister* lectures we read:

> This poet's poetizing does not revolve around the poet's own ego. No
> German poet has ever achieved such a distance from his own ego as
> that distance that determines Hölderlin's own hymnal poetry. This is
> the real reason why we of today—who despite all "community" remain
> metaphysically, that is historically, entangled in subjectivity—have such
> difficulty in bringing the right kind of hearing to encounter the word of
> this poetry. . . . The poet is the river. And the river is the poet. (GA53,
> 203/165)

The river spoken of here is not a metaphor, allegory, or symbolic image; but neither is it therefore to be taken literally. It is outside or prior to the metaphysical opposition between the literal and the merely figurative. This river spoken of here is "something else" (GA54, /166). And only by being heard and repeated in this way, as something else, can this river lead to Greece, can it lead the Germans to the Greeks, so that the Germans might first find themselves as Germans. Hölderlin's river poems poetize the same as what is poetized in the choral ode of Sophocles' *Antigone.* This sense of the same, however, is grounded for Heidegger first of all in a *difference:* "the same is truly the same only in what is truly different" (GA54, /123). This difference makes up the historical difference that spans between the Germans and the Greeks: each is not at home and thus encounters a coming to be at home in a different way but also in a relationality to each other. The river thus says something properly German, by virtue of difference. The river is the *Ortschaft*, the placed character of human life that prevails throughout human dwelling upon the earth. It determines where such human dwelling belongs, where and how it is at home. In this way, Heidegger says, the river "brings the human into the proper and maintains the human in it" (*Der Strom bringt so den Menschen ins Eigene und behält ihn im Eigenen*) (GA53, 23/21). And then also: "The river is the journeying of human beings as historical in their coming to be at home upon this earth" (GA53, 37–38/32). The *Ister* lectures are thus a sustained reflection upon this way of not being at home, this being out of place or non-belonging. But it is the attentiveness to precisely this lack of the home that also makes apparent the possibility of a coming to be at home upon the earth, certainly for the Germans, but also for human life as such, as it finds itself constituted in the modern age.

> This coming to be at home in one's own, in the proper, entails in itself that human beings are initially, and for a long time, and sometimes forever, not at home. And this in turn entails that human beings fail to recognize, that they deny, and perhaps even have to deny and to flee what belongs to the home. Coming to be at home is thus a passage through the foreign. And if the coming to be at home of a particular humankind sustains the historicality of its history, the law of the encounter between the foreign and one's own is the fundamental truth of history, a truth from out of which the essence of history must unveil itself. For this reason, the poetic meditation on coming to be at home must also for its part be of a historical nature and, as poetic, demand a historical dialogue [*Zwiesprache*] with foreign poets. (GA53, 60–61/49)

Thus, at the same time, such coming to be at home has to be regarded as deeply enigmatic. The enigma consists in the fact that the journey home is always a passage through the foreign or strange (*ein Durchgang durch das Fremde*). It is at this point that the precise character of Hölderlin's relation to the Greeks comes into focus, as Heidegger sees it. But it is also at this point that one must exercize the greatest caution in interpreting or translating this relation. For without such caution it would appear that here the strange is merely put into the service of the return home. In such

a case, one should already recognize the most familiar trope of both speculation and storytelling: the hero's journey home, the *nostos* that recovers,
after the adventure, the safety of the hearth. The journey through the
strange would become, then, a process of assimilation and recuperation,
the production of consummate ownership. One might even see here implicitly the articulation of a possible overcoming of death itself, through
the greatest sacrifice: the greatest loss or expenditure only makes more sa-
cred, recuperates everything and then some. At the same time, such a sense
of homecoming, if left unquestioned, can also be heard to articulate and
support, therefore, the crudest and most chauvinistic sense of the national:
the identity of a people grounded in simple nature, understood as what is
proper being. Now I would like to bring to bear upon such a logic or teleology of recuperation the greatest suspicion possible, precisely in order to
hold to the sense of the task of translating *Innigkeit* as I have presented it.

According to Heidegger, because Hölderlin and Sophocles poetize "the
same," this means that the Germans and the Greeks are bound together.
But they are bound together in the greatest difference. What is at issue,
therefore, in this difference that binds the Germans and Greeks together
is a certain *Innigkeit*.

> Because Hölderlin's relationship to the Greek world is, to put it in catch-
> words, neither classical, nor romantic, nor metaphysical, Hölderlin's tie
> [*Bindung*] to the Greek world is not looser but rather just the opposite,
> it is *inniger*. For only where the foreign, the strange, is known and ac-
> knowledged in its essential oppositional character does there exist the
> possibility of a genuine relationship, that is, of a uniting [*Einigung*]
> that is not a confused mixing but a joining in holding apart. (GA53,
> 67–68/54)

Here *Innigkeit* names not simply the belonging together of what must
remain apart but more precisely the belonging together in an essential op-
positionality (*wesenhafte Gegensätzlichkeit*). Without question the most
important Hölderlinian text for Heidegger concerning such an oppositional relation is the well-known letter to his friend Böhlendorff from December 4, 1801. Heidegger returns to this letter repeatedly in all three of
the lecture courses he devotes to Hölderlin. The first of these lectures, in
fact, from 1934–35, concludes with what is arguably the most decisive
statement from the letter: "We learn nothing more difficult than the free
use of the national" (*Wir lernen nichts schwerer als das Nationelle frei ge-
brauchen*) (GA39, 294).

Let me conclude with a brief discussion concerning the way in which the letter articulates the difference between the Germans and the Greeks (or between the moderns and the Greeks) by opening up a difference within nature itself. This will allow me to close by posing a question.

What the letter says is that what is natural for us (Germans?) is the *Klarheit der Darstellung,* or "clarity of presentation," whereas what is natural for the Greeks is *das Feuer vom Himmel,* or the "fire of heaven." The letter characterizes these two manifestations of nature in an inverse and oppositional relation to each other: distance from one means a proximity to the other. But nature or what is proper also has here a sense that needs to be given careful consideration. What is proper is not simply given but must be learned; and nothing, says Hölderlin, is more difficult. What is *most difficult,* the greatest burden, *das Schwerste,* is the free use or free relation to what is one's own, *das Eigene.*

Now we have already seen how the relation between these two—the clarity of presentation and the fire of heaven—amounts to a difference of what must be held together. This relation, as such a differing and belonging together, can be said, therefore, to be a kind of *Innigkeit.* But let me also say—or rather put it forward as a question for discussion—that what is said in these two phrases, if said *together,* also itself says the difficulty of thinking and saying *Innigkeit,* if, that is, the fire from heaven is heard as the unity that obliterates or destroys all singularity and individuality, all *difference,* while the clarity of presentation is heard as precisely the difference that sustains things in their discrete singularity and individuation. Not only is the relation between the two a relation of *Innigkeit,* but the two together, *when said and thought together,* say something that cannot be said, except perhaps tragically. The difficulty here is that these two *cannot be said together and yet must be said together.* The two together say, in other words, the belonging together of the strange, in the sense that would awaken us precisely to the loss of the proper *in* the proper itself, the proper itself as most strange and thus also, perhaps, most difficult.

Notes

Epigraphs: Jacques Derrida, *The Politics of Friendship,* trans. George Collins (New York: Verso, 1997), viii; Philippe Lacoue-Labarthe, *Typography: Mimesis, Philosophy, Politics* (Cambridge: Harvard University Press, 1989), 247; Martin Heidegger, *Hölderlins Hymnen "Germanien" und "Der Rhein"* (Frankfurt am Main: Vittorio Klostermann, 1980), 293. Hereafter, GA39.

1. GA4, 195–97. The editor of the *Gesamtausgabe* volume, Friedrich-Wilhelm von Hermann, states that this short text was originally written for the recording "Martin Heidegger Reads Hölderlin" (GA4, 205).

2. The poetic fragment reads: Alles ist innig / das scheidet / so birgt der Dichter / Verwegner! möchtest von Angesicht zu Angesicht / die Seele sehn / gehst du in Flammen unter.

3. *Theaetetus* 189e–190a.

4. "Dies will sagen: Eines ist in das Andere vereignet, aber so, daß es dabei selber in seinem Eigenen bleibt, sogar erst in dieses gelangt: Götter und Menschen, Erde und Himml. Die Innigkeit meint kein Verschmelzen und Verlöschen der Unterscheidungen. Innigkeit nennt das Zusammengehören des Fremden, das Walten der Befremdung, den Anspruch der Scheu" (GA4, 196).

5. "[T]he mystery (*Geheimnis*) is the Innigkeit; this is however being itself, the belligerence of the conflicting powers, in which belligerence the decision comes to pass over the gods and the earth, the human and all that is created" (GA39, 250–51).

6. GA53, 91/74.

7. See "Heidegger's Ear: Philopolemology," in *Reading Heidegger: Commemorations*, ed. John Sallis (Bloomington: Indiana University Press, 1993), 169. Although Derrida is concerned with the problem of how to translate another group of words, it is also the case that Heidegger clearly states that the word is not to be thought in this way.

8. Heraclitus, fr. 50.

9. "Der Streit ist kein Riß als das Aufreißen einer bloßen Kluft, sondern der Streit ist die Innigkeit des Sichzugehörens der Streitenden." Martin Heidegger, *Holzwege* (Frankfurt am Main: Vittorio Klostermann, 1980), 49. Hereafter cited as HW.

10. Is Aristotle's friend of wisdom not also a friend of myths? Does he not say that both share in the wonder proper to beginnings?

11. *Republic*, 424a, 449c. *Phaedrus*, 279c. *Lysis*, 207c.

12. There is another remarkable passage that appears in *Basic Problems of Phenomenology* where Heidegger takes up the originary sense of *Dichtung*.

13. See Schelling's *System of Transcendental Idealism*. Schelling Werke III, 629.

14. HW 58–59.

15. GA4, 7.

16. Dennis Schmidt, *On Germans and Other Greeks: Tragedy and Ethical Life* (Bloomington: Indiana University Press, 2001).

17. "The poet does not mean that Germany of those poets and thinkers imagined and wished for by the rest of the world: the simple dreamers and idiots who are easily persuaded with regard to what is decisive and who would be the fools for all the others. Instead he means that poetizing and thinking that breaks into the abysses of being, not satisfied in the shallow waters of a universal world reason, that poetizing and thinking, which in its work brings forth beings anew into appearance" (GA39, 290).

5 Heidegger's Philosophy of Language in an Aristotelian Context: *Dynamis meta logou*

Günter Figal

On the Way to Language—with this title, Heidegger has not only aptly characterized the contributions of his late book; the title characterizes his philosophy as a whole. There has never been a turn to language in Heidegger; at the beginning of his independent philosophizing he was already concerned with the question of language, in a manner that, basically, applies or ought to apply to each philosophizing: philosophy, as thinking that articulates itself in language and that has to endeavor to reflect its actualization, is always already more or less expressly an engagement with its linguistic character (*Sprachlichkeit*). However, Heidegger pursues this engagement with particular intensity. Already in his earliest lectures he is carried by the conviction that language as possibility of philosophy is at the same time its endangering; thus it is essential to gain philosophically the language of philosophy against the tendency of language itself—particularly a linguistic form that gives the impression of being appropriate to philosophy. But in the course of time Heidegger has understood ever more clearly that the possibility of philosophical articulation is located in the essence of language itself. It arises from language itself, provided that one corresponds to that essence without ever being able to appropriate it. Language is always prior to philosophizing, and it always stays ahead of it. Heidegger's thinking as a whole can demonstrate that philosophy is a path in language, a being-toward-language without available beginning and without a goal within reach.

Already from the very beginning, Heidegger's reflection on language is a discussion with the traditional understanding of philosophy. What is inherent to it as possibility and endangering is, as Heidegger calls it, "the theoretical."[1] By this is meant the attitude in which the world as a whole or some of its particular aspects become an object, and in which that which can be asserted becomes an object of assertion. What is concealed by this is that the world is primarily experienced in significance and that life in the world is actualized in a worldly manner. Accordingly, a turning away from assertions and the development of a language is required in order to do justice to this primordial experiencing of world. Heidegger finds a model of this turning away in the expression and manifestation of Christian life, as they are realized in Paul's *Epistles*—Heidegger thinks that precisely there something that has never been seen in the philosophical tradition, especially not in ontology, becomes effective: "history and life."[2] This expression means an existing that actualizes in temporal openness: in a present that is extended between the having-been of revelation and the futural return of the Lord and that is thus temporal in a transparent manner. Since the "expressive forms of ancient science" that were adopted in later Christianity distort this mode of experience, it is essential to "radically get rid of" its formative power.[3] What would be in theological terms a repetition of early Christianity in its primordiality Heidegger has attempted philosophically and for the sake of philosophy: in analogy to the linguistic form of the *Epistles* he develops the concept of a philosophical discourse that does not objectify life, thereby treating it as an indifferent given, but rather interprets and communicates the temporally and "factically" actualized life. Heidegger's name for this attitude and mode of articulation of life is "hermeneutics of facticity."[4]

Now it would have been obvious to work out the program of such a hermeneutics in terms of a turning away from the "expressive forms of ancient science" and the very conception reflecting it. Over and above an orientation toward the Pauline *Epistles* this would have helped the fundamental themes of Christian theology to achieve new significance, and it could have led to an understanding of language stimulated by the former. But this possibility was seized not by Heidegger, but only by his student Gadamer: Against the forgetting of language that he diagnoses with regard to Greek thought, Gadamer, in his opus magnum, falls back to the thought of Incarnation in order to come to an understanding of the true being of language. In contrast and despite his critique, Heidegger remains committed to Greek thought—above all to the one among its representatives who, in a manner authoritative for the tradition, establishes the understanding of philosophy as theory and also of language as medium of determining and establishing: Aristotle. Just as Heidegger criticizes the ontological tradition by reflecting on Aristotle as its originator and by attempting to gain from his thought the possibility of a different "ontology of facticity"[5] truly corresponding to life or existence, he remains also, as a thinker of language, an Aristotelian criticizing Aristotle. In the elaboration of his hermeneutics of facticity Heidegger engages with the Aristotelian examination of language as the possibility of determining and establishing, as *logos apophantikos,* that is not in the sense of a negative critique, but rather in an integrative manner. Heidegger's hermeneutics of facticity takes up the Aristotelian program of a "logic," "of the categories of this addressing and interpreting."[6] Thus understood, logic "needs to be brought back to . . . the original unity of facticity"; it is an "offshoot," that is, an emerging part of the hermeneutics of facticity.[7] One can reverse this: If logic belongs as one part to the hermeneutics of facticity, one has to articulate it "logically"; it does not abolish the Aristotelian examination of *logos apophantikos,* but it renders it effective in a new manner when understood in a comprehensive context.

Heidegger's attachment to Aristotle is obvious in his thought of the twenties up to *Being and Time;* anybody who describes it does not discover anything new anymore, but at best contributes to a better understanding of basically familiar facts. But Heidegger, by recognizing the failure of the program of *Being and Time,* in no way leaves Aristotle behind. Heidegger's attachment to Aristotle is also not limited to his early project of a hermeneutic ontology of Dasein. On the contrary, even the revision of his thought leading Heidegger away from the approach of his opus magnum and bringing him to the realization regarding the irretrievable pre-givenness of language goes back essentially to an engagement with Aristotle. This is neither inconsistent nor an expression of a bias regarding Aristotelian thought. Rather, it is Heidegger's only possibility not to give up his earlier conception as simply having missed its point. This conception can be revised only if there can be a different interpretation of the very context that was worked out by it. On condition that the hermeneutics of Dasein actually includes a "logic" in the Aristotelian sense, a new, more appropriate conception of this hermeneutics is dependent on a different understanding of this "logic." We shall now see what all this means in greater detail.

*   *   *

Heidegger's "logic," as it is developed thoroughly for the first time in the lecture from the winter semester 1925–26, has a clearly formulated intention. It discusses the Aristotelian definition of *logos apophantikos* in order to show that the statement "is not the locus of truth, but truth the locus of the statement."[8] Not least because this interpretation was included with minor modifications in *Being and Time,* it is known in its essential features. Something as something can be brought to language only because there is always already the possibility of discovering it as something. By coming to language in an assertion, something becomes accessible in a particular manner. But the effecting of this accessibility, the *apophainesthai* of *logos apophantikos,* is due to the previous accessibility of worldly relations. To take up Heidegger's example from *Being and Time:* in order to be able to articulate the statement "the hammer is heavy," one has to have experienced the hammer as too heavy and thus unsuitable while working with it. If the "apophantical as" that becomes effective in the assertion of something (the hammer) as something (heavy) is founded in the "hermeneutical as," in the interpretation of something (the hammer) as something (too heavy for this particular purpose) occurring in dealing, then Heidegger can rightly claim that logic as "the interpretation of the categories of this addressing and interpreting" belongs in the context of the interpretation of worldly relations and of life or existence in them, and thus into hermeneutics.

In the unfolding of this train of thought Heidegger is by no means sparing in critical remarks regarding Aristotle. Aristotle has "failed" to ask about the "structural phenomenon" of the hermeneutical as;[9] he "has not freed himself from the orientation towards language"[10] and therefore holds on to the "logos in the sense of determining"[11] as a main idea that has been authoritative for the entire tradition. On the other hand, Heidegger sees in the Aristotelian determination of *logos apophantikos* itself nonetheless the signs for the dependence of linguistic truth and falsity on a previous uncovering: When Aristotle states that only the one *logos* is expounding "in which being-true and being-false comes forth," "coming forth" (*hyparchein*) originally means "from the outset being objectively present" or, in an added explanation, "laying the foundation for something so that everything else is carried by means of this being which is objectively present from the outset."[12] In the context of this determination the critique of Aristotle can be limited to the point that, instead of Dasein and its worldly relations, he understands the objectively present, that is, being in its essential determinateness and identity (*ousia*) as that which "lays the foundation."

This is certainly a central difference; it is the one from which Heidegger's program of a fundamental ontology of Dasein—that is to prove an ontology of objective presence as something derivative and at the same time is to found it in its possibility—receives its justification in general.

But Heidegger can put human Dasein at the ontological locus of *ousia* only if he leaves the very frame unchanged in which he carries out this replacement. This is the very way in which the claim of *Being and Time* is formulated: the "unity of being in contrast to the manifold of 'categories'" that, according to Heidegger, Aristotle has discovered but not explained in a satisfactory manner[13] is shown vis-à-vis Dasein. Since Dasein is not only "ontic," a being, but, due to the understanding of being essential to it, also "ontological,"[14] it can be the One all manifold exhibiting is to relate to. Accordingly, Dasein, like *ousia* conceived by Aristotle, has to be accessible in its unity such that it carries the multiplicity of "categorial" determinations and renders them comprehensible. In other words, Dasein has to be understood as that which is already from the outset accessible, without which nothing belonging to it can be exhibited, brought to language and thus to explicit attention.

This is the real point of Heidegger's critical interpretation of the Aristotelian *logos apophantikos:* at most, it is of secondary importance to him to show that the assertion is an abstraction becoming independent vis-à-vis a context that is experienced primarily in everyday taking action. Rather, what is crucial is that with everyday taking action the very unity that is Dasein itself comes into play. Everyday taking action belongs to a Dasein that interprets itself in the multiplicity of the diverse aspects of worldly life, but that is essentially—Heidegger would say: authentically—the immediate apprehension of its own being. This immediacy of Dasein does not communicate itself in the articulating language linked thus with the manifold, and it can by no means be shown and asserted. If it comes to be expressive, then this takes place all at once, in a moment. And provided that it is the matter of philosophy, there is already a name for it in Heidegger's first lecture from 1919: "hermeneutical intuition."[15]

Although hermeneutical intuition does not communicate itself in asserting, it is not without language, and in order to understand its linguistic character, Heidegger again falls back on Aristotle, more exactly, on his determination of the *nous* and the *noein,* on, as Heidegger calls it in *Being and Time,* "the simple sense perception of something."[16] Since in it the simple is grasped, it is not an asserting of something as something, but a touching lightly and saying, a *thigein kai phanai,* as Aristotle calls it (*Met.* 1051b 24). Here one should not think of a simple addressing as it occurs with naming, but rather of a saying of the simple accessibility as it prevails more or less explicitly in each articulated discourse. In Aristotle, simple saying corresponds to a revealed being (*on alethes, Met.* 1051b 1) in Heidegger, to the being of Dasein that, hermeneutically, is to come to language in its simplicity and immediacy. It uncovers the truth that lays "the foundation" or each saying and that is concealed, if the perceived, as Heidegger says at one point, is "disperceived" (*Auseinandervernommen*):[17] as Dasein in the dispersion of the worldly life and not in the simplicity of its being.

It is precisely through the very way in which Heidegger here introduces the alternative of truth and coveredness (*Verdeckung*) that the notion of a perceiving and saying prevailing in discourse becomes problematic: The unity and simplicity is purely perceived at most in a moment so that it, inhering in the manifold, emerges as if in a puzzle picture and disappears again immediately; since the articulated and manifold cannot be removed, the unity that can be grasped only immediately is always obscured or covered by it. But this difficulty need not be due to the matter, but may have its reason in the intention to realize the simplicity of perceiving and saying immediately and as much as possible by itself. This intention could for its part cover the essence of language, if the simple and the manifold in language do not contradict but rather complement each other.

* * *

Heidegger draws this conclusion in his lecture during the summer semester of 1931 that attends to the first three chapters of Book Θ of the Aristotelian *Metaphysics*. Language itself is here determined as unity and multiplicity; it is no longer the articulation of a primordial simple, but the possibility for the unification of the manifold and at the same time the enabling of multiplicity leading necessarily to this unification. Language understood as *logos* is, as Heidegger himself says, "to glean, to harvest, to gather, to add one to the other, and so to place the one in relation to the other"; it is itself "the relation, the relationship" that "holds together that which stands within it." It is "the *ruling structure,* the *gathering* of those beings related among themselves."[18] This holding together and relating is, however, actualized always only in certain regards. The gathering takes place in a selective manner; it is, Heidegger says, "only partially a taking into possession of something because that which is to be possessed always remains other."[19] By placing the one in relation to the other, "it is always a this or that which is decided upon and separated out."[20] That which is separated out, that which is kept apart from the particular gathering, is not the diffuse and chaotic multiplicity of a prelinguistic, wholly non-articulated world, but the non-bounded yet explorable space of the negative, of the sayable, that is excluded from the particular saying yet encloses it. In Heidegger's formulation: The space of the negative is a dispersing "into a *multiplicity* of expository sayings and assertions," in which language understood as *logos* "is always already found split up and scattered."[21] For this reason Unity is "always a winning back,"[22] the winning back of a unity that is essential to language and in which it always again and essentially loses itself.

In this rough characterization of *logos* Heidegger develops determinations that form the center of his later thinking of language. The considerations of *On the Way to Language* as well as the interpretations of Heraclitus's understanding of *logos* are here prefigured, and this shows that Heidegger does not gain them only in the context of a reflection on the poetic character of language or of his engagement with Heraclitus's fragments. That *logos* as a relating is something Heidegger unfolds with regard to the apophantical as he had recovered it in his discussion of Aristotle: By saying something about something, this something comes not only to language in its immediate particularity, but gets also related to something that is not identical with that which it is in itself. Moreover, the assertion stands in a relation to that which is not ascribed to it. In each ascribing, "it is always a this or that which is decided upon and separated out"; something is something as that which is addressed, always in the context of particular other, not yet realized possibilities, so that the determinateness of the assertion belongs together with the indeterminateness, the multiplicity of being-other.

Despite these characteristics of the assertion, Heidegger does not see the assertion as the locus in which the essence of *logos* becomes most effective. For him, it is in a knowledge of producing (*episteme poetike*) that the relation of unity and multiplicity is developed in a more decisive form. Here, *logos* is to grasp as the reason why the form—Heidegger says: "outward appearance"—of the work to be produced not only can be regarded as end and completion of producing, but, in the actualization of production, also can be related to that which essentially "lies over and against."[23] According to this interpretation, producing is tantamount to "forging something into its boundaries, so much so that this being-enclosed is already in view in advance,"[24] and this being-enclosed forms itself in the "unbounded" standing over and against it, lying opposite of it. That is, the *eidos* becomes effective in the material that, taken on its own, is unbounded, and it becomes effective by becoming form (*morphe*). Heidegger summarizes his considerations: "Because this proximity of *eidos* and *hyle* lies in the essence of producing, producing necessarily, at each step along the way, is constantly excluding and enjoining, fitting in and, at the same time, leaving out."[25] And since the relation of the enclosed unity of *eidos* that has the effect of enclosing and the boundlessness of the unformed are brought together in *logos*, Heidegger can say that "the being-gathered-together of production is at play in the gathering [*legein*] of the discussion and of the cognizance."[26] If the *eidos* regulating producing is given in *logos*, so that it has to be understood as *logos*, and if the forming of *eidos* in the material is to be understood as fitting in and excluding in terms of *legein*, producing can indeed be characterized as "a talking to oneself and letting oneself talk."[27]

It is doubtful whether Heidegger's reflections constitute accurate assessments of the Aristotelian train of thought in *Met*. E 2. When Aristotle determines the understanding of producing as a capability that is accompanied by *logos* (*dynamis meta logou*) and therefore can say of it that it is not only directed at a singular, that is, its end, but also at its contrary, he thus thinks of this contrary as material, but also as a condition opposed to the end; more precisely, he thinks of a condition that is characterized by the being-out-of-reach (*Entzogenheit*) of that which, as end, would be actuality. In this sense, the art of healing deals with sickness *and* health; both are present in it, whereas the "alogical" capability of the warm has no immanent relation to the cold, but is directed only at making warm (*Met*. 1046b 2–7). The fact that Heidegger misses this point by reading the question of the relation of *eidos* and *hyle* into the Aristotelian discussion does not prevent him from grasping precisely Aristotle's insight: that *logos* is the possibility and the locus of the different and opposite.

However, Heidegger is not primarily concerned with a clarification of *dynamis meta logou*. Its determination in Aristotle is for him simply a point of departure and a turning point toward a different conception of human existence as such. Consequently, the distinction between *dynamis meta logou* and *dynamis alogos* fades in Heidegger's interpretation. He is no longer concerned only with distinguishing a capability that realizes itself in an actuality belonging to it from a capability regulated by *logos* and actualizing itself in the recognition of a lack and its compensation. That *logos* keeps present the lacking is just one possible formation of its essence: in *logos* everything that is not immediately there can be there, and something that is there can be related to something different from it. Thus *logos* is the play-space of the relational and the possibility to comport oneself in it. Or, in Heidegger's expression, *logos* is "the perceiving exploration of . . . , and the conversant relating to . . . ,"[28] and, already before this, "the possibility of exploring and becoming conversant and so being conversant."[29]

* * *

For Heidegger, *logos* is therefore now the essence of human existence; in the terms from *Being and Time,* it is its disclosedness and that which has to be comprehended philosophically against the very tendency of self-concealment. But this no longer amounts to rendering effective against language a "hermeneutical intuition." The attempt to bring Dasein into language originates from language itself. Correspondingly, philosophy can be attentiveness toward language—articulation of the essence of language that neither reveals itself in each discourse nor eludes discourse altogether.

Heidegger can claim the concept "hermeneutics" not only for the interpretation and communication of Dasein to be grasped intuitively, but also for this very manifest attentiveness toward language, since it is as far from the reification of its matter as Heidegger had insisted it is for the hermeneutics of facticity. The manifestation of the attentiveness toward language belongs to language itself; it does not deal with what-is-the-case, but, in Heidegger's later formulation, it is itself "what-is-the-case,"[30] in which a case fore-gives the possibility of comportment, a "relation"[31] that has no enclosed and bounded opposite, but rather is the adopting of a giving-itself. This giving-itself is the possibility of discourse in and out of language experienced as such, the non-objective fore-given that is not reached with any naming of a particular, but is already experienced in each as play-space of the relational. It can be explored only hermeneutically since it is as the "hermeneutic"[32] already "the bearing of message and tidings."[33] Language as the play-space of the relational founds also the relation to itself. It is the very mediation that mediates itself in a discourse open for its own being-possible. The engagement with and discussion of Aristotle had a preparatory function for these thoughts that form the center of Heidegger's later thinking of language. One can thus understand it as a dialogue in which the essence of language becomes effective in the mediation of reading and interpreting.

Translated from the German by Drew A. Hyland and Erik M. Vogt

Notes

1. Martin Heidegger, *Towards the Definition of Philosophy,* trans. Ted Sadler (London: Continuum, 2000), 50.

2. Martin Heidegger, *Grundprobleme der Phänomenologie,* GA 58 (Frankfurt am Main: Vittorio Klostermann, 1993), 146.

3. Heidegger, *Grundprobleme der Phänomenologie,* 61.

4. Martin Heidegger, "Phenomenological Interpretations in Connection with Aristotle: An Indication of the Hermeneutical Situation (1922)," in *Supplements: From the Earliest Essays to Being and Time and Beyond,* ed. John Van Buren (Albany: SUNY Press, 2002), 111–45, 121.

5. Heidegger, "Phenomenological Interpretations," 121.

6. Ibid.

7. Ibid.

8. Martin Heidegger, *Logik. Die Frage nach der Wahrheit,* GA 21 (Frankfurt am Main: Vittorio Klostermann, 1976), 135.

9. Ibid., 141.

10. Ibid., 142.

11. Ibid., 159.

12. Ibid., 129.

13. Martin Heidegger, *Being and Time,* trans. Joan Stambaugh (Albany: SUNY Press, 1996), 1–2.

14. Ibid., 10.

15. Heidegger, *Towards the Definition of Philosophy,* 99.

16. Heidegger, *Being and Time,* 29.

17. Heidegger, *Logik,* 185.

18. Martin Heidegger, *Aristotle's Metaphysics Θ 1–3: On the Essence and Actuality of Force,* trans. Walter Brogan and Peter Warnek (Bloomington: Indiana University Press, 1995), 103.

19. Heidegger, *Aristotle's Metaphysics,* 123.

20. Ibid.

21. Ibid., 124.

22. Ibid.

23. Ibid., 119.

24. Ibid., 118.

25. Ibid., 119.

26. Ibid., 124.

27. Ibid.

28. Ibid., 108.

29. Ibid., 104.

30. Martin Heidegger, *On the Way to Language,* trans. Peter D. Hertz (New York: Harper and Row, 1971), 11.

31. Ibid., 32.

32. Ibid., 11.

33. Ibid., 29.

6 Toward the Future of Truth

William J. Richardson

Anyone who is not a native of Greece will have one or other standout memory of his or her first experience of that remarkable place that is Athens. For me, it was the first visit to Marathon. Propelled by a longtime adolescent fantasy as old as high school days, I took off alone one summer afternoon only to find this singular monument to the Marathon dead closed down tight as a drum—not a human being in sight, neither vendor, nor visitor, nor even a watchman to bribe. The funeral mound itself was barely visible through the padlocked iron gate shouldered by a ten-foot-high iron picket fence mounted with angry spikes. But I finally found a spot where I could slither through a small opening between the end of fence and adjoining concrete wall. With deep breath, risky hope, and six-foot leap, I was soon utterly alone with . . . the dead, and nothing to interrupt the silence but the chatter of the crickets.

It was quite wonderful. I tried to recall the facts of the battle but details were hazy. By a brilliant deception, Miltiades caught the Persians by surprise before their cavalry had assembled and drove them back into the sea. Over 6,000 Persians died in the battle while the Greeks suffered only 192 casualties of their own. The remains of the fallen were disposed of in a mass cremation, followed by animal sacrifices and funeral banquet. Then the spot of cremation was covered by the immense mound of earth, which, somewhat eroded by the centuries, is what we still see today. The dead were venerated as heroes, their names carved somewhere in stone. It was easy to feel close to them, as if the almost 2,500 years that separated us had dissipated long enough to leave us together in a strange way with what happened there at the dawn of Greece's Golden Age. Such is the power of the tradition of language and culture that binds us still, the sense of which Martin Heidegger has helped us to understand better, perhaps, than anyone else.

Fast forward to our own day: to another funeral monument honoring dead from another war—the war that America waged in Vietnam almost forty years ago. This is not a huge mound of earth covering ground made holy by the blood of those who died there. It is rather a long black granite wall that lies like a huge scar in the green hillock of an urban park in Washington, D.C. Almost five hundred feet long, the wall consists of two wings set at an angle to each other, one stretching toward the Washington Monument, the other toward the Lincoln Memorial—both of them rich with traditional meaning for Americans. The only decoration on the wall is name after name of the fallen in Vietnam, listed in the grim democratization of death—not according to rank or age or years of service but simply in the order of their dying. There are similarities here to Marathon, of course, but one major difference: the cause for which the Athenians fought was clear and unambiguous. Not so for everyone who fought in Vietnam. The moral justification for fighting there remains debatable even today. What is honored in the monument is the courage and fidelity of those who gave their lives because the country asked it of them.

Interesting, perhaps!—but what has it to do with Heidegger and the Greeks? I begin this way for two reasons: (1) apologetic; (2) propaedeutic. I say "apologetic" in the sense of offering an "apologia." Some keep asking for an explanation of why my own interest appears to have shifted from Heidegger and philosophy to psychoanalysis and Freud-Lacan. When I returned home after finishing studies in Europe in the early 1960s, I was plunged into the turmoil of the time: the assassinations, the Vietnam War, student protests, conscientious objection, and so on. One could talk the talk about the Being question, ontological difference, event of appropriation, and the like, but to walk the walk with the students it was necessary to make clear the relevance of all this to them as embodiments of Dasein. This led to a focus on Dasein as an indispensable component of Heidegger's experience of the reciprocity between human being and Being as such. I was especially sensitive to Heidegger's insistence at the beginning of *Being and Time*:

> The roots of the existential analysis, for their part, are ultimately *existentiell*—they are *ontic*. Only when philosophical research and inquiry themselves are grasped in an existentiell way—as a possibility of each existing Da-sein—does it become possible at all to disclose the existentiality of existence and therewith to get hold of a sufficiently grounded set of ontological problems.[1]

This led to requests to explain the relationship between Heidegger and what was then called "existential psychoanalysis," and this in turn led to confrontation with Freud, then with the "French Freud," Jacques Lacan, about whom I had heard in philosophical circles while still in Europe. This was not a turn away from Heidegger's basic insight but an effort to extend its influence to ontic disciplines badly in need of an ontological base. What interested me most in Lacan was his effort to develop an ethics of psychoanalysis—it correlated nicely with a long-term interest in the ethical dimension of Heidegger's thought. Would it be possible to consider the thought of these two thinkers as complementary to one another rather than, as seemed to be the case, irreducibly opposed?

Lacan had a longtime interest in Heidegger. He personally translated Heidegger's essay on the *Logos* of Heraclitus (1954) into French for his students, and during the fifties several French analysts tried to arrange an encounter between the two men. This effort was led by Jean Beaufret, one of Lacan's analysands, who, after having been the occasion for Heidegger's famous "Letter on Humanism" had become a close friend of Heidegger and the most prestigious Heideggerian in France. Surely he saw a value in such an encounter. Eventually Heidegger and Lacan did meet, but there was no real exchange between them. What might have happened if they could have listened to each other and engaged in real dialogue? This is a question that has perdured over the years, though any answer is still waiting out its future. In a genuine sense, it is the question that lies behind the present reflection.

So much for apologia. Now a word of propaedeutic. Reference to the Vietnam Memorial seems suggestive of the principal parameters of Lacan's entire enterprise. His basic conception of the human phenomenon is that of a "being" (*être*) that "speaks" (*qui parle*), that is, a *parlêtre*. The term itself would come later, but from the beginning he was impressed by the fact that Freud's deepest insight into the nature of the human unconscious was not the hypothesis of some hidden hydraulic system of the psyche but the insight into the way that language works (witness, for example, *The Interpretation of Dreams* [1900], *The Psychopathology of Everyday Life* [1901], *Jokes and the Meaning of the Unconscious* [1905]). Lacan's project was to return to this original insight of Freud and expand it. He did so by postulating that *parlêtre* is constituted by three basic components, deeply intertwined. These components he called the "symbolic," the "imaginary," and the "real." How he could claim to have found these components in

Freud, how his conception of the symbolic had been mediated through the work of C. Levy-Strauss, who had turned to the linguistics of F. de Saussure to develop a new methodology for his own cultural anthropology, how it was a disciple of Saussure, R. Jacobson (1956), who first noticed the similarity between metaphor and metonymy as figures of speech in linguistics and "condensation" and "displacement" as formations of the unconscious in the construction of dreams for Freud—all such elaborations, however helpful in themselves, we must leave for another venue and summarize Lacan's fundamental position by citing only his signature principle: "the unconscious [discovered by Freud] is structured like a language." In the triad that constitutes the basic structure of *parlêtre*, the term "symbolic" refers to the specifically linguistic component of that structure. In the War Memorial, the symbolic function plays an important role in generating the monument's power, for there is no embellishment other than the names of the dead. But proper names are forms of language that mean much more than the carving of letters in stone. In this case the names signify more than fifty thousand modes of human existence, many of them polyglot in origin, each name pointing to the same hopes, loves, and fears that mark every human life. Now, through the inscription of these names in stone, all this rich panoply survives the disintegration of physical bodies through the sheer power of language.

The second component of Lacan's triadic structure of *parlêtre* he calls the "imaginary"; that is, it is characterized chiefly by images and imaging. His fundamental model for the imaginary is the infant's first discovery of himself as a quasi-unified image in some reflecting surface such as a mirror, that is, a visual representation of itself, essentially other than itself but with which it cannot help but identify. This imaged self-representation will accompany all symbolic representation when the child begins to speak and will impose an inescapable narcissism on all its human activity throughout the rest of life. In the War Memorial, this inevitable self-imaging that accompanies the symbolically structured world is suggested by the highly polished black stone into which the names are carved. It serves to mirror ourselves to ourselves as we read these symbolic names, signaling to the viewer the inevitable interaction of imaginary and symbolic in all human experience. As background for the names, the shining stone itself seems to speak to us through our own image in it, saying: "Where were you in all this?" Or "Where would you have been had you been here when it all happened?"

The third component in the triadic structure of *parlêtre* Lacan calls the "real"—not "reality" but the real. Reality we already know as what is represented to us by the symbolic and the imaginary, but the real is what is left over as "impossible" to represent—it is the enigmatic, the unimaginable, and the unspeakable in experience. In this War Memorial, the real would be, I suggest, what is not represented by the names nor imagized by reflections but rather the horrible enigma of the war itself that cannot be represented but can only be pointed at with horror in the dumb silence of the stone.

Symbolic, imaginary, and real—these are the essential components of human being as a "speaking" being (*parlêtre*) for Lacan, at least in the context of psychoanalysis, and the last ten years of his teaching were devoted to conceptualizing the indissoluble unity of them. He conceives of them as a single knot of three cords/circles/"holes" that are so intertwined that if one of the cords is broken, the entire knot falls apart. He calls it the "Borromean Knot." It is his ultimate formula for the triadic paradigm that in fact guided his thought from the start.

Heidegger, too, has a summarizing formula that crystallizes his own experience from the beginning. We know that that beginning was the discovery of the Being-question in reading Brentano's dissertation on the manifold meaning of being (*on, Seiendes*) in Aristotle. We know the long trajectory that began with the publication of *Being and Time* (1927) and came full circle in the lecture "Time and Being" (1962): "What remains to be said? Only this: Appropriation appropriates. Saying this, we say the Same in terms of the Same about the Same. . . . This Same is not even anything new, but the oldest of the old in Western thought: that ancient something which conceals itself in *A-letheia*" (1972, p. 24/24–25). The question to be raised here is: are these two franchise formulae compatible? I do not mean "conflatable," that is, reducible one to the other, but rather can each throw light on the other for those who respect both modes of human experience? More precisely, may they be thought of as somehow complementary, as in the language of *Being and Time* "ontic" and "ontological" are complementary dimensions of the same phenomenon? To engage the discussion, I ask whether Lacan's correlation of symbolic and imaginary might not be the analogue of the alpha-privative (*Entbergung*) of Heidegger's conception of *aletheia,* and whether Lacan's real might not be analogue to *lethe* (*Verbergung*) in Heidegger's understanding of *aletheia.* There is no way to make the full case for this hypothesis here, but I propose to sketch the argument in at least general terms and conclude by suggesting briefly the possible utility of such an effort.

World as Revelation

Lacan's correlation of symbolic and imaginary is analogous, I suggest, to Heidegger's conception of the alpha-privative of *aletheia,* because both generate the disclosure of the world. Heidegger speaks early in *Being and Time* of the "disclosedness" (*Erschlossenheit*) of the world, discerned phenomenologically as "horizon" of total meaningfulness. He takes a fresh approach to the problem two years later in his lecture course of 1929–30, *Fundamental Concepts of Metaphysics* (1995), where he justifies the claim that the world is given shape by human being (as *Weltbildend*) insofar as human being is capable of language. His argument is based on an analysis of Aristotle's use of the word *logos.* The seminar itself is long and complex, but the focus here will be confined to this theme only.

> To begin in the simplest terms, what did Aristotle understand by *logos?*
>
> We shall first consider what Aristotle says in general about the *logos.* *Logos* means discourse (*Rede*). The Greeks really have no word corresponding to our word, "language." *Logos* as discourse means what we understand by language, yet it also means more than our vocabulary taken as a whole. It means the fundamental faculty of being able to talk discursively and, accordingly, to speak. The Greeks thus characterize man as *zoon logon echon*—that living being that essentially possesses the possibility of discourse. The animal as the living being that lacks this possibility of discourse is *zoon alogon.* (305/442)

For Aristotle as read by Heidegger, then, human being must be understood as *parlêtre.* "It is in the *logos* that man expresses what is most essential to him, so as in this very expression to place himself into the clarity, depth and need pertaining to the essential possibilities of his action, of his existence" (303/439).[2] The first task of *logos* for Aristotle is to permit human beings to share with one another meaning (*semantikos*) (*On Interpretation* 4, 17a1), that is, to give something to be understood by others so as to facilitate dealings with the things about them with which all are involved and thus arrive at some form of agreement (*kata syntheses*) (306/443) that would permit them to get along.

And the basis of such agreement? Aristotle is clear: the establishment of a *symbolon* (*On Interpretation* 2, 16a28). Heidegger expatiates:

Symbole means throwing one thing together with another, holding something together with something else, i.e., keeping them alongside one another, joining them to and with one another. *Symbolon* therefore means joint, seam, or hinge, in which one thing is not simply brought together with the other, but the two are held to one another, so that they fit one another. Whatever is held together, fits together so that the two parts prove to belong together, is *symbolon*. (307/445)

Thus discourse (*logos*) has as its task to form a "sphere of understandability" whenever a being held together occurs in which agreement may be found. That sounds (*phone*) are emitted in such a process goes without saying, but what distinguishes human from animal sounds is the occurring of the *symbolon* as basis for agreement. It is only fundamental agreement of this kind that makes meaning (and the exchange of meanings) possible. "Sounds which emerge out of and for this *fundamental relation of letting something come into agreement and holding it together* are words. Words, discourse, occur in and out of such agreement with whatever can be referred to from the beginning and can be grasped as such" (308/446, Heidegger's emphasis).

The signifiers we call words, then, emerge from the primordial agreement among humans through which in their being with one another they are together open toward the beings around which they can agree (or, for that matter, disagree). "Only on the grounds of this originary, essential agreement is discourse possible in its essential function: *semainein*, giving that which is understandable to be understood" (309/448).

With this much said about *logos* as discourse in general, Heidegger focuses, as Aristotle does, on one form of it in particular, one that simply points out, or exhibits (*apophantikos*) something to be the case (e.g., "a is b"). There are many other forms of language, of course (expressions of wish, command, imprecation, affectivity, etc.), but all may be seen as different ways of proposing something and in that sense fundamentally (though reductively) as forms of statement.

Reduced to bare bones, the argument proceeds thus: what the exhibiting statement "a is b" points out is the experience of a *as* b, already apprehended (*noesis*) in some antecedent comportment. Thus the *logos apophantikos* brings a and b together into a unity (*synthesis*) while still maintaining their difference, that is, by keeping them apart (*diairesis*) as distinct terms (*noemata*), in affirming the "is" that unites them. Hence:

The "as"-structure itself is the condition of the of the *logos apophantikos*. . . . The "as" is not some property of the *logos,* stuck on or grafted onto it, but the reverse: the "as"-structure for its part is in general the condition of the possibility of this *logos*. (315/458)

But what does the "is" as copula of the proposition add to the a and b that are conjoined by it? It adds something (*prossemainei*), to be sure, but not some new third thing. Of course, there is an undifferentiated manifold of possible meanings that the word "is" elicits, but Heidegger reduces them to three that he deems essential: the "what-being" (*Was-sein*), taken in a very loose sense ("what kind of a thing" is affirmed); its "that-being" (*Dass-sein*), that is, the presence at hand of what is being affirmed; and its truth valence (*Wahr-sein*), that is, the intimation that what is affirmed is "true" (326–33/474–83).

But for this truth valence to emerge, the *logos* must allow itself to be determined by what is to be affirmed. *Logos* in affirming "is" must allow itself to be guided by the comportment through which the "as" was experienced. This supposes both the manifestness of what is to be affirmed and the docility of *logos* that lets itself be bound by it. This docility Heidegger describes as freedom on the part of Dasein. "Being open for . . . is from the very outset a free *holding oneself toward* whatever beings are given there in letting oneself be bound" (342/496, Heidegger's emphasis).

But there is one more step for Heidegger's argument to take. The task, after all, is to discover the role of Dasein in its function of forming a world (*Weltbildend*). He takes as example the remark: "the blackboard is poorly positioned." This could be the purely subjective judgment of the lecturer, but that would take no account of the fact that the blackboard is only one element in the complex structure of a multifunctional auditorium. But if the auditorium were not already pre-predicatively manifest, there would be no way to say that the blackboard is improperly positioned with regard to it.

More specifically, the pre-logical being-open out of which every *logos* must speak has in advance always already expanded the scope of beings in the direction of a completeness that is experienced "as-a-whole." "By this *completion* we are not to understand the subsequent addition of something hitherto missing, but rather the *prior forming of the 'as-a-whole' already prevailing*" (348/505, Heidegger's emphasis). Every assertion occurs on the basis of the prior formation of this as-a-whole. It is this prior formation of the "as-a-whole" already prevailing that constitutes the formation of Dasein's world.

Heidegger concludes with a reflection on the meaning of world as he has just discerned it. "Its essence resides in what we call the prevailing (*Walten*) of world, a prevailing that is more originary than all those beings that press upon us" (351/560). The appropriate response of Dasein to such a prevailing would involve three moments: holding oneself toward something that binds it; stretching out toward completion of a whole out of which it functions; unveiling the being of beings. These three moments are unified in what Heidegger calls "projection" (*Entwurf*): "*World prevails in and for a letting-prevail that has the character of projecting*" (362/527, Heidegger's emphasis). "*In projection there occurs the letting-prevail of the being of beings in the whole of their possible binding character in each case. In projection, world prevails*" (365/530, Heidegger's emphasis).

There is much to say about all this, and we must restrict ourselves to the essentials. In the first place, note the relationship between Dasein and *logos* that appears through the whole analysis. In orchestrating Aristotle's use of *logos* as *apophantikos*, Heidegger has offered warrant for his claim that the term *logon* in the Greek conception of human being as *zoon logon echon* should be understood as "discourse" rather than "reason," that is, human being as *parlêtre*, rather than as "rational animal." What would have happened to the metaphysical tradition if *logos*, as Aristotle understood it, had been translated originally as "discourse" (or its equivalent) rather than as *ratio*/"reason"/*Vernunft*, must remain pure speculation, but it is very clear that for Heidegger any new inception of philosophy should include that kind of question as grist for its mill: an other beginning "can only happen . . . by our taking upon ourselves the effort to transform man, and thereby traditional metaphysics, into a more originary existence, so as to let the ancient fundamental questions spring forth anew from this" (350/508).

With this the *Fundamental Concepts of Metaphysics* (1929–30) comes to an end and we become aware of what a remarkable watershed in Heidegger's thinking it records. The concept of world as manifestness, that is, openness (*Offenheit*) that prevails (*Walten*) over a Dasein that "projects" it (lit. "throws it open" [*Entwerfen*]) looks both backward and forward. Retrospectively, the course makes clear that the world disclosed phenomenologically in *Being and Time* (1927) as *Nichts* (Nothing), that is, as *Nicht-Seiendes* (No-thing)—terminology repeated famously two years later in Heidegger's inaugural lecture at Freiburg of 1929, "What Is Metaphysics?"—is not a declaration of nihilism but an insistence upon the non-ontic character of the world. This can be articulated now positively as openness that prevails over all beings, beginning with Dasein. Prospectively, the course anticipates the pivotal essay, "On the Essence of Truth" (1997), which appeared only in 1943 but had begun its long gestation with a first formulation in lecture form in 1930, just as the formal course concluded. In other words, this course offers a surprising opportunity to watch the so-called "turn" (*Kehre*) in Heidegger's thinking come about. However one understands this turn, it seems to have been fully functioning by the spring of 1930.

So far so good. Lacan would certainly be happy with the recognition by Heidegger's Aristotle that human being is in its most profound essence a *parlêtre*. He would be happy, too, to learn that for Aristotle the basis of all language is *symbolon* (with its structures) that makes any form of human agreement possible. But what is more interesting here is to see how the conception of world with which the 1929–30 course ends (the sense of a wholeness that prevails over human being which projects it in turn) soon becomes paradigm for the coming to pass of truth as *aletheia*.

The first lecture version of "On the Essence of Truth" begins by repeating the argument Heidegger has made before that truth in the sense of concordance between knower and known must presuppose a prior truth, that of revelation. Heidegger repeats the argument this way:

> What is stated by the presentative statement [i.e., *logos apophantikos*] is said of the presented thing in just such manner as that thing as presented is. The "such-as" has to do with the presenting and what it presents. . . . To present here means to let the thing stand opposed as object. As thus placed, what stands opposed must traverse an open field of opposedness and nevertheless maintain its stand as a thing and show itself as something withstanding (*ein Ständiges*). This appearing of the thing in traversing a field of opposedness takes place within an open region (*Offenen*), the openness (*Offenheit*) of which is not first created by the presenting but rather is only entered into and taken over as a domain of relatedness. The relation of the presentative statement to the thing is the accomplishment of that bearing (*Verhältnis*) that originarily and always comes to prevail as comportment. But all comportment is distinguished by the fact that, standing in the open region, it in each case adheres to something opened up as such. What is thus opened up, solely

in this strict sense, was experienced early in Western thinking as "what is present" and for a long time has been named [a] "being" (*Seiendes*). (1997, 144)

A few lines later, Heidegger adds "Western thinking in its beginning conceived this open region as *ta alethea,* the unconcealed. If we translate *aletheia* as 'unconcealment' rather than [as] 'truth,' this translation is not merely 'more literal,' it contains a directive to rethink the ordinary concept of truth in the sense of correctness of statements and to think it back to that still uncomprehended disclosedness and disclosure of beings" (144).

The sense here, of course, is that *aletheia* means a *lethe* (concealment) that has been taken away (alph'a privative). The full import of this we shall return to shortly. For the moment it is important only to insist that the world, experienced as domain of primordial openness, is not just the sum total of these beings that are encountered within it but the Open as such that makes this encounter possible—and not just for the individual thinker but for an entire people.

To gain a better sense of how *aletheia* serves as the Open within which the world of an entire people may be disclosed, let us return to Heidegger's description of the Greek temple at Paestum, Magna Graecia, the land of Parmenides himself:

We pose now the question about truth with the work [of art] in view. In order, however, to become more aware of what the question involves, it will be necessary to make the happening of truth in the work visible anew. For this attempt, let us choose a work that cannot be regarded as a work of representational art.

A building, a Greek temple, portrays nothing. It simply stands there in the middle of the rocky, fissured valley. The building encloses the figure of a god and within this concealment, allows it to stand forth through the columned hall within the holy precinct. Through the temple, the god is present in the temple. This presence of the god is, in itself, the extension and delimitation of the precinct as something holy. The temple and its precinct do not, however, float off into the indefinite. It is the temple work that first structures and simultaneously gathers around itself the unity of those paths and relations in which birth and death, disaster and blessing, victory and disgrace, endurance and decline acquire for the human being the shape of his destiny. The all-governing expanse of these open relations is the world of this historical people.

From and within this expanse the people (*Volk*) first return to itself for the completion of its vocation.

Standing there, the building rests on the rocky ground. This arresting of the work draws out of the rock the darkness of its unstructured yet unforced support. Standing there, the building holds its place against the storm raging above it and so first makes the storm visible in its violence. The gleam and luster of the stone, though apparently there only by the grace of the sun, in fact first brings forth the light of day, the breadth of the sky, the darkness of night. The temple's firm towering makes visible the invisible space of the air. The steadfastness of the work stands out against the surge of the tide and, in its own repose, brings out the raging of the surf. Tree, grass, eagle and bull, snake and cricket first enter their distinctive shapes and thus come to appearance as what they are. Early on, the Greeks called this coming forth and rising up in it and in all things *physis*. At the same time, *physis* lights up that on which man bases his dwelling. We call this the *earth*. . . .

Standing there, the temple first gives to things their look, and to men their outlook on themselves. This view remains open as long as the work is a work, so long as the god has not fled from it. . . .

To be a work means: to set up a world. . . . World is not a mere collection of the things—countable and uncountable, known and unknown—that are present at hand. Neither is world a merely imaginary framework added by our representation to the sum of things that are present. *World worlds*, and is more fully in being than all those tangible and perceptible things in the midst of which we take ourselves to be at home. World is never an object that stands before us and can be looked at. World is that always nonobjectual to which we are subject as long as the paths of birth and death, blessing and curse, keep us transported into being. Wherever the essential decisions of our history are made, wherever we take them over or abandon them, wherever they go unrecognized or are brought once more into question, there the world worlds. . . . (2002, 20–23, passim)

e claim being made here is that such a world, which for Heidegger ild be an instantiation of Being as *aletheia* in its moment of revealment, he world of "reality" that Lacan claims to be constituted by collusion he symbolic and the imaginary. As a physical monument it can be scru-zed, analyzed, and pawed over by archeologists, architects, and hard ntists of all description; as a witness to the history of religion it can be examined by historians, sociologists, theologians, philologists, or even lin-guists who may study the language in which its history is recorded or even the signifiers with which Heidegger describes it. But these are all ontic dis-ciplines that do not touch the truth (*aletheia:* revealment) of the world it instantiates and makes the ontic exercises possible. So, too, with the triadic structure with which Lacan conceptualizes the way in which the human subject relates to the phenomenon of unconscious experience in a psycho-analytic context. This is a completely ontic enterprise that supposes—and must suppose—the disclosure of world as such that Heideggerian thinking is uniquely equipped to discern.

World in Concealment

Returning to Heidegger, we ask: if *aletheia* is the privation of *lethe,* what of the *lethe* that survives? In a first reading it means "concealment," but hereby hangs a tale. The problem poked up its head in the lecture course when Heidegger paraphrased Aristotle (*On Interpretation* 4, 17a3–4) to say that only in exhibitive discourse is truth (*aletheuesthai*) or un-truth (*pseudesthai*) to be found. Heidegger refuses to translate the latter as "falsity," for this is only the contrary to truth in the sense of correspon-dence. He calls attention rather to the fact that *pseudesthai* is the medial form of the Greek verb, suggesting that the activity in question is in the truthing process itself, which makes it inherently deceptive, that is, reveal-ing something as what it is not. Heidegger prefers to translate *pseudesthai* as "concealing," which of course is the proper complement to *aletheuein,* if this be taken to mean "revealing" as he intends (1929–30, 310/449).

This thematic is orchestrated in "On the Essence of Truth," where the non-truth proper to truth as revelation takes the form either of mystery (*Geheimnis*), the concealment of concealment (148–49), or of errancy (*Irre*) (150–52):

> Errancy is the essential counter-essence to the originary essence of
> truth. Errancy opens itself up as the open region for every counter play
> to essential truth. Errancy is the open site of and ground of error. Error
> is not merely an isolated mistake but the kingdom (the dominion) of
> the history of those entanglements in which all kinds of erring get
> interwoven.
>
> In conformity with its openness and its relatedness to beings as a
> whole, every mode of comportment has its manner of erring. Error ex-

tends from the most ordinary wasting of time, making a mistake, and miscalculation, to going astray and venturing too far in one's essential attitudes and decisions. . . . By leading them astray, errancy dominates human beings through and through. (150–51)

This passage is puzzlement. Whence comes the power of errancy? We know from the 1929–30 lectures that the world exercises a kind of power (*Walten*). We know from the 1935 course, *Introduction to Metaphysics* (2000), that *physis, logos,* and *dike* exercise different modalities of power; the power of errancy is negative in form—a power to seduce, subvert, or sabotage: "By leading them astray, errancy dominates human beings through and through." Is this just a rhetorical ploy, or is something specifically new being said here?

Heidegger attacks the problem frontally in his course on *Parmenides* (1997), delivered at the same time that "On the Essence of Truth" was given its final redaction before going to press (1943). The course was devoted to a meditation on the philosopher's dogmatic *Poem,* with special focus on the meaning of *lethe* as counter-essence (*Gegenwesen*) to the essence of truth. Given the general sense of "concealment," this sense is strummed out in every possible way: as forgetting, falsifying, covering-up, veiling, dissembling, hiding, misleading, detouring, sheltering, and so on. Of these senses, the most fundamental is "forgetting."[3]

Daughter of strife (*eris*) and night (*nyx*), *lethe* must be understood as "oblivion," a cloud that enshrouds everything in "signlessness," a withdrawal into concealment that conceals itself (1992, 82). In this context, Heidegger dismisses any subjective or psychological interpretation of "forgetting" but does insist that this "oblivion" affects what another language would call both "theoretical" and "practical" dimensions of human activity. This becomes clear when this activity finds its place in the social context of the *polis:*

> The *polis* is neither city nor state and definitely not the fatal mixture of these two inappropriate characterizations. . . . The *polis* [is] the abode, gathered into itself, of the unconcealedness of beings. If now, however, as the word indicates, *aletheia* possesses a conflictual essence, which appears also in the oppositional forms of distortion and oblivion, then in the *polis* as the essential abode of man there has to hold sway all the most extreme counter-essences, and therein all excesses, to the unconcealed and to beings, i.e., counter-beings in the multiplicity of their counter-essence. Here lies concealed the primordial ground of that fea-

ture Jacob Burckhardt presented for the first time in its full bearing and manifoldness: the frightfulness, the horribleness, the atrociousness of the Greek *polis*.[4] Such is the rise and fall of man in his historical abode of essence—*hypsipolis-apolis*—far exceeding abodes, homeless, as Sophocles (*Antigone*) calls man. It is not by chance that man is spoken of in this way in Greek tragedy. For the possibility, and the necessity of "tragedy" itself has its single source in the conflictual essence of *aletheia*. (1992, 90)

Whence comes the subversive power of *lethe*? It derives from the force generated by the conflict between concealment and non-concealment in the very nature of *aletheia*. The disorder and even disaster that lurk in the *polis* are essential to the dwelling of historical Dasein because every unconcealment of beings is engaged in conflict with concealment and, consequently, with dissemblance and distortion. If *lethe*'s drag toward self-concealing concealment were given full sway, total withdrawal of *lethe* would result in an absolute void. Heidegger grapples with this very conception when he meditates on the myth with which Plato closes the *Republic*, the story of Er (1961, 614b2–621d3). In Heidegger's paraphrase of 621a2–5 we read:

> The warrior narrates that the way to the field of *lethe* leads through a blaze consuming everything and through an air that asphyxiates everything. . . . This field of concealment is opposed to all *physis*. *Lethe* does not admit any *phyein*, any emerging and coming forth. . . . The field of *lethe* prevents every disclosure of beings, of the ordinary. In the essential place of *lethe* everything disappears. Yet it is not only the completeness of the withdrawal of the presumed quantity or the concealment that distinguishes this place. The point is rather that the "away" of the withdrawn comes into presence itself in the essence of the withdrawal. The "away" of what is withdrawn and concealed is surely not "nothing," for the letting disappear that withdraws everything occurs in this place—in this place alone and presents itself there. The place is void—there is nothing at all that is ordinary in it. But the void is precisely what remains and what comes into presence there. The barrenness of the void is the nothing of the withdrawal. (1997, 118–19)

*   *   *

The task here has been to ask whether the conception of human being according to Lacan (as *parlêtre*, structured by symbolic, imaginary, and real) and that of Heidegger (as the There of Being understood as locus among beings for the event of *aletheia*) are compatible enough to permit one to throw light on the other. We have responded with the hypothesis that the revealment (alpha-privative) component of *aletheia* in psychoanalytic conceptualization, as revelatory of the world, is analogous to Lacan's correlation of symbolic and imaginary. Now we are suggesting that *lethe* for Heidegger (that self-concealing, signless oblivion, intolerant of any living thing and stretching toward the void) is analogous to Lacan's real—the "impossible" real, impossible because incapable of (and hostile to) access of any kind, whether imaginary or symbolic.

But so what? As analogies go, it seems to work and leaves each style of thinking (so different one from the other) to be itself. But of what good is that? Is it anything more than a set of acrobatic moves that provide a curious philosophical exhibition but leave us no wiser than before? In fact, I propose it as one possible scenario of the dialogue that might have taken place if the two thinkers had been able to hear each other out and the dialogue allowed its time with a future that still may await it. In the blunt language of *Being and Time*, Lacan's problem, it would seem, is an ontic one and Heidegger's an ontological one. Such apparent complementarity, if true, might prove helpful to both.

For his part, Lacan would seem to have real need of Heidegger's conception of *aletheia*. His early attraction to Heidegger's notion of language as "speaking" human being (*die Sprache spricht*) is based on the latter's interpretation of *logos* in Heraclitus as Being itself, that is, as language in its most originary, primordial form. As Heidegger reads Heraclitus, *logos*, like *physis*, is another modality of *aletheia*—all three, as is evident in *Introduction to Metaphysics* (2000), different versions of Being itself. To be sure, Lacan insists that there is "no Other of the Other" (as if Being might be taken as such a second "Other"). He clarifies this immediately, however, by explaining that he means only that there is "no metalanguage," that is, no system of signifiers beyond ("other" than) the one we already have—and equally as ontic. But [Being-as-] *aletheia*, the Open, is in no sense an ontic metalanguage. Rather, the Open (as Being/*logos*/*aletheia*) lets language itself be in such a way that Lacan (and the rest of humanity) may have access to it. Without Being/*logos*/*aletheia*, there would be no language at all and—rather more disconcerting—no one to speak it.

Aletheia also means "truth" as revelation, and Lacan needs the concept badly to escape an *aporia*. On the one hand, he insists on the importance of discovering and honoring the "truth," say, of the subject's desire, and "truth" as a function in his analysis of the four different modes of human discourse (1991). On the other hand, he emphasizes the impossibility of truth that does not simultaneously negate itself: "The discourse of error—its articulation in action—could bear witness to the truth against evidence itself" (2002, 113). Only a conception of truth that includes its own counter-essence (non-truth) in some form such as mystery and errancy suggest would seem able to resolve the problem.

Finally, in 1959–60 Lacan pleaded the cause for an "ethics of psychoanalysis" (1992)—a bold task indeed, for it implies that the subject of psychoanalysis (subject of the unconscious) is capable of posing an ethical, that is, morally responsible, act. This is a tall order. In a text contemporary with this proposal, the subject of the unconscious is described in these terms: it is "caused" by the signifier whose only task is to represent it to another signifier, "beneath" which it "disappears," so that, apart from its transference from one signifier to another, the subject is described as "absolutely nothing" (1995, 265). The uninitiated will find this language strange, indeed if intelligible at all. An astute hermeneutic may situate it in its proper context to clarify its coherence and plausibility, but what hermeneutic can find in it the ingredients of a moral agent capable of positing an ethical act? Whether a Heideggerian concept of Dasein could help meet the rigorous demands of the problem is a question that at least may be raised. As a formalized conceptualization, however, Dasein would be more than "absolutely nothing" to begin with, for as "ek-sistence" it would already be, and be structured (in part) by the existential component of *logos* that in turn would be eminently determinable by the symbolic order. Whether such an apparent correspondence has any viability must remain an open question for now that only the future can decide.

But psychoanalysis à la Lacan can be of service to philosophy à la Heidegger as well. At least it can help to keep it honest. The centrality of language in its own project forces the Heideggerian thinker to remain aware that ontological thinking, even when it aspires to be inceptive, must continue to be rooted in the ontic experience of human existence. This means that the effort of the later Heidegger to reflect on the *logos* as aboriginal language must respect, whatever its reserves about Freudian metapsychology, the seriousness of the ontic claim that "the unconscious is structured like a language." More precisely, Heidegger's own efforts to illumine the creative power of the poets (such as Hölderlin, George, Trakl, and Celan) should take seriously the effort of the later Lacan to formalize the creative genius of a James Joyce by finding in it the supreme instantiation of the triadic paradigm for *parlêtre:* the Borromean Knot (1975–77).

Epilogue

In the 1950s an important dialogue between Martin Heidegger and Jacques Lacan was arranged but failed to materialize, and it was left to a future that is still to come. We have sought to address that future by postulating a first moment in such a dialogue in exploring the possibility of a basic complementarity between the two thinkers. Specifically, this became a reflection on the role of *aletheia* in their work. How to measure the success of the effort? Obviously there can be no measure of success beyond *aletheia* itself: "the evidence for evidence is evidence," and in this case the evidence is still to come. Perhaps the surest sign of success is simply continuing to explore, "until we arrive where we started and know the place for the first time."

Notes

1. Martin Heidegger, *Being and Time,* trans. Joan Stambaugh (Albany: SUNY Press, 1996), 13.

2. Aristotle's influence on Heidegger's own phenomenological analysis of Dasein is evident from the role he assigns to *Rede* (*logos,* "discourse") as an "existential" component of Dasein's structure in *Being and Time* (1996, 28–30, 150–56). For Heidegger, too, then, Dasein is clearly a *parlêtre.*

3. *Lethe* is a nominative form derived from *lanthano,* which, according to Liddell and Scott, means: (1) to escape notice; (2) to make one forget. In the middle voice it means: (3) to forget, to forget purposely, to choose to forget, etc.

4. Note the similarity between this language and that of the "Letter on Humanism," which speaks of the "malice of rage" (*Bösartigen des Grimmes*) as deriving from the fact that Being itself is contested (*das Strittige*). "Letter on 'Humanism,'" in *Pathmarks,* ed. W. McNeill (Cambridge: Cambridge University Press, 1998), 260.

7   What We Owe the Dead

Dennis J. Schmidt

To speak of "Heidegger and the Greeks"—to speak, that is, of a single contemporary thinker who volatized inherited forms of thinking (forms largely owing to how "the Greeks" have been read) and of a collective designation for a diverse group of ancient thinkers now canonized—is to speak, among other matters, of the relation of the present to the past. A large theme, summoning far too much at once, like the ghosts who flock around Odysseus when he goes to the underworld to speak with Tiresias, this theme can overwhelm: history, memory, tradition—all that comes with the passage of time—start to emerge as necessary topics. They are topics not by chance central to Heidegger's own concerns; topics that have come to define who Heidegger is for us. When Heidegger takes up these themes in ancient Greek contexts, when he places himself in conjunction with "the Greeks," he not only does so with Greek philosophers in mind, but searches out a Greek sensibility that is not found only—or even always—in Greek philosophers. He reminds us always that "the Greeks" is a designation that does not at all limit itself to those we call philosophers. Indeed, the philosophers might be the ones who opened the door to something that would no longer be deemed "Greek."

   In what follows, my intention is to unfold one small, yet telling, theme crucial to that ancient sensibility that I take to be at the heart of those themes at stake in the topic of "Heidegger and the Greeks," namely, the question of what it is that we owe the dead.

*   *   *

Corpses are uncanny things. Pure ambiguities, they are no longer bodies of singular beings marked by self-consciousness as a possibility, but, as effigies of such a being, they are not yet "mere" nature.[1] Before this body dissolves into the natural world, leaving the person alive only in the memories of the living, the corpse stands as a memento of just how peculiar, just how enigmatic, a human being is insofar as it is a being belonging to a body. It poignantly reminds us that we both are and are not our bodies. Above all, the dead body, strangeness in material form, is the emblem of how the passage between life and death challenges our comprehension of who we are. We go to great lengths to invest the corpse with some residue of life, or at least to treat it as the repository of the memory of life. Rituals surround the dead body, ceremonies seek to preserve that which natural processes will inevitably reclaim. Corpses are liminal bodies, transitions into what we do not understand. As such, our relation to the corpse helps give definition to what we hold to be true and valuable about ourselves. In the end, one might extend this claim and suggest, as does Hegel, that our treatment of the corpse is among the founding acts of community.[2]

Much can be said of the culture surrounding the treatment of the dead body and even of how culture itself is founded on such rituals. However, my interest in this general topic is much less ambitious than such sweeping concerns with the relation of culture and the corpse might open up. I am simply interested in thinking about the peculiar significance of corpses in ancient Greece and in marking a difference on this point in the present age. More precisely, I am interested both in looking at how dead bodies play such a vital role in the literature of Greek tragedy and in noting why it is that this role is so difficult for us to understand today. The important role of corpses is especially evident in two of the greatest works of antiquity, Homer's *Iliad* and Sophocles' *Antigone*.[3] Significantly, these corpses are the result of wars. In the *Iliad*, it is Achilles' passion to recover and bury the dead body of his dear friend, Patroclus, that animates the rage and great battles eventually leading to Achilles' own death. Likewise, Antigone's quarrel with Creon is over the rights of burial for the corpse, and, like Achilles', Antigone's own death is precipitated by her desire to *save* a corpse. One also finds dead bodies very much at the center of such works as the *Odyssey*,[4] Plato's *Republic*[5] and *Laws*,[6] and Pericles' *Funeral Oration*.[7] The list of such examples could be extended, but rather than offer further instances of prominent roles granted to the corpse, let me simply make my special concern with this prominence more precise by suggesting that what needs to be noted is that such instances invariably point to a decidedly *ethical* interest. The Greeks understood that a quite peculiar form of our consciousness of mortality is found in the concern with the dead bodies of others, and I believe that there is something to be learned from the Greeks by following out the character of this consciousness. In the end, we come to see something of how the limits and stakes of ethical life need to be conceived. So, the first part of the question I want to address concerns this matter of the ethical import of the consciousness of death and of the manner in which we conceive our relation with the dead. Is it fair to say that *in the way we understand what it is that we owe the dead we are answering an elemental question that says much about how we are to be with the living*? It is a question very much at the heart of the consciousness of mortality animating Greek tragedy.[8]

But, as soon as one reflects on this question with reference to our own times one soon realizes that the manner in which death is given for reflection today is powerfully mediated by images (on television and in print media) and by words. Significantly, as the Greeks well knew, this is especially true in times of war, when the corpse most directly poses a question to the character of community. Above all, one needs to acknowledge that there is a difference between the ancient and modern forms in which the role of the corpse, this material presence of mortality, will be present for us. Susan Sontag has taken up this question of how one witnesses death in her book on the relationship of photography to images of war, *Regarding the Pain of Others,* and I believe that there are some points she makes that cannot be avoided by one who would take up this ancient question in the present age. More precisely, Sontag opens her book by challenging Virginia Woolf's assumption that in seeing horrible images of death humans cultivate a moral repugnance toward war. Woolf's assumption expresses the same view that we find in Aristotle's *Poetics,* where he suggests that to witness suffering and death (importantly, Aristotle is referring to witnessing something on a *stage, not in a photograph*) is to be overtaken by the moral emotions of pity and fear. But, after pointing out that so much of our understanding of death in war is mediated by photographic images, Sontag raises the question of the possibilities that such images carry. She suggests both that we risk being *numbed* rather than moved by the proliferation of such images and that such images are also able to be enlisted for ideological rather than moral reasons, such that we are *incensed* and driven to retaliation rather than pity by such images. In short, her claim is that we can no longer take for granted that the dominant form in which death is presented to us today summons an ethical, rather than a manipulated, response from us. Without attempting to take up all of Sontag's rich analysis of this matter, let me say that I do want to take her remarks as an inspiration for the second part of the question I want to address today, namely, *how is it that the living are best able to bear witness to the dead*? In other words, how does our consciousness of mortality present itself to us and how does the form of its presentation and communication shape the way that consciousness reverberates in our lives?

Those are my two questions. In what follows, my intention is to answer these questions in three stages. First, I want to clarify the different natures of the two chief forms in which contemporary philosophers typically locate a lived consciousness (rather than a simple cognition) of mortality, namely, *anxiety* and *mourning*. Second, I want to discuss the attitude toward death and our relation to the dead that we find in some ancient texts, in which a sense of *debt* to the dead is expressed. In the third part, my purpose is to address remembering and bearing witness and to ask what sort of acts best accomplish those tasks.

But before engaging those questions, let me announce the conclusions I will draw in each case. First, I will argue that yes, we do find something elemental and original for ethical and political life in thinking through this question of what we owe the dead; in fact, I will argue that, as we move beyond presentations of anxiety and mourning, and as we approach a sense of our debt to the dead, we draw close to the founding event of community. Second, I want to suggest that *art* is better suited to figuring this debt and to bearing witness to the phenomenon of death than is philosophy; indeed, I will argue that the tradition of philosophizing that gets its first inspiration from the singular case of the death of Socrates is, by virtue of some of its most cherished assumptions, poorly equipped to take up the topic of death. In light of my first conclusion this will imply of course that I also take philosophy to be poorly equipped to deal with the elements of ethical life.

* * *

Let me begin then with Heidegger, who makes the question I want to address exceedingly difficult insofar as he argues that we cannot have an original experience of the death of others, but that all consciousness of death is rooted ultimately in a consciousness of *my own* death and that even the most deeply felt grief traces itself back to anxiety, which is already a difficult and rather displaced consciousness of death.

This is the argument he makes in *Being and Time* where, after suggesting that it is in death that any sense of the wholeness of life is first to be found, he asks how it is that we know of death. He begins by noting the great paradox of any discussion of death; namely, that strictly speaking, no phenomenology of death is possible. I survive the death of the other, and I can have no experience of my own death. Nonetheless, he argues that even if no experience of death as such is possible, even if it constitutes the non-phenomenal par excellence, it still remains true that knowing and feeling oneself to be mortal form the foundation of the experience that the human being has of itself. It is not the *cogito sum* that opens up my being to me, but the *sum moribundus* that opens me to my *I am*. In order to account for this, Heidegger undertakes an analysis of anxiety, which he contends is the sole manner in which we have what knowledge is to be found of the real nothingness of death. Establishing the priority of anxiety is crucial for Heidegger, and so while he says that all we can think and say of life is mediated by our being toward death, he also claims that we do not experience the dying of others in a genuine sense; we are at best always just "there" too.[9] In other words, Heidegger argues that *mourning is not an original relation to death, that anxiety is more original than mourning, and consequently that from our mourning the death of others we cannot draw original conclusions.* Heidegger's contention is simple: that even if the death of the other is suffered as an irreparable loss, the loss that the other suffered has still not become accessible. However much we may suffer, the force and meaning of the death of the other escapes us. We are fated to die alone, and our lamentations for the dead, which might seem to be a residue of our solidarity with others, are really expressions of our own solitude. Indeed, one can mourn only insofar as one has already been disclosed to oneself and has already constituted oneself as finite. Mourning is a sort of sublation of death in which I also experience my own survival rather than an original consciousness of mortality. So runs Heidegger's argument in a nutshell.

Two points need to be noted regarding this analysis: first, that while death itself radically eludes all presence, in anxiety it nonetheless confers upon all appearance the character of finitude; and second, that in anxiety each of us is radically singularized. Finitude and ipseity are the real meaning of death for us. The fragility of the world and the untranslatable singularity of my being are what is given to me by my consciousness of my own mortality. In the end, because it is disclosed to itself in anxiety, Dasein, Heidegger's name for the sort of being that we are, is an *idiom*. Or in the words of Nietzsche: *Ich bin eine Nuance*. For my purposes, let me say that despite Heidegger's own allergy to speaking of ethics, I believe one can find a profoundly ethical sensibility in Heidegger at this point. In the ipseity of Dasein we find a powerful sense of both freedom and responsibility—I alone am answerable for myself—and in the singularity of Dasein we find something akin to Kant's notion that I am an end unto myself and that I need to understand myself as living in a kingdom of such ends.

But I want to think about this claim and challenge it. I do not at all want to dispute Heidegger's analysis of anxiety, nor its significance for us. This somewhat Kantian ethical sensibility is something I want to preserve for the full answer to the question of the ethical significance of our consciousness of mortality. But I do want to dispute Heidegger's claim that it is the *sole original form of our consciousness of death.* In other words, I want to suggest that the realm of our consciousness of mortality is wider than that which Heidegger describes. While I believe that Heidegger is right to identify anxiety as a fundamental disposition, I also believe that to fully grasp the import of our consciousness of mortality, mourning needs to be recognized as a genuinely *different* yet equally *original* form of that consciousness. Much is at stake in the decision to grant anxiety a priority over mourning as the basic experience of the finitude and singularity of being. The stakes are above all evident in the ethical significance of this difference. In the end, I will suggest that even mourning does not go far enough to answer the question of how we are to think our relation with the dead. But I do want to claim that it is only by passing through mourning that we arrive at the most ethically significant form of that answer, and so asking about mourning is the first step toward the point I want to make today.

Here beginning with Freud is helpful. In his effort to distinguish anxiety and mourning as reactions to loss, Freud twice notes that one characteristic of mourning remains completely obscure, its special painfulness.[10] He only begins to elaborate that pain in his further attempt to distinguish mourning from melancholia. He makes this distinction by arguing that there is a special sort of *work* through which mourning can be overcome. It is a work with a double task: the adjustment of one's sense of reality to accommodate the loss of the other and the abandonment of the libido relation to the lost other (something one does not do easily). The failure to accomplish this work, being stuck with that special painfulness, is the consequence of an idealization of the other such that reality can never recover from this loss of the other. The result is a sort of chronic condition of mourning, and that is what he calls melancholia. It is in the contrast between mourning and melancholia that Freud sharpens his presentation of the work of mourning and the dynamic of that consciousness of mortality proper to it. Most importantly, he suggests that at the end of the work of mourning, the self is returned to itself free and unimpaired. Famously, he says that in mourning, the world is impoverished, in melancholia it is the self that is emptied.[11] What I want to emphasize is that, in contrast to Heidegger, Freud argues that mourning is essentially a different form in which the consciousness of mortality shapes us. In it we struggle to form a sense of reality and the self by confronting the great enigma of death in a way that anxiety does not; namely, in mourning we face the great affront of death that life goes on and that life so easily absorbs death into itself. I believe that this is the locus of the "special pain" of mourning to which Freud cryptically alludes: the heartbreak, the heartlessness of death, is that I must go on. The "work" of mourning is, to use the language of Hegel, to sublate the monstrous negative of death and to take it up into life; to "accept" it and its reality. This "sublation" of death, this taking it up into the movement of life, is what anxiety does not accomplish.

To make the decision that it is indeed the case that there is something irreducible in our consciousness of being mortal to be found in mourning is to suggest that others belong to the constitution of myself in an original manner. Anxiety is a liminal experience, an experience that opens up the radical finitude of the world in a manner that *constitutes* something like a self that is then responsible for itself. Mourning is a liminal experience in which the limits of the capacity of the self to define itself by itself are exposed. It entails an acknowledgment that we belong to, and are constituted by, a world that is larger than that which we can either define or control—a world that continues even when there is a death that I must absorb. A different sort of finitude is opened up here: it is the finitude proper to the capacity of the self to become conscious of itself by itself. This is the finitude proper to what I want to call the porosity of the self, which is that character of the self that is always in a tension with its own ipseity. We are this struggle to find ourselves in this aporia of being both singular and engaged, being both individuated and wedded to others. Hegel, who suggests that self-consciousness achieves the satisfaction of its desire for recognition only in another self-consciousness[12] and who identifies the act of burial as the first decisive act in the formation of community, is interesting on this point by virtue of the extent to which he acknowledges both the singularity and the essential belonging together of consciousnesses. We are torn between our being an idiom and belonging to the common, and for Hegel the dialectic of this contradiction in our own natures propels us to ever-deepening forms of self-consciousness.

My intention is not to move into this dialectic of self-consciousness as such, but to stay focused on my original question about the ethical import of our consciousness of mortality. In order to do this I want to make two points, one regarding anxiety, the other regarding mourning. About anxiety, my point is simple: it instructs us about *responsibility.* In anxiety I learn that I alone am answerable for myself; that there is some *inalienable task* that I cannot pass along to another and that is mine alone. In anxiety I understand that death is mine alone and that in the end I am always returned to myself in such a way as to make evident to me that this "self" rests upon nothing but itself. It "is" only in this "return." Simultaneously then, I learn the ineluctability of my *responsibility* and the bottomlessness of my *freedom.* This experience of freedom and responsibility is, as Schelling saw in his *On the Essence of Human Freedom,* the condition of the possibility of any possible ethical life. And it is, as Nietzsche saw in so many places, the condition of being able to speak of the realm of ethical life beyond the polarities of good and evil, and the calculus of that economy.

But the full story of the ethical import of our consciousness of death is not told by understanding this truth of anxiety. The truth of mourning also needs to be taken into account. Here what I want to argue is that the real truth of mourning is that it is *impossible,* that we *cannot* complete the task of mourning because the other, like me, is an idiom, a singular being, and no adjustment of reality can accommodate that loss. It is final. It is the fate of finite being that such loss cannot be recuperated. Homer tells a story that beautifully illustrates this great gulf that separates the living and the dead. It is found in the eleventh book of *The Odyssey,* where the story is told of Odysseus's descent into the realm of the dead. He goes there to speak with Tiresias, who, though blind, is the one who can see the route Odysseus must take to find his way home. There is a complex ritual, involving the drinking of blood, which enables the living and the dead to speak. Odysseus is crowded in, terrifyingly, by scores of the dead who long to drink the blood he brought with him. He guards it, but then, after speaking with Tiresias, he sees the shade of his mother. He had been gone from home for about fifteen years at this point and did not know that she had died. He weeps and longs to speak with her. She drinks the blood and they trade stories. As the time for them to speak draws to a close Odysseus, tears now streaming down his face, having learned the fate of his mother and the rest of his family, moves to her in order to embrace her. He tries three times to hold her in his arms. But she is only a shade and cannot be held. He asks her why he cannot hold her and she answers, powerfully, that "it is the justice [*dike*] of mortal life." She explains this by saying that "sinews no longer bind the flesh and bones together, the fire in all its fury burns the body down to ashes once life slips from the white bones, and the spirit flitters away . . . like a dream."[13] Much is illustrated about how the Greeks thought the relation of the living and the dead in this story of Odysseus's journey to the underworld (it is a story that Plato will rewrite in the final book of the *Republic*, "The Myth of Er"), but for my purposes the point it most illustrates is that the separation of the living from the dead is final and, in the end, cannot be crossed. The reason is important: it is by virtue of the absent body that this divide is inscribed as absolute.

I will return to this point about the body later. Now let me simply say that here we are reminded in a poetic image that the truth of mourning is lodged in its impossibility. There are two reasons for this: one, as I just indicated, is that the body—the real locus of idiomatic being—is absent; the other reason that we cannot finish with its work is because the dead are still among us. They are never completely fugitives, even if they are beyond our reach.[14] They reside in our language, in our monuments, in our texts, our memory; the earth's crust is full of the dead, so much so that we must say that we are closer to the dead than to the stars that also powerfully inspire thinking. So it is the task of the living to understand this peculiar presence. In a very real sense, I have already been constituted by those others who are now dead, and this makes mourning complicated. Strictly speaking, it makes mourning *impossible*. But it is important to see that it is not impossible in the way that Heidegger would have us believe (i.e., that mourning is, in the final analysis, rooted only in anxiety). Nor is it the case as Freud would have us believe—namely, that such a failure to complete the work of mourning leaves one with melancholia and its narcissism that is so thoroughly indexed to the dead past. There is rather a way of seeing the task of mourning as somehow "translated" or as handed over to a sense of a *debt* that is indexed not to the past, but to the future. This is a difficult point to make, but it is central to my concerns. In order to explain this notion of our "debt" to the dead we should begin to talk again about *bodies* of the dead, and here Greek tragic consciousness is especially instructive.

Dead bodies and burials form the heart of two of ancient Greece's most enduring texts: Homer's *Iliad* and Sophocles' *Antigone*. Corpses are also very much at the heart of two of Plato's most detailed and important dialogues: *The Republic* and *The Laws*. Homer and Sophocles present us with characters who somehow seem to want to "save" the dead. Plato takes issue with such a point of view. Let me briefly indicate how these texts speak of dead bodies and the task of the living regarding such bodies.

The *Iliad* is the story of Achilles' rage and grief, and of how the alchemy of these emotions drives him to go back into battle and to murder Hector. I will not rehearse the story, but simply remind you that it is in order to save the corpse of Patroclus that Achilles returns to the fight, which he had previously abandoned because of his dispute with Agamemnon. Achilles knows from a prophecy that to kill Hector will mean his own death; nonetheless, the rage that emerges out of grief drives Achilles to kill Hector. Hector's last words to Achilles, just before dying, are the request that Achilles not mutilate his body, but that he return it to the city for proper burial. Achilles refuses. Indeed, he sets for himself only two tasks before his own death: to desecrate Hector's body and to bury the body of Patroclus. The funeral of Patroclus is a celebration of sorts full of competitions. But the body of Hector will not rot, and it does not show any sign of Achilles' desperate efforts to mutilate it. Eventually, Hector's father, Priam, comes to Achilles to plead with him to permit the city to bury his son. Achilles sees in the eyes of Priam the memory of his own father and the grief that he knows he will suffer, and so he relents, returns the body, and permits a funeral. The Trojan War, which had raged at this point for a decade, stops while the Trojans bury Hector. It should be noted that this strange respect for the bodies of the dead is something that still animates modern wars. Article 15 of the First Geneva Convention stipulates in great detail the rules of the treatment of the dead. It says, for instance, that "at all times both parties must search for the dead and prevent their being despoiled." In short, some echo of the Greek sensibility is still present with us.

Two plays by Sophocles make dead bodies and burial their central theme: *Antigone* is the drama that plays out as a struggle for possession of a corpse and *Oedipus at Colonus* is the drama of the blind Oedipus looking for a place where he might die and be buried. *Antigone,* which begins in the aftermath of a civil war, is about Antigone's efforts to bury her brother Polynices. The only real "action" of the play is that Antigone twice sprinkles dirt over the corpse of her brother (and even that is concealed from view). Creon insists that the city still retains jurisdiction over the body, while Antigone argues that in death we leave the community of the living and its laws and that we return to that pure singularity which is outside the law of the common, the laws of the *polis*. Like Achilles, she charts a course that she knows will result in her own death, and, like Achilles, she does this to "save" a corpse. One reason for this is that at an earlier phase of her life Polynices had asked her to care for him if he should die in the war to come. When he made this request of her she had been leading her father, Oedipus, now blinded, from city to city, as he looked for a place to die and be buried. No city would have him. But Oedipus tells Theseus, the king who finally consents to permit his burial, that his corpse will protect the city from harm so long as the site of his grave remains a secret.

Plato too has a pronounced concern with the dead, even a concern with corpses and with burial (he even, in a provocative passage, describes written language as "the corpse of a thought"[15]). But among the many examples one might give, let me refer you to just two. First, the entire dialogue of the *Republic* is sandwiched between two quite potent images of death: Socrates meets Cephalus, a very old man, and Socrates rather rudely asks him what it is like to be so close to death. Cephalus, the head of the household, sitting on a "head" chair (his name too means head, in short he is the very image of the cerebral life without a body) answers with three comments. First he cites Sophocles, saying that he has finally lost all *eros,* "that mad monster." Then he says that as *eros* has departed from his body he has taken up two new interests: he now has more time for *logos,* and a newfound concern with justice has taken root in him. Despite his newfound love of discourse, Cephalus wears out, lacking all energy for conversation, and totters off to sleep. But before he leaves he bequeaths the conversation to his son, Thrasymachus, who, he says, will inherit his fortunes and so might begin by inheriting this conversation. Two consequences of this opening should be noted: first, that the question of justice is opened and framed by a concern with death; second, that the questions both of justice and of death are bound up with the notion of inheritance. This concern with death will saturate the *Republic.* Two more passages illustrate just how prominent a matter it is for Plato's understanding of how we are to form the ideal *polis.* When Socrates and Glaucon set out to found the city in words, their very first act is to exile the poets from the discussion regarding the city. The reason given for this, which is the focus of all of Book III, is simple: the poets cultivate an unhealthy attitude toward death. Socrates criticizes Homer and specifies several passages—all about the presentation of death in Homer—as illustrative of what is wrong with the poetic image of death. Among these passages is one drawn from the eleventh book of the *Odyssey,* Odysseus's descent into the realm of the dead, in which Odysseus speaks with the dead image of Achilles. Plato complains about the propriety of Achilles' comment that he would rather be a poor slave living a life of poverty than be even the king of the realm of the dead (386c). The second passage in which we see how death plays a decisive role in the task of founding the *polis* is found in the tenth book, more precisely, in the "Myth of Er," which tells the "story of what awaits the dead." Socrates begins to tell that story by describing how it is that "Er was slain in battle, and when the corpses were taken up on the tenth day already decayed, his was found intact, and having been brought home, at the moment of his funeral, on the twelfth day as he lay upon the pyre, revived and related what he had seen in the world beyond" (614b).

In *The Laws* Plato is similarly centered on matters of our mortality, especially the question of what to do with dead bodies. So, for instance, after discussing how our debts are to be paid and the penalties for those who do not pay their debts, the Athenian Stranger launches into a lengthy and rather detailed discussion of burial and the rules for the treatment of corpses. It is a strange discussion, one easily passed over, but it is also one in which Plato lets his hair down when he argues that "one ought never to squander one's substance in the belief that this lump of flesh being buried especially belongs to the one who was alive" (959c). This is because "the soul is altogether different from the body; that in life itself, what constitutes each of us is nothing other than the soul, the body following each of us as a semblance. It is a noble saying that the bodies of corpses are images [*eidolon*] of the dead" (959b).

I could supply many more examples, and not just from these texts. For instance, one might refer to the *Phaedo*, which is the story of Socrates' own death. But the point is that once one begins to see how a concern for death drives Plato, one begins to see it everywhere; one sees it even in the *Theaetetus*, which opens with the dying body of a now elderly Theaetetus being carried back from war. But for now let me simply assert this: that a concern with death, with our consciousness of being mortal, is at the heart of Plato's way of conceiving the possibility of the *polis*. That should not entirely be a surprise in light of the celebrated claim Socrates makes in the *Phaedo* that "those who pursue philosophy are practicing how to die" (67e). But there is an important difference between *how* this consciousness of our mortality is presented and thought in Plato, and in Homer and Sophocles. In Plato death never really makes an appearance. What we find is always only the aftermath of death, and then every effort is made to *conceal the dead, to efface the body, to hide the violence of death.* Plato is aware of this difference between how he wants us to think and speak of death and how this is done by the tragedians, and this will be the reason he is so insistent on criticizing poetic practices. This is fully in line with the argument we find in the *Phaedo* that philosophy is a discipline that trains the soul to be separate from the body, that is, it is a training for what will be called death when the body truly dies. Consequently, philosophers are, says Plato, those who have no fear of death. The real fear is of being too attached to the body and the life of the senses. A sort of homology is set up between philosophy and a rather special conception of death: philosophy is like death in that both are about the separation of the soul and the body. But it is a conception of death that conceals the dead body and has mortified it in advance of its real death. I will return to the significance of the concealment in a moment.

Let me now answer my claim that there is a sense of a "debt" to the dead that one can find in some ancient works—above all in Homer and Sophocles—and that in this notion of some debt to the dead we find something of great import for our ethical lives that is effaced in philosophy. It is, I believe, no accident that in Homer and Sophocles we are asked to be witnesses to bodies, corpses, violence, and burials. In short, the *bodily* meaning of death is very much present. Aristotle recognizes this and so defines tragedy as "the presentation of death and great suffering and wounds" and "of actions causing destruction and suffering" (1452b 11–13). Of course, the corpse, which is the bodily image of death, is a strange thing: a purely liminal presence, full of ambiguity, and a reminder that every bond that unites us will be interrupted. To think the bonds that unite us means that we need to think the possibility, the inevitability, of those bonds being severed. And yet, because the other has already constituted us, that severance can never be complete, at least as far as memory can take us. The other resides in memory as an idea. *Psyche,* which is the seat of memory and intelligence, can, after a fashion, be recalled by another memory and intelligence even if this recollection is only partial, only in the form of mourning. But the body cannot be summoned back. This is what is lost. This is the idiom of the other concentrated in the most extreme form. In life, flesh is not only a limit that separates us, but is, when the body is in love, an ecstatic site in which I belong with the other. The body in love, the erotic body, is an opening, a reception of the other. The dead body is a pure closure. In it we find the riddle of our being and the most pronounced expression of the enigma of death. Any real consciousness of our mortality must face this enigma. Any real consciousness of death must come to terms with the dead body. If it is true—and I believe that it is—that mortality does not signal the end of the question of ethical life but rather marks its incipient possibility, then the struggle to think the dead body belongs to the beginning of ethical consciousness. I might understand something of what this means in my own anxiety, but it seems clear that for me to understand what it means for the death of the other I must bear witness. I owe the other this look, this seeing that is so painfully difficult. What will be lost and, in the end, beyond the reach of even memory, is this body. Before I can even mourn, before I can be in the position of knowing what this death means, I must have *seen* something of it. Philosophy has always had a difficulty granting the body its place. It has, in effect, buried the body in advance of its real death. It has a tendency to mortify the body. But art, a form of thinking that disturbed Plato precisely because it is so wedded to images and to bodies, is better at this bearing witness. It has always been better at rendering visible the face of the dead. Of course, in saying this I am suggesting that art has always been better than philosophy at getting close to the conditions that render ethical life possible, insofar as those conditions are rooted in a genuine consciousness of mortality. Aristotle's treatment of the work of art in his *Poetics* demonstrates a great sensitivity to this point, especially in his scant, but crucial and typically misunderstood, remarks on *katharsis*. Kant too comes close to recognizing this capacity of art to reach deep into the heart of the ethical in his Third Critique. Nietzsche, who suggests both that "we have art, lest we perish of the truth" and that thinking needs to move beyond "good and evil," comes closer still.

But I believe that we do this natively for those we know and love: we bear witness. It is painful, but something we do. From out of this experience a genuine mourning, a real sense of what reality has lost, is almost possible. We almost know what has left the world. And yet we somehow know as well that what has been lost is ultimately not able to be known. It is far more than this dead body, and yet it the body that helps me remember that memory will not grasp the truth of the life now gone. It is an incalculable loss. I would like to suggest that all ethical sensibility begins with this sense of the incalculable.

* * *

Let me begin to move to my conclusion by returning to my beginning and make a comment about the difference between the ancient and contemporary worlds on this point. Today we tend to hide the face of the dead; we refuse to see and bear witness to what war means. An article in the *New York Times* on Monday, April 7th, 2003, acknowledges this.[16] It surveys the images of the war that the United States has just waged and notes that most everywhere there are "pictures of soldiers, battles, rubble, but no corpses."

Susan Sontag points out that "ever since cameras were invented in 1839, photography has kept company with death."[17] But, as she also points out, letting such images be seen in a time of war has always been controversial, even prohibited. The American Civil War was among the first wars fully documented by the camera. But Matthew Brady's images were so shocking that the people who saw them vilified him for showing them. He never printed some fifteen thousand images, which remained only on glass plates. There destiny is a remarkable irony: after a point, those glass plates with images of the Civil War dead where sold as building materials for a greenhouse on Long Island. At the start of World War I, that greenhouse was demolished and the glass—once the glass negatives of the Civil War dead—was used to make the lenses for gas masks used by soldiers in that new war.

Sontag contends that memory is the province of images, and so photography has a special lock upon how it is that we remember. Her view implies that looking is sufficient for us to understand. I will end by saying that here I am not so sure that this is true. I do tend to believe that images, especially painful images of the dead, might finally be an element of what gives birth to something like an ethical consciousness. But I also believe that those images alone do not suffice to educate that consciousness about its possibilities. Our first debt might be to see, to bear witness. But that debt is not taken up until we find the words that match those images and let them be understood in the best way we can understand. Nothing redeems a death. No replacement is possible. But, once we have seen I do believe that we need to search for the words that give some sense to the senselessness of war, and perhaps even, against all odds, bring it to a halt.

Notes

1. Though in a sense the body is always struggling to preserve itself against this eventual transition to "mere" nature. See John Vernon, *A Book of Reasons* (Boston: Houghton Mifflin, 2000), 149: "We are in life, walking, talking crematoriums and incubators. Cells in our bodies and bacteria just along for the ride continually die, while others, their offspring, are born and multiply. Microorganisms are dead when they've irreversibly lost the ability to reproduce. We're killing them all the time by washing our hands, by brushing our teeth, by ingesting antibiotics. They die so we can live, but when *we* die, they thrive. Like a clan of never-ending Snopeses, they throw a perpetual house party in our bodies, and inevitably wind up burning the place down. Decay produces heat, after all. Dr. Brouardel of turn-of-the-century Paris pricked his corpses with

needles to let the gases escape, then set fire to the holes and watched the long bluish flames burn off the products of decomposition." Among the strangest conceptions of how the dead body is to be thought is that which we find in Jeremy Bentham's book on the preservation of corpses, *Auto-Icon*. Bentham, about whom Foucault writes for his invention of the panopticon, was never buried, but had himself preserved. His body still remains on display at University College in London.

2. See Hegel, *Phaenomenologie des Geistes* (Hamburg: Meiner Verlag, 1952), especially the discussion of "ethical culture" which is founded by an act of burial. See also J. Assmann, *Tod und Jenseits im alten Ägypten* (Munich: C. H. Beck, 2003), for a discussion of this claim with respect to Egyptian culture.

3. On this see my *On Germans and Other Greeks: Tragedy and Ethical Life* (Bloomington: Indiana University Press, 2000).

4. See especially Book XI where Odysseus makes his descent into the realm of the dead, where the blind see clearest and where the dead are bodiless shades.

5. See Book X, the *Myth of Er*, which is a tale told by Er, who learns of the realm of the dead while his corpse is lying upon a battlefield.

6. See especially Book X.

7. On this, see N. Loreaux, "The Invention of Athens: The Funeral Oration in the Classical City," in M. H. Hausen, *The Athenian Democracy in the Age of Demosthenes* (Oxford: Oxford University Press, 1991), 73–85.

8. I would not suggest that this consciousness is completely absent from later cultures. For instance, one needs to read Lincoln's *Gettysburg Address*, given on the occasion of the reburial of the dead (as was Pericles' *Funeral Oration*), as driven by such a consciousness.

9. Martin Heidegger, *Sein und Zeit* (Tübingen: Niemeyer Verlag, 1972), 239.

10. Sigmund Freud, "Trauer und Melancholie," in *Psychologie des Unbewussten* (Frankfurt: Fischer Verlag, 1975), 194.

11. Ibid., 200.

12. Hegel, *Phänomenologie des Geistes*, paragraph 175.

13. Homer, *Odyssey*, Book XI, lines 215 ff.

14. See Sarah Iles Johnston, *Restless Dead: Encounters between the Living and the Dead in Ancient Greece* (Berkeley: University of California Press, 1999).

15. Plato, *Phaedrus*, 264.

16. "Telling War's Deadly Story at Just Enough Distance," April 7, 2003, p. B 13. Another relevant article is "Is the Body More Beautiful When It's Dead?" June 1, 2003, p. 37 of "The Arts."

17. *Regarding the Pain of Others* (London: Penguin Books, 2004), 24.

8   Beyond or Beneath Good and Evil? Heidegger's Purification of Aristotle's Ethics

Francisco J. Gonzalez

Es gilt nicht Neues zu sagen, sondern das zu sagen, was die Alten schon meinten.

Martin Heidegger (GA18, 329)

Published for the first time in 2002 but originally delivered in 1924, Heidegger's course *Grundbegriffe der aristotelischen Philosophie*[1] has without question been very eagerly awaited. Though some knowledge of the course was possible earlier through the Walter Bröcker transcript in the Marcuse Archive, and though apparently Heidegger's own manuscript survives for approximately only one-third of the course, the *Gesamtausgabe* volume nevertheless provides the most complete picture of the course currently possible. That it was worth the wait cannot be denied. What most impresses initially is Heidegger's ability to free Aristotle's texts from layers of metaphysical dogma deposited on them throughout the course of two thousand years. Yet the goal here is not some archeology of the past for its own sake, but the opening up of future possibilities within the past. The methodological presupposition according to which history and the past have *Stoßkraft* (jolting-power) for the present and future is, in Heidegger's words, the very air in which philology breathes (334). Heidegger can thus claim that the goal of the course is neither the history of philosophy nor even philosophy but *philology*, understood as the *passion* for *logos* ("die Leidenschaft der Erkenntnis des Ausgesprochenen," 4): specifically in this case, the passion for making the Aristotelian *logos*, the Aristotelian fundamental words, *speak again*.

What accordingly also impresses in the course is its existential urgency: the insistence that what is at stake here is not the learning of abstract philosophical concepts, but our becoming who we are. At one point Heidegger exhorts his students not simply to learn, repeat, and apply Aristotle's concepts, but to imitate what he does, to *see* the matter itself with the same genuineness and originality. This is the fundamental earnestness of the course. If Heidegger at one point dismisses the word *Lebensphilosophie* as a redundancy comparable to "botany of plants" (242), this is because for him philosophy and life are not two distinct things: philosophy *is* life, indeed, as will emerge from the course, life in the fullest and most genuine sense. An explicit presupposition of the course is that Dasein is capable of standing completely on its own (*sich einzig auf sich selbst stellen*) in the genuine interpretation and determination of its possibilities (334), without, that is, the help of faith, religion, or the like (6). Here we can see how the course is not just a discussion of Aristotle's basic concepts, but an exhortation to live the life Aristotle himself considered the most free: the life of *theoria*. One can understand why, according to Gadamer, students had a hard time telling whether it was Aristotle or Heidegger speaking:[2] instead of the scholarly discussion of Aristotle's philosophy to which they were accustomed in other courses, what they encountered here was an Aristotle *redivivus*[3] exhorting them to the autonomous and genuine realization of the possibilities of their existence.

I emphasize this way in which the very performance of the course appears to be an appropriation of Aristotelian ethics because my focus in the present paper is precisely how Heidegger in the content of the course transforms Aristotle's basic *ethical* concepts. This might seem an odd focus, given that a cursory glance at the table of contents in the *Gesamtausgabe* volume shows that Heidegger devotes only a small part of the course to a reading of Aristotle's *Ethics;* more time is devoted to the *Physics, Metaphysics,* and *Rhetoric* (though the habit of referring to the course as a course on Aristotle's *Rhetoric* greatly exaggerates the amount of space devoted to this work). Furthermore, Heidegger devotes more time to the *Ethics* in the *Sophist* course offered the next semester (WS 1924–25) where he provides a detailed analysis of Aristotle's treatment of the "dianoetic virtues" in Book 6. However, in the SS 1924 course Heidegger provides interpretations of some of the most fundamental concepts in Aristotle's *Ethics: agathon, telos, hexis, arete, hedone, lype,* and *proairesis;* interpretations that are presupposed, rather than repeated, by his turn to the dianoetic virtues in the *Sophist* course. Furthermore, these interpretations demand both our reflection and a critical distance of which the original auditors were perhaps incapable, because the transformations to which they subject Aristotle's ethical concepts in the move from the originally planned book on Aristotle to its final form as *Being and Time* are not only highly questionable on philological grounds but deeply disturbing for what they reveal about the direction of Heidegger's own thought. It is not just that Heidegger "ontologizes" these concepts, as has been argued before:[4] these concepts emerge from Heidegger's transformations with the ghostly remnant of an ethical connotation—as one can infer from the exhortatory and imperative character of Heidegger's course—but one that is a complete inversion and perversion of their ethical meaning in Aristotle.

Heidegger and Aristotle on the Human *Agathon* and *Telos*

Let us begin at the beginning, that is, with *the good.* The first text of the *Nicomachean Ethics* to which Heidegger turns in the course is appropriately the opening chapters of Book 1, devoted to a discussion of the *agathon.* Heidegger has been reflecting on the characterization of the human being in the *Politics,* according to which human beings differ from other animals in the possession of *logos* and, specifically, of a *logos* that aims at revealing the advantageous and the disadvantageous, the just and the unjust (*Pol.* A2, 1253a 9 ff). It is the presence of the terms *sympheron* and *blaberon* (which I have translated as "advantageous" and "disadvantageous," and which Heidegger translates as *Zuträgliche* and *Abträgliche*) in this determination of human being that leads Heidegger to an examination of how Aristotle understands the *agathon* to which human beings are essentially related in their very being. Heidegger makes clear from the very beginning that he will give a strictly *ontological* account of the *agathon.* He asserts, before even turning to the text, that the *agathon* is a *way of being, "the genuine character of man's being"* (65). To see what exactly it means to characterize the *agathon* in this way and what such a characterization might exclude, we need to turn to Heidegger's reading of the very first line of the *Ethics.*

The initial translation of this line must leave the key terms untranslated, since they are precisely what is at issue: "Every *techne* and every procedure [*methodos*], as well as [*homoios de*] *praxis* and *proairesis* appear to aim [*ephiesthai*] at some good." As is often the case with Heidegger, his interpretation already begins his translation/paraphrase of this sentence. Most significant, and most essential to his subsequent claims, is the way in which Heidegger translates the terms that appear to be contrasted in Aristotle's sentence: on the one hand, *techne* and *methodos,* on the other, *praxis* and *proairesis*. Heidegger translates *techne* as *Auskenntnis im einem Besorgen*, know-how in taking care of something (67). That in itself is unobjectionable. But what of the translation of *praxis* as *Besorgen*, taking care of something, and *proairesis* as *das Sichvornehmen von etwas als zuerledigendes, als zu besorgen, zu Ende zu bringen*, the taking-in-hand of something to be settled, taken care of, brought to an end. The effect of such translations is to suppress the distinction implied by the phrase *homoios de*, "as well as, on the other hand," by assimilating or subordinating *praxis* and *proariesis* to *techne*, making them only the taking-care and bringing-to-completion for which *techne* provides the know-how.

This translation is not a slip but is rather essential to what Heidegger wishes to conclude from this opening sentence of the *Nicomachean Ethics*. He approaches this passage with the following question: in what or where is the *agathon* expressed and made manifest (65)? The answer at which Heidegger arrives through his reading of the first sentence of the *Ethics* will not surprise any reader of his translation, but must surprise any reader of the Greek: the *agathon* is expressed and made manifest (*ausdrücklich sichtbar wird*) in *techne* (68). As a result, the distinction between *techne* and *praxis* suggested by Aristotle's sentence, a distinction of which Heidegger is well aware and which he even briefly summarizes on pages 70–71, is simply ignored in this conclusion. Here and, as we will see, throughout the rest of the course, *techne* becomes the sole and guiding perspective in Heidegger's account of the *agathon*.[5]

But why is this important? In *techne* the good appears as the end result of an action, as something produced, finished; and as we have seen, this is exactly the kind of language that Heidegger imports into his translation/paraphrase of the first sentence of the *Ethics*. Therefore when Heidegger, following Aristotle's discussion of the good in the opening chapters of the *Ethics*, proceeds to discuss the good as *peras* and *telos*, he clearly understands these terms from the perspective of *techne*: "'Ende' im Sinne des Eine-Fertigkeit-Ausmachens" (79): the good is an "end" in the sense of being finished, completed, taken care of. But it is at least questionable whether the good appears this way in *praxis*. Does the "end" of being generous, being just, or even seeing have the character of *Fertigsein*, of something "finished"? A house produced by a builder is *fertig*, and it is this being-finished at which the builder aims. But the aim of being courageous is not to make something *fertig*, nor does being courageous itself ever have simply the character of being finished or complete. As Aristotle insists, while in the case of *techne* the perfect tense rules out the present tense, this is not the case with *praxis:* for example, while the sentence "I have built the house" cannot be true at the same time as the sentence "I am building the house," the sentences "I have seen" and "I am seeing" *can* be true at the same time. One can perhaps put the crucial point this way: *praxis* is complete without being complet*ed* in the sense of *finished;* if the good therefore appears in *praxis* as *telos,* this cannot be in the sense of *Fertigsein* or *am-Ende-Sein.* Heidegger himself much later in the course, and apparently forgetting for the moment the conception of the good he is defending here, insists that virtue is *not Fertigkeit* (188), by which he clearly means both that it is not a *skill* (the normal meaning of *Fertigkeit*) and that it is not something fixed or finished (he insists that it is not the "bringing-into-play of some fixed and set skill [*einer festsitzende Fertigkeit*]," 189). How Heidegger positively understands virtue will be considered later. Here we can conclude with the un-Heideggerian suggestion that courage is an "end," not in the sense of being "finished" or "completed," but rather in the sense of being pursued, desired, and chosen for its own sake.

That this suggestion is indeed un-Heideggerian is shown by the other peculiarity of Heidegger's interpretation of the first sentence of the *Ethics.* Here again we need to consider specific translations: *proairesis,* normally translated in English as "choice" or "decision," is translated by Heidegger as *das Sichvornehmen von etwas als zu erledigendes, als zu besorgen, zu Ende zu bringen* (67), taking in hand something to be finished, taken care of, brought to an end; *ephiesthai,* normally translated in the sense of "aiming" at the good, is translated by Heidegger as *Hinterhersein einem Guten,* to be behind the good, in the direction of the good. To these translations we should add Heidegger's translation of the characterization of the good in the *Politics* as that which is *haireton* in itself and for its own sake: Heidegger translates *haireton,* usually translated as "chosen," instead as *ergreifbar* (61), graspable. What is common to all of these translations? Clearly the exclusion from our relation to the good of any deliberate choice, desire, or decision. This should not surprise us since this is precisely what Heidegger must do in order to interpret the *agathon* ontologically as *a way of being.* Our relation to the good is to be located in our *existing,* not in our acting, desiring, deliberating, or choosing. Heidegger's reading of the very first sentence of Aristotle's *Ethics* has already succeeded in transforming ethics into ontology, and a very determinate ontology according to which Being means being-finished, being-completed, being-delimited.

This disassociation of the *agathon* from ethical *praxis* and all that is involved in such *praxis,* that is, choice, deliberation, and desire,[6] is only completed when Heidegger, in a move very characteristic of this course, turns to *Metaphysics* Δ 16 for help in interpreting the terms *telos* and *teleion* (80–91; §11). What he concludes from this digression into Aristotle's *Metaphysics* is, not surprisingly, that *telos* does not at all mean "goal" or "aim" nor has it any relation to moral goodness: it means end (in the sense of "at-an-end") and outermost limit. "*Telos* is not 'goal,' but *eschaton*, character of a limit, 'outermost.' Goal and aim are determinate ways in which *telos* is 'end,' but they are not primary determinations; instead, goal and aim are grounded in *telos* as 'end' as in the original meaning" (85; see also 82 and 88). At one point Heidegger goes so far as to write: "Activity pursuing some aim [*Zwecktätigkeit*] or desire directed at some goal [*Zielstrebigkeit*] are at this level of our investigations a complete misinterpretation [*eine völlige Misdeutung*], and encourage the impression that Aristotle was one of those primitive people who lived in the nineteenth century" (82–83). Leaving out of consideration for the moment the questionable move from the *Ethics* to the *Metaphysics*, a move that of course greatly facilitates an ontological reading of the *Ethics*, to what extent are Heidegger's conclusions supported by the text of the *Metaphysics* itself?

In this text Aristotle distinguishes between the following meanings of *teleion*: (1) something can be *teleion* in the sense that nothing lies outside it; for example, time is *teleion* in the sense that there is no time outside of time; (2) something is *teleion* when it lacks nothing with regard to its proper virtue or good; for example, a good doctor or a flute player can be *teleios* in this sense; (3) something can be *teleion* in the sense of having reached its outermost limit, being finished and at an end; for example, it is this sense of the word that enables us, through a transfer of its meaning (*kata metaphoran*), to speak of a *teleion* destruction and to characterize death as a *telos*; (4) *telos* can finally mean the ultimate or final for-the-sake-of (*hou heneka eschaton*).

It should by now be clear that it is the third sense, *teleion* as what has reached an end or outermost limit, that is for Heidegger the original and primary meaning of the word. But I wish to consider briefly what Heidegger does with the second and fourth meanings in particular. The second meaning associates *teleion* with being virtuous or good. Do we not have here a meaning quite distinct from the one on which Heidegger focuses? Heidegger emphasizes the passage (1021b 17–20) in which Aristotle says that we *transfer* (*metapherein*) to those who are bad (*kakoi*) the meaning of *teleios* found in our speaking of a *teleios* doctor, when, for example, we speak of a *teleios* thief, that is, a "complete" or "perfect" thief. Heidegger takes this transfer as evidence that the word *teleios* has originally no moral connotation: "In the case of the fully accomplished doctor, it is not a matter of moral goodness, but in this *telos* lies the bringing-to-an-end. The *metapherein* makes clear what is actually meant by *teleion*" (84; see also 86). But does the "transfer" of *teleion* from the doctor to the thief show that no other sense of goodness is at issue in this sense of *teleion* beyond the being-at-an-end with one's distinctive possibilities? What Heidegger appears to ignore is that we still have a *transfer* here. If *teleion* has nothing to do with moral goodness—or with whatever goodness it is a thief lacks— then why should its meaning need to be *transferred* to those who are bad? Why should not a thief be *teleios* in as original a sense as a doctor? In discussing later Aristotle's description of how we *transfer* the word *telos* to death, Heidegger writes: "but we are dealing here with a transfer. This means that in the calling of death a *telos* the genuine meaning of *telos* and *teleion* is in a certain sense lost" (89). And yet in the case of the other transfer from *teleios* doctor to *teleios* thief, Heidegger recognizes no loss, or at least says nothing about what is lost.

But the major stumbling block to Heidegger's interpretation is the fourth meaning, since here Aristotle is listing as distinct from *telos* in the sense of end or outermost limit (third meaning) *telos* in the sense of that-for-sake-of-which. Do we not obviously have here a sense of *telos* as aim or goal for desire? Heidegger indeed feels compelled for once to introduce desire into his characterization of the *hou heneka*: "The *hou heneka* is that being which *exists in a willing*, with which I willingly have to do, that which I am out towards in some form of *orexis*" (88). So do we not have here a conception of *telos* as aim or goal, the conception most relevant to the *Ethics*? With one quick and simple move Heidegger evades this conclusion: in the next sentence he asserts that the *hou heneka* is a *telos only because it is something ultimate or final*, so that *telos* does not at all mean goal or aim, but only what is at an end or limit. In other words, Heidegger reduces the fourth meaning to the third. But does not Aristotle present them as distinct meanings? This is precisely Heidegger's hermeneutic violence: he reduces to some ultimate meaning what Aristotle presents as different meanings. And since the difference Aristotle wishes to preserve is partly a difference between ethical, *praxis*-oriented meanings of *telos* and ontological meanings, it is precisely the collapse of any distinction between ethics and ontology that not only results from Heidegger's reading, but also is presupposed by the way in which he moves back and forth between the *Ethics* and *Metaphysics* without so much as seeing a possible objection here. By a collapse of the distinction between ethics and ontology is meant not that ethics is simply put aside for the moment in favor of ontology, but rather that ethics is denied any autonomy in its basic concepts or questions.[7]

This is not to suggest that ethics and ontology have nothing to do with each other for Aristotle. On the contrary, a result of ignoring the distinctiveness of ethical practice and of reducing all meanings of key terms to one "original" meaning may be an impoverished ontology. And it is precisely such an impoverished ontology that Heidegger ends up attributing to Aristotle *as a result* of his own hermeneutical violence. Heidegger's discussion of the text of the *Metaphysics* concludes: "*Telos* has the determination of *limit.*" He then clarifies: "*Telos* means originally: *being at an end in such a way that this end constitutes the genuine There, genuinely to determine a being in its presence [Gegenwärtigkeit]*" (89–90). Here we can see what Heidegger is aiming at with his insistence on being-at-an-end-or-limit as the original meaning of *telos:* that, as he states the point explicitly later in the course, "Being for the Greeks means being-present [*Gegenwärtigsein*], and indeed always-being-present [*Immer-Gegenwärtigsein*]" (113; see also 93). Yet, as we have seen, Heidegger can attribute this conception of Being to the Greeks only by reducing *praxis* to *techne*, abstracting from desire and deliberation, and reducing the multiplicity of meanings of *telos* to one. And it becomes perfectly clear later in the course that *poiesis* has been made the determining perspective for the interpretation of being: "That is the genuine meaning of *poiesis*. Being-there [*Da-Sein*] is in the genuine sense *being-produced* [*Her-gestelltsein*], that it, *being-finished* [*Fertig-Dasein*], *having-come-to-an-end* [*Zu-Ende-Gekommensein*]. *Telos = peras*" (214; see also 329 and 381). Perhaps most revealing is the following passage from Heidegger's notes for the course: "The question of *ti tini* is drawn out of the determinations of *poiesis* and of *being-present* [*Gegenwärtig-Daseins*]—*poiesis* as primary Being-in-the-world, *praxis*" (329). Here *praxis* is simply listed beside *poiesis*, which is again asserted to determine the question of being, as if there were no difference between them.[8]

Since Heidegger's account of Greek ontology is another story for another time,[9] let us return to the *Ethics*, as Heidegger himself does after the digression into the *Metaphysics*, in order to see further effects of his reading on ethics itself. Two important things are worth noting in Heidegger's reading of chapters 5–6 of Book 1 of the *Ethics*, the chapters in which Aristotle arrives at a final determination of the human good. First is his startling interpretation of Aristotle's characterization of the human good in chapter 5 as *haplos teleion*, "an end without qualification." Aristotle's argument in this chapter is that happiness is *haplos teleion* and therefore the human good because, according to the common translation/interpretation, happiness is always chosen or desired (*haireton*) for its own sake and never for the sake of something else. Heidegger of course cannot allow choice, desire, or preference into the picture here without going back on his interpretation of *telos*. We therefore find this extraordinary paraphrase of what Aristotle says: "With a view to the *kath' auton*, what is *teleioteron* is that which *medepote di' allo* and *aiei kath' auto haireton*, the kind of *di' auto* that 'enduringly' [*beständig*], 'always' is what it is" (94). Note how the phrase *aiei kath' auto haireton*, which many of us might be tempted to translate as "is always chosen or preferred for its own sake," becomes in Heidegger's paraphrase "*always is what it is*"! A more violent transformation of the ethical content of what Aristotle says into a purely ontological content is hard to imagine.

But Heidegger does not stop here. To keep *telos* distinct from any goal or aim, it is necessary not only to disassociate it from any desiring or choosing, but also to rid it of any determinate ontic content. Heidegger sees the opportunity for this move in the following claim Aristotle makes in justifying his identification of the human good with happiness. "Honor and pleasure and virtue we indeed choose [*hairoumetha*: Heidegger leaves the word here untranslated] for their own sake, ... but we also choose them for the sake of happiness" (1097b 2–4). This suggestion of a *telos* beyond honor, pleasure, and virtue (the three candidates for the human good earlier in the *Ethics*) gives Heidegger the opening for an extraordinary conclusion, which he immediately proceeds to draw: "These *tele* can have in the background yet another *telos*, the one that *genuinely concerns man* [wobei es *darauf dem Menschen eigentlich ankommt*]: this *telos* is Dasein itself" (94–95). Thus the ultimate *telos* for human existence turns out to be human existence itself, Dasein existing for its own sake. Heidegger is quick to draw out of this conclusion what will become a central thesis of *Being and Time*: Dasein is the kind of being that is in its being concerned, expressly or not, with its own being (95).

Whatever one thinks of this claim in *Being and Time*, as an interpretation of Aristotle's ethics it is an evident distortion. First of all, we have here an absolutization of human existence that runs completely counter to Aristotle's ethics. Despite considering the earth on which we live the center of the world and defining "up" and "down" accordingly, would Aristotle accept Heidegger's assertion, made later in the course and presupposing what he says here, that "there exists nothing from the perspective of which my Dasein would be relative" (266)? What seems clear is that at least in the case of ethics Aristotle would not make human existence its own end, despite the emphasis he gives to self-sufficiency. We only need to recall Aristotle's concluding words in Book 10: the life of complete (*teleia*) happiness is "one lived not insofar as one is a human being, but insofar as there is something divine in one. . . . It is therefore not necessary to follow the words of those who exhort us to think only human thoughts being human or only mortal thoughts being mortal, but we should to the extent possible strive to be immortal and do everything we can to live according to the greatest thing in us" (1177b 9–34).[10] But the second and related objection to be made here is that while *eudaimonia* is certainly *a way* of being of human beings, it cannot be identified with human being (Dasein) as such. *Eudaimonia* is a specific and determinate way of being that has yet to be defined. This is why Aristotle believes that the ultimate human *telos* remains undefined even after it has been shown to be *eudaimonia*. We still need to determine what specifically constitutes *eudaimonia*. When Aristotle, in the passage quoted by Heidegger, says that virtue is chosen for the sake of *eudaimonia,* he is not excluding the possibility that virtue will later prove to be not something external to happiness as a mere means to an end, but rather its essential defining characteristic. If Aristotle were to agree that the ultimate human good and *telos* is Dasein, he would do so only with the qualification that the human *bad* is also Dasein.

Aristotle of course proceeds to give a definition of the human *telos* that goes beyond his identification of it with what is without qualification a *telos* and with *eudaimonia*. We must therefore look very carefully at how Heidegger interprets this final definition. Aristotle's argument in chapters 6–7 is well known, and the main steps can be briefly summarized as follows: the good of something is to be located in its distinctive *ergon* and can be identified with performing this *ergon well* (*eu*); for example, the distinctive *ergon* of a lyre-player is to play the lyre, but a *good* lyre player is not simply one who plays the lyre, but one who does so *well*. Aristotle next argues that human beings as such have a distinctive *ergon* that distinguishes them from other living beings, namely, *practical life according to reason* (*logos*). Aristotle can now conclude that the distinctive and highest human good is such a life conducted *well,* or, in other words, "the soul's activity according to virtue [*kat' areten*]" (1098a 16–17). One should already be able to guess which part of this definition Heidegger will downplay and to the extent possible ignore, namely, precisely the part that is of greatest importance to Aristotle and that has been the *telos* of his argument because the *telos* of human life itself: virtue, or *arete*. What Heidegger emphasizes is that the definition makes human life itself, human being (Dasein), the *ergon* and therefore *telos* of human life: "Therefore, insofar as the *telos* of man does not lie outside himself, but *in himself* as *his possibility of being*, the *anthropinon agathon* is *zoe* itself, 'life' itself" (100). But the human good is such a life lived *according to virtue*. What has become of *arete* in Heidegger's account? Heidegger takes advantage of Aristotle's description of the lyre-player who plays well as being *spoudaios* in order, by way of an extremely literal and reductive translation of *spoudaios* as "serious" (*ernsthaft*), to characterize the difference between the excellent lyre-player and the bad one as a difference between one who "has become serious about his possibility of being" (*der mit seiner Seinsmöglichkeit Ernst gemacht hat*) and one who has not (100). This then enables Heidegger to interpret the crucial phrase in Aristotle's definition, *energeia kat' areten*, as "putting-to-work [*Ins-Werk-Setzen*] as *eu*, seriously (*spoudaiou*) grasped [*ergriffen*], in such a way that the ultimate possibility of being is grasped in its end" (100–101). In this sentence we see again some of the moves we have seen before: the use of the word *ergriffen* to avoid any talk of choice or desire and the identification of *telos* with what is brought to an end in the sense of an outermost limit. But what has to be especially noted here is the reduction of *arete* to "seriousness": virtue has become taking seriously one's utmost possibility of being, which means grasping it as ultimate; one of Heidegger's paraphrases can thus even suggest that *arete* is nothing more than the *genuine being-there* of one's possibility of being.[11] This interpretation of *arete* persists throughout the course, so that, for example, on page 165 he can, without explanation, simply translate it as *Ernst*.

That this conception of *arete* is not Aristotle's hardly needs saying. But then we must ask what Heidegger's conception of *arete* would *mean* on the level of concrete ethical *praxis*. This of course is not Heidegger's concern, as he makes clear when he breaks off his discussion of the *Ethics* with the following words: "We will not follow [Aristotle's] consideration of the *aretai*. The concrete development [*Ausgestaltung*] of the interpretation of Dasein does not interest us here" (103). But we must ask: is Heidegger simply refraining here from something he could have pursued if he had wanted to? *Could* he have turned to a concrete consideration of specific virtues on the basis of his account of virtue and the human good in Book 1 of the *Ethics*? It is certainly hard to see how, after reducing the human good and *telos* to Being-there-at-an-end and virtue to "seriousness," one could "return" to a consideration of concrete deliberation and choice in the different spheres of generosity, justice, temperance, courage, and the like. If Book 1 of Aristotle's *Ethics* is meant to open the way to philosophical reflection on concrete human *praxis,* Heidegger's violent "ontologization" of this book clearly *blocks* the way to such reflection. Since, furthermore, what Heidegger claims not to interest him *here* will interest him *nowhere* in the subsequent half-century of his lecturing and writing, we have additional reason for suspecting that the occasional suggestions of a later return from ontology to ethics represent a *permanent* postponement. It is not that Heidegger simply puts ethics aside while he does ontology; instead, what we see in the present course is Heidegger so radically transforming key ethical concepts as to render them utterly incapable of guiding and sustaining a concrete ethics.[12]

Heidegger and Aristotle on *Hexis* and *Arete*

Matters will prove more complicated, however, since Heidegger, despite what he says on page 103, does not leave the *Ethics* for good at this point in the course. Instead, he later provides a reading of Aristotle's definition of virtue in Book 2 and even of a couple of specific virtues. And yet this will not prove to be the ever-delayed "concrete development [*Ausgestaltung*] of the interpretation of Dasein" since Heidegger's reading of Book 2 takes place on the same ontological level as, and is no more concrete than, his reading of Book 1. One can already imagine that the results of such a reading will be strange, but they are in reality much stranger than one can imagine. To the extent that Aristotle's account of *arete* is more specific, determinate, and concrete in Book 2, Heidegger's reading will become only more violent. The strangest, and most disturbing, result of such violence is an ethics so distorted as to become the absolute negation of itself: an ethics that is an anti-ethics.

It is in the context of a reading of Aristotle's *Rhetoric* on the question of how *ethos* and *pathos* contribute to persuasion (165–72) that Heidegger turns to the discussion in the *Ethics,* Book 2, chapter 4, of the distinctions between *dynamis, pathos,* and *hexis,* distinctions Aristotle makes on the way to the definition of *arete* as a *hexis.* After a brief summary of this text and a return to the *Rhetoric,* Heidegger insists that *pathos* and *hexis* can be characterized, *anhand von Aristoteles,* as "*fundamental concepts of Being*" (172). This opens the way for Heidegger to turn once again to *Metaphysics* Δ, this time chapters 20 and 23 on the different meanings of *hexis* and *echein,* with even a brief discussion of chapter 19 on the meaning of *dia-thesis.* Heidegger's analysis is too dense and cryptic to be examined here in detail; indeed, even after several careful readings, Heidegger's final characterization of *hexis* still strikes me as a sudden and unexplained leap. Claiming that all the different meanings of *echein* constitute a characterization of beings as in their being existing out toward a possibility of being (174; Heidegger again reduces Aristotle's different meanings to one fundamental one),[13] then pointing to meanings of *hexis* that supposedly suggest that it is the presence of a having and being had, and finally using Aristotle's identification of *hexis* in one of its meanings with a *diathesis* to suggest that having/being-had is here an articulated ordering, Heidegger somehow concludes: "*Hexis* is the determination of the authenticity [*Eigentlichkeit*] of Dasein in a moment of being in control and collected [*Gefaßtsein*] for something: the different *hexeis* are the different ways of being capable of being collected [*Gefaßtseinkönnens*]" (176). As Heidegger makes clear in the sentences that follow, *hexis* is being understood here as a possibility of being that is in itself directed at the possibility of my being (176); in other words, we have here again the idea that my *telos* is my own being. What is new is the characterization of my relation to my being as a *Gefaßtsein*, a characterization presumably derived from Heidegger's reading of the verb *echein.*

Before considering the meaning and implications of Heidegger's conclusion, we need to recognize just how *strange* it is by citing in contrast the last major meaning of *hexis* Aristotle discusses in *Metaphysics* Δ, chapter 20, the one clearly relevant to ethics, which is also the last one Heidegger discusses in the apparent belief that it somehow supports his conclusion: "*Hexis* is a disposition (*diathesis*) according to which what is disposed can be well or badly (*kakos diakeitai*) disposed, in itself or in relation to something else" (1022b 10–12). If we compare this definition with Heidegger's, the most obvious difference—and unfortunately this can no longer surprise us—is that there is nothing in Heidegger's corresponding to the words "well or badly" in Aristotle's. We presumably cannot identify Heidegger's *Gefaßtsein* with "being *well* disposed" for the simple reason that this word is meant to define *hexis as such*. So what has happened in Heidegger's account to the distinction between a good and a bad *hexis*?

One might be inclined to insist on another difference by objecting that there is not even an indirect reference in Aristotle's definition to being "collected," "in control," "*gefaßt.*" But Heidegger would not be impressed by such an objection since he informs us at one point in the course that "interpretation is perhaps nothing other than the bringing out [*Heraus-stellen*] of what is not there [in the text]" (66). But what is perhaps more productive is to point out an important *tension* between Aristotle's definition and Heidegger's. In the *Ethics* one of the ways in which Aristotle argues that virtues and vices are not *feelings* (*pathe*) but rather *hexeis* is by pointing out that we are *moved* in our feelings, while in the cases of our virtues and vices we are *not moved, but disposed a certain way* (*ou kineisthai alla diakeisthai pos*, 1106a 4–6). Unlike a feeling, a disposition (*diathesis*) is not a movement but something constant and enduring. Therefore, this is how Aristotle is characterizing *hexis* when he defines it as a *diathesis*. Thus in the *Ethics* we find the virtuous person described as acting while *bebaios kai ametakinetos echon*: "'having' in a stable and unchanging way" (1105a 33). Yet when we look at Heidegger's concluding definition of *hexis*, this characterization of *hexis* as a stable and unchanging disposition, which is of course what links it to *character*, appears to be altogether absent. What we find instead is something that looks like the *opposite* of Aristotle's characterization: *hexis* is located in *a moment* of being collected for something.

Yet these differences between Aristotle's and Heidegger's characterizations of *hexis* could conceivably be only preliminary. Heidegger now proceeds to discuss the parts of Book 2 of the *Ethics* where Aristotle examines how virtue develops and what it is, that is, what kind of a *hexis* it is. This reading presents Heidegger with the opportunity of following Aristotle in distinguishing between a virtuous *hexis* and a vicious one, a possibility opened up by Heidegger's claim, cited earlier, that there exist different *hexeis* as different forms of *Gefaßtsein*; it also gives him the opportunity to bring in *character* as the central locus of Aristotelian virtue. But what is remarkable is that Heidegger does not take this opportunity. On the contrary, his reading of the central chapters of Book 2 only completes what he has already begun: purging Aristotle's ethics not only of any reference to character, but of the very distinction between virtue and vice. This strange spectacle merits our full attention.

Let us first consider Heidegger's interpretation of Aristotle's definition of virtue. As is well known, according to Aristotle's account, though both virtue and vice are *hexeis*, what distinguishes a virtuous *hexis* from an unvirtuous one is *mesotes*, that is, being disposed in such a way that one inclines toward neither excess nor deficiency in one's feelings and actions. This of course is not a recommendation of mediocrity: the correct "middle" for the feeling of anger could be *rage* in a situation where one sees one's kin assassinated before one's eyes; as Aristotle points out, the "middle" here is not an absolute but varies according to the situation: this is why the notion of the *kairos*, the appropriate moment, plays such an important role in Aristotle's *Ethics*. What Heidegger does is to use the relative character of *mesotes*, and its association with the "moment," as an opportunity for ridding it of any determinate content whatsoever. Thus his interpretation concludes that *mesotes*, being-in-the-middle, "means nothing other than *seizing the moment*" (186). Heidegger's only defense of this reading is the bizarre suggestion that the only alternatives are the attribution to Aristotle of mediocre, bourgeois morality (179–80) or the invocation of absolute norms (186). However relative the "mean" or "middle" is, it is not arbitrary; Aristotle's detailed accounts of the individual virtues show that much can be said about the virtuous way to act in specific kinds of situations without invoking some absolute norm or measure. To reduce the "mean," and therefore virtue, to being *only* a "seizing of the moment" with no determinate content is to rid this "outline" of virtue of all the concrete content with which Aristotle wants us to fill it.

But we should also note the rather inconvenient *consequences* of Heidegger's interpretation. One is that on this interpretation *mesotes* adds nothing to *hexis*, since the latter has already been interpreted as being in itself "a *Gefaßtsein* of Dasein as oriented towards the moment" (180). Heidegger somehow manages to swallow this consequence since in the course—and this will become only clearer later—he uses *hexis* and *arete* interchangeably, clearly seeing them as the same thing. *What*, then, has become of *vice* on Heidegger's reading? It has simply disappeared as a *hexis* distinct from virtue. But surely Heidegger must give some account of the excess and deficiency to which Aristotle contrasts virtue? Of course he does, and this is what he says: "Dasein on average and for the most part remains in extremes, in 'more or less', in too-much and too-little" (180). Aristotle's "vice" has been transformed into average, everyday existence! Such existence not only cannot be virtuous: it is not even a *hexis* in Heidegger's sense of *Gefaßtsein*, since it is a mere letting-go, losing-oneself, being-carried-away. Of course, that Aristotle *does* characterize the vice of excessive indulgence in certain feelings as a *hexis* can be seen as refuting conclusively Heidegger's interpretation of *hexis* as *Gefaßtsein*. But let that pass. What Heidegger does with his misreadings is more interesting than these misreadings themselves: and what could be more interesting than the identification of vice with everyday existence?

Another inconvenient consequence is that the characterization of virtue as "the seizing of the moment" seems hard to reconcile with the importance Aristotle gives to habituation and character formation in the development of virtue. Heidegger initially gives a very abstract and noncommittal paraphrase of Aristotle's account of the genesis of virtue (181–84), but he returns to it later precisely in order to minimize, or eliminate altogether, the role habituation plays in it. Consider the following extraordinary sentence: "The manner and way of habituation [*Gewöhnung*] in the case of action [as opposed to *poiesis*] is not practice [*Übung*], but *repetition*. Repetition does not mean: the bringing into play of a stable ability, but *acting anew each moment from out of the corresponding decision*" (189). Thus virtue exists only in the moment, and what Aristotle describes as an enduring, unchanging state acquired through practice and habituation is really nothing but the *repetition* of a decision and resoluteness (*Gefaßtsein*) that is completely new each moment. But is there not some constant *telos* the desire for which guides the decision and action? No, because the *telos*, as Heidegger's interpretation of *mesotes* already implies, *is nothing but the moment itself.* "The action itself has its *telos* in the *kairos*" (189). On Heidegger's reading of Book 2, to appropriate the *hexis* of virtue means that "man puts himself in a position of *being gefaßt for each moment;* no routine, but keeping oneself free, *dynamis* in the *mesotes*" (190). This virtue is rare, Heidegger explains, not in the sense that few people have it (which is of course Aristotle's meaning), but in the sense that *it cannot be had at all as a stable state, but can only be repeated* (*Widerholung*) (191). "What is at issue is the *momentary* [*jeweilige*] resoluteness [*Entschlossensein*] and appropriation of the moment" (191; my emphasis). Aristotle's account of the *genesis* of virtue has, in a few pages, been completed inverted.

There is yet another inconvenience. Though Heidegger will not make this perfectly clear until later in the course, that in relation to which we are resolute, in control, *gefaßt*, is our *feelings* (*pathe*) and our potential dispersion in them. Apart from the mistaken view that this self-possession is *hexis* as such, that there cannot be a *hexis* of giving way to excessive indulgence in feelings or appetites, this idea of being in control of our feelings sounds Aristotelian enough. The problem is that the interpretation of virtue as a "being-in-control with respect to feelings in the moment" turns it into what Aristotle *distinguishes* from virtue and calls *enkrateia*. Heidegger does not discuss *enkrateia*, and how could he when his interpretation completely undermines the distinction between *enkrateia* and *arete*?

As readers of *Being and Time*, we can of course see where Heidegger is heading with this reading of Aristotle's *Ethics:* the distinction between virtue and vice is transformed, or rather *dissolved,* into a distinction between authentic resoluteness and inauthentic everyday existence, between resolutely confronting one's possibility of being in the moment of decision and losing oneself in the objects of everyday concern. Yet if we are interested in anything more than the genesis of *Being and Time,* we must ask: *at what cost* is Heidegger proceeding in this direction? I am referring to the "philological" cost not only in the narrow sense of the word but also, and more importantly, in the broader sense Heidegger gives it:[14] the passion of knowing what is expressed. The greatest cost is not what is amputated from Aristotle's text but what is amputated from what Aristotle's text is trying to express: concrete human existence. This cost will become particularly evident when we turn to Heidegger's interpretation of what he has appeared to avoid so far: choice, decision, *proairesis.* But before we turn to this, two other aspects of Heidegger's interpretation merit some attention: (1) what he makes of the distinction between pleasure and pain that plays such a central role in Aristotle's account of virtue; (2) his very revealing choice of which specific Aristotelian virtues to take into consideration.

Heidegger and Aristotle on *Hedone*

One entire chapter—chapter 3—of Aristotle's account of virtue in Book 2 is devoted to pleasure and pain because, as Aristotle explains, pleasure and pain reveal character: for example, the person who takes pleasure (*chairon*) in refraining from physical pleasures is temperate (*sophron*), while the person who suffers in refraining from physical pleasures is not (is *akolastos*) (1104b 5–7). In short, Aristotle claims that virtue of character (*ethike arete*) is to be found in pleasures (*hedone*) and pains (*lype*) (1104b 8–9). Since, as we have seen, Heidegger's reading has effectively eliminated virtue *of character* and thereby the distinction between *arete* and *enkrateia,* one wonders what he could possibly have made of such claims. Wisely, he does not discuss this part of Book 2. Later, however, in the context of discussing the *pathe,* and specifically, Aristotle's claim in the *Rhetoric* that every *pathos* is accompanied by *hedone* or *lype* (1378a 20ff), Heidegger turns to Aristotle's discussion of *hedone* in the first five chapters of Book 10 of the *Ethics* (241–48). Predictably, Heidegger insists that "*hedone* is not so-called 'Pleasure', but a *determination of being in itself as life*" (244). From Aristotle's claim that *hedone* is not a motion (*kinesis*) and does not occur "in" time, Heidegger infers that it is not something that arises occasionally and is not the result of determinate conditions, but rather is *life itself* (244–45). *Hedone* is being-in-the-world *as had,* how we *find ourselves* in the world. What *hedone* "adds" to *pathos* is nothing other than Dasein itself in its character of self-having (where this self-having is prior to any self-reflection): "*Hedone* is disposedness [*Befindlichkeit*] *in the manner of the self-having of a Dasein*" (246). The obvious problem with this definition is not only that it equates *hedone* with *hexis,* as the emphasis on the word "having" makes clear, but also that it ignores the distinction between *hedone* and *lype,* since the latter must presumably also be a way of being-in-the-world. Yet Heidegger finally turns to this distinction, with results that are shocking to any reader of Aristotle's text but probably predictable to any reader of Heidegger. There are indeed, Heidegger proceeds to tell us, two kinds of *Sich-befinden:* one is characterized by *hairesis,* that is, Dasein taking itself in hand, seizing and grasping its own being; the other is characterized by *phyge,* that is, Dasein fleeing from itself. It is in this distinction between seizing upon and fleeing one's own existence that Heidegger locates the distinction between *hedone* and *lype* (247). One cannot help but admire the breathtaking audacity with which Heidegger transforms Aristotle's distinction between *hedone* and *lype* into a distinction between authenticity and inauthenticity! The goal again is to turn *hedone* and *lype* into purely ontological determinations; "*Hairesis* and *phyge* are fundamental *movements of Daseins*" (247). Proving that this cannot be sustained as an interpretation of Aristotle need not detain us; practically any claim Aristotle makes about *hedone* and *lype* picked at random would suffice as a refutation. I will only note one of the interesting consequences of this interpretation: when Heidegger turns next to an interpretation of the *pathos* of *fear,* he must, since fear is a *lype,* interpret it as a *flight from one's own being* (250–51); in other words, he must transform fear into *Angst* (see 261).

Heidegger and Aristotle on Courage and Truthfulness

In Heidegger's interpretation and conflation of *hexis* and *arete* as the "resolute seizing upon one's own being in the moment," there certainly appears to be *no place* for many of the specific virtues Aristotle discusses, such as generosity, justice, friendliness, and right honor, not to mention "wit" (Book 4, ch. 8). There are, however, two specific virtues that are named and discussed by Heidegger, and one could probably guess which ones they are: *courage* and *truthfulness* (261ff). Yet even these two virtues have to be radically reinterpreted to find any place in Heidegger's account. Courage (*Mut*) is transformed from the confronting of the ultimate danger of death *for the sake of what is noble* (*tou kalou heneka, touto gar telos tes aretes*, 1115b 12-13) into the resolute laying-hold of one's being in the face of *Angst* (261). What of course disappears in this transformation is "the noble" as the *telos* of courage and of all the other virtues. But even more extraordinary and momentous in its implications is Heidegger's interpretation of Aristotle's account of "truthfulness" (*aletheuein*) in Book 4 of the *Ethics*, chapters 12-13 (Aristotle actually discusses here two different, though related, virtues, each lacking a proper name). Heidegger first describes the state of vice in a way that reveals how he is going to characterize the contrasting virtue: "Dasein in its everydayness remains in the 'more or less,' it moves in extremes, it is not very exacting in its dealings with itself; it is *unsachlich* to a certain degree. Man is *unsachlich* in relation to himself" (264). Here we see again the identification of what Aristotle calls vice with everyday existence. Thus Heidegger sees the vice of boasting (the *alazon*) as the way in which human beings exist "immediately and for the most part" (*zumeist und zunnächst*, 264). What is new here is the characterization of this everyday state of existing in extremes as *Unsachlichkeit*. This enables Heidegger to characterize the contrasting virtue as *Sachlichkeit*: "Now the possibility arises of coming to a determinate *Sachlichkeit*, which in a certain way pushes back [*zurückstellt*] the way of seeing the world indicated by the *pathe*. Only when one sees being [*das Dasein*] in this way, can one push back [*zurückstellen*] the *pathe*" (262). This "pushing back" of the *pathe* to which Heidegger refers is of course how he earlier characterizes *hexis* as such. The virtue of "truthfulness" then becomes simply the application of this *hexis*, qua *Sachlichkeit*, to our relations with others: it is thus "being in control of Dasein with respect to its unconcealedness [*Entdecktheit*], presenting oneself in such a way that this self-presentation and being-with-others is not a self-concealment, a self-misrepresentation, *presenting oneself as one is and as one thinks*" (264).

Two momentous results of this analysis need to be noted, though they will not emerge fully into the light of day until later in the course. Heidegger has identified existing in extremes *as such*, being swept away by the *pathe as such*, with *Unsachlichkeit*, while *hexis* as such, defined as the holding back of the *pathe* (*Gefaßtsein*) and made equivalent to virtue, has been identified with *Sachlichkeit*. In this way the difference between vice *as a whole* and virtue *as a whole* becomes a difference between *unsachlich*, self-fleeing, self-obstructing, inauthentic everyday existence, on the one hand, and the *sachlich* confrontation of one's being in its unconcealment. What Heidegger here calls *Sachlichkeit* and *aletheuein* is not *one* virtue, but the whole of virtue. The other consequence is what one might provisionally call, for want of a better word, the "intellectualization" of virtue. *Sachlichkeit* is of course the virtue that Heidegger often identifies with the philosophical life. So is he not here turning virtue into philosophy? That this is the direction in which Heidegger is heading is shown by an extraordinary move he now makes. He concludes his account of the virtue of *aletheuein* in chapters 12–13 of Book 4 of the *Ethics* by informing us that Aristotle will treat thematically the different possibilities of *aletheuein* in Book 6 (265). This is a move that must leave one dumbfounded: the virtue discussed in Book 4 is what Aristotle calls a "virtue of character," concerned, as Heidegger himself notes, with our relation to others, while the virtues discussed in Book 6 are the "dianoetic" virtues, which Aristotle sharply distinguishes from the virtues of character. It is perhaps precisely to avoid any confusion here that Aristotle, unlike Heidegger, does *not* call the virtue, or rather virtues, of truthfulness discussed in Book 4 *aletheuein* but instead tells us that they have no name (1127a14).

What Heidegger is doing here must astonish: he first implicitly reduces all the virtues of character to one virtue he, but not Aristotle, calls *aletheuein;* he then identifies this virtue, as if the social dimension were inessential to it, with the *dianoetic* virtues (something facilitated, of course, by Heidegger's complete abstraction of virtue of character from character and habituation). What is in preparation here is what will prove to be the final coup de grace of Heidegger's interpretation: the elimination of the distinction between virtues of character and dianoetic virtues. Furthermore, the latter themselves will be reduced to *theoria*.[15] It is significant that Heidegger makes here the claim that he makes repeatedly throughout the course: that "*aletheuein* as the *bios theoretikos* represents *the authentic* [*eigentliche*] and highest possibility of Greek existence" (265). Furthermore, Heidegger's earlier account of *hedone* implicitly identifies it with *theoria:* "The authentic being of man, the highest possibility of being, lies in *theorein*— the possibility of being there in the most radical sense. *Hedone* is, in short, nothing other than the determination of the presence [*Gegenwärtigkeit*] of Being-in-the-world, that is there in finding-oneself [*Sichbefinden*] as such" (246). Such an identification is of course facilitated by the characterization of *hedone* as the pursuit and confrontation of being.

146   *Francisco J. Gonzalez*

Heidegger and Aristotle on *Proairesis*

Finally, it is in Heidegger's extraordinary interpretation of *proairesis* that all of his cards are put on the table. It is also in this interpretation that we see just how great the gulf between Heidegger and Aristotle has become. First, a brief reminder is needed of how Aristotle characterizes *proairesis*. In Book 3 of the *Ethics* Aristotle defines *proairesis* as "deliberative desire [*bouleutike orexis*] concerning things that are up to us" (1113a 11). The discussion that precedes this definition makes clear why both deliberation and desire are essential to *proairesis*. As Aristotle points out, the very word suggests that *proairesis* is a choosing of something *for* (*pro*) something else: "And the word itself appears to connote being chosen for other things [*pro heteron*]" (1112a 16–17). This makes deliberation essential to *proairesis* because deliberation is precisely deliberation about what contributes to or promotes certain ends (*ta pros ta tele*, 1112b 34). But if *proairesis* and deliberation concern what is *for* a certain end, then the end must be given prior to deliberation and choice; in other words, it cannot be itself an object of deliberation and choice (see 1111b 26–29 and 1112b 33–34). This is what makes desire essential to *proairesis:* only if an end is already given as an object of desire can we deliberate about and choose what is *for* this end. Put simply, we desire a certain end and we deliberate about the means; once deliberation discovers something that promotes the end we desire and is "up to us," that is, in our power, *proairesis* takes place.

Heidegger's interpretation of *proairesis* is not be found in the context of a reading of the relevant part of Book 3 of the *Ethics* or of any other specific text. Instead, it arises in the very important context of taking the interpretation of Aristotle's fundamental concepts back to an interpretation of Dasein as the ground of all conceptualization (*Begrifflichkeit*). In the context of arguing that Dasein is *being-possible* and most fundamentally a being-possible *against* instead of *for*, Heidegger says the following: "We already know that the Dasein of human beings is characterized in terms of *proairesis*. A 'deciding-onself' [*Sichentschließen*] is always determined in this manner: that it decides *against something*, and that therefore presumably even the formation of conceptuality [*Begrifflichkeit*] grows out of a kind of being of Dasein that *precisely goes against* this conceptuality" (272). Here we see the most striking feature of Heidegger's interpretation of *proairesis* and the one that represents the most complete inversion of the Aristotelian interpretation: while for Aristotle the most important feature of *proairesis*, and the one that makes deliberation and desire essential to it, is that it is *for* (*pro*) some end, Heidegger insists that *proairesis* is at the most fundamental level decision *against* something. This move should not surprise us since it is only the natural culmination of Heidegger's reading of the *Ethics*. Having already excluded from his interpretation of virtue and the human good deliberation and desire in relation to specific means and ends, Heidegger must now eliminate the *pro* from *proairesis*.

As the cited passage shows, however, *proairesis* is still on some level *for* something. But what requires our reflection here is *what proairesis is for* on Heidegger's interpretation and how what it is for is a *result* of what it is *against*. What *proairesis* is for is what Heidegger calls here "*Begrifflichkeit,*" which is essentially the equivalent of what he called "*Sachlichkeit*" in his interpretation of virtue. We decide ourselves for the explicit disclosure and articulation of our being. The following remarkable passage makes this point clear as well as reiterating that this decision can take place only as a decision *against:* "When science [*Wissenschaft*] is something for which Dasein can resolve itself [*sich entschließen*], *hexis*, then what characterizes this *hexis* is that it is *pos echomen pros allon, pos,* that which it is, *pros,* 'against' [*gegen*], 'in relation to' something which it works itself out of" (274). A number of things need to be noted here. First, that *science* is what *hexis* decides for. Here we have the final outcome of what I called earlier Heidegger's "intellectualization" of virtue: virtue was reduced to *aletheuein* in the sense of the intellectual virtues of Book 6, and now it is equated with a decision for science. Another thing to note is that this decision is simply called *hexis:* this is because Heidegger has earlier simply identified virtue with *hexis* in the sense of "*Gefaßtsein.*" Indeed, the most extraordinary feature of Heidegger's reading of the *Ethics* now becomes clear: the *identification* of *arete, hexis,* and *proairesis,* so that the possibility of a *bad proairesis* or *bad hexis* is completely eliminated. In addition, we now have the implicit identification of all three terms with *theoria:* the only real decision is the decision for science, and the only genuine way of being in possession of one's being is the life of science. Anything else is not *hexis* or *proairesis* at all.[16] Finally, we have again in the cited passage Heidegger's insistence that decision is decision *against,* an insistence that goes so far as to translate the word *pros* in Aristotle's characterization of *hexis* as "against" (*gegen;* in the manuscript the word is implicitly identified with *das Wogegen,* 356). This insistence can be explained in terms of Aristotle's own characterization of *proairesis.* Since what Heidegger calls *proairesis* is clearly not a deliberation about means toward determinate ends, it cannot have the character of *pro-airesis* and therefore can be characterized only negatively as *against* something.

But against *what*? What is it that runs against conceptuality and science and therefore is that *against which* Heideggerian *proairesis* defines itself? The answer should not be hard to guess by this point: *proairesis* is always *hairesis against average and everyday existence as such*. *Proairesis* is the possibility Dasein has of "*appropriating in a genuine sense* the conceptual (*das Begriffliche*) out of everydayness and against it in *hexis*" (277). The occurrence of the word *hexis* here is significant: as we have seen, Heidegger characterizes *hexis* as a being-in-control or being-collected (*Gefaßtsein*) and as such identifies it with virtue. Now we see that what we are collected *against* in *hexis* is average and everyday existence. What characterizes such existence is not a bad *hexis* or *proairesis*, but the complete absence of these. One cannot decide for average everyday existence since it is simply the absence of all decision, resolution, self-possession, courage, and truth (where all these terms are synonymous). Aristotle's deliberative desire about practical means toward practical goals has thus been transformed into a resolution defined *negatively* as directed *against* the average and everyday and therefore, one could argue, against the social sphere as such.[17]

Ethics without Ethics

It would not be productive to insist that we have in Heidegger's reading of Aristotle's *Ethics* probably the most thorough distortion and misinterpretation of a Greek text in the history of philology. But what then do we conclude? Here, of course, I have not considered much that is highly impressive in the Aristotle course. Heidegger's interpretation of life as being-in-the-world and of the *pathe* as ways of being-in-the-world, for example, is a lightning flash that illuminates huge areas not only of Aristotle's thought but of Greek thought in general. So why not simply grant the course its brilliant discoveries on the level of ontology and allow that such discoveries required Heidegger to disregard for the moment the specifically ethical content of Aristotle's texts? After all, Heidegger explicitly says, as early as the 1922 prospectus of the book on Aristotle he was working on during this time, that his reading of the dianoetic virtues in Book 6 of the *Ethics* will proceed "with preliminary disregard for the ethical problematic."[18] This furthermore fits the picture of a Heidegger merely postponing ethics as something to be done *after* ontology through some move to "metontology."[19]

But a careful reading of the Aristotle course seriously brings this picture into question. Heidegger's interpretation of Aristotle *could* have focused on texts from the *Metaphysics, Physics,* and *De Anima,* leaving Aristotle's *Ethics* alone or discussing only those passages of the *Ethics* that have nothing explicitly to do with the distinction between the virtuous and the vicious life (this of course would not leave much, except maybe the intellectual virtues of *sophia* and *techne;* as for *phroneis,* how could *it* be adequately interpreted "with preliminary disregard for the ethical problematic"?[20]). But we have seen that this is not what he does. He offers interpretations of Aristotle's ethical concepts and in language that certainly continues to sound ethical: resoluteness, self-possession, truthfulness, courage, authenticity, and so on. That Heidegger should arrive at these notions through an interpretation of Aristotle's ethics supports those who have found it difficult to take Heidegger at his word when he insists in *Being and Time* that notions such as "authenticity" and "inauthenticity," "guilt" and "conscience," have no ethical connotation there.[21] But we have also seen that there is some justification for this insistence: if Heidegger appropriates Aristotle's ethical concepts, it is only by sucking all the ethical blood out of them. What we have in Heidegger is neither no ethics at all nor a determinate, concrete ethics; instead, what emerges from Heidegger's misreading of Aristotle is something unique and extremely strange: an ethics with strong imperatives of truthfulness, courage, resoluteness, and authenticity, but completely lacking determinate content, the content, that is, that would distinguish virtue from vice, goodness from wickedness.[22] What we can conclude is that the "ontologizing" of ethics that takes place in the Aristotle course sharpens and intensifies the *rhetoric* of ethics while at the same time ridding it of any determinate content. And what could be more *dangerous* than such an ethics? Except, that is, a similar *politics.*[23]

Heidegger's reading of Aristotle's *Ethics* demands our reflection not to the extent that it is a misreading of Aristotle—there are many misreadings of Aristotle, of which most must leave us philosophically indifferent—but to the extent that it is a misreading of human life. What gets assassinated in Heidegger's reading is not just the text of the *Ethics,* but the very possibility of reflective ethical life.[24] In Heidegger's notes for the course we find a revealing critique of Karl Jaspers that was presumably not delivered: "Dasein is to be experienced overall as an ontological task. One believes that what one has to deal with here are consciousness, personhood and life. One thus fails to grasp anything [*Hier versagt alles*]. Cf. *Jaspers*" (381). Since Aristotle apparently believed that experiencing human existence has to do with desire for determinate ends, deliberation between competing means, and enduring moral character, Heidegger had to purify him to save him from the fate of Jaspers: that is, the fate of being shallow and beside the point, the fate of being—and this is what has turned out to be for Heidegger the greatest, indeed the *only* vice—*unsachlich*.

Notes

This paper was written with the support of the Alexander von Humboldt-Stiftung and the National Endowment for the Humanities.

1. *Grundbegriffe der aristotelischen Philosophie, Gesamtausgabe* 18 (Frankfurt am Main: Vittorio Klostermann, 2002); hereafter GA18. All translations of the course are my own.

2. Describing the Marburg years, Gadamer writes: "Aristoteles wurde einem derart auf den Leib gerückt, daß man zeitweise jeden Abstand verlor und nicht einmal realisierte, daß Heidegger sich nicht selber mit Aristoteles identifizierte, sondern am Ende auf einen eigenen Gegenentwurf zu Metaphysik zielte. Vielmehr lag die Auszeichnung dieser frühen Aristoteles-Deutung darin, daß die verfremdende scholastische Überformung abstreifte und geradezu ein Vorbild hermeneutischer 'Horizontverschmelzung' wurde, die Aristoteles wie einen Gegenwärtigen zu Worte kommen ließ," *Gesammelte Werke* 3 (Tübingen: J. C. B. Mohr, 1987), 286.

3. ". . . er uns fast wie ein Aristoteles *redivivus* erschien," H. G. Gadamer, *Gessamelte Werke* 2 (Tübingen: J. C. B. Mohr, 1993), 486.

4. Especially by Franco Volpi: see his *Heidegger e Aristotele* (Padova: Daphne Editrice, 1984), 102–103, 111–15; "Dasein as *Praxis*: The Heideggerian Assimilation and the Radicalization of the Practical Philosophy of Aristotle," in *Martin Heidegger: Critical Assessments*, vol. 2, ed. Christopher Macann (New York: Routledge, 1992), 90–129; and "*Being and Time*: A 'Translation' of the *Nicomachean Ethics*?" in *Reading Heidegger from the Start: Essays in his Earliest Thought*, ed. Theodore Kisiel and John van Buren (Albany: SUNY Press, 1994), 195–211. See also Enrico Berti, who closely follows Volpi's reading, in *Aristotele nel Novecento* (Rome: Laterza, 1992), 91–98. In the 1994 article Volpi describes as follows one of the two alterations the Aristotelian concepts undergo in their Heideggerian reappropriation: "The most notable alteration seems to me to be the emphasizing and indeed absolutizing of the ontological feature of the determinations, that is, their interpretation as ways of being in the strict sense, such that all ontic meaning is excluded in principle" (201). Yet Volpi appears to assume that this alteration can be simply reversed: thus he interprets Heidegger's claim that "only Dasein is constituted as a to-be" as meaning that "only Dasein comports itself to itself in an eminently practical-moral sense" (204); Dasein's "to-be" is identified with its "practical-moral determination" (208). In this way, Volpi misses just how radical and distorting Heidegger's ontologization of Aristotle's ethical concepts is. Ted Sadler rightly emphasizes, in reply to Volpi, what this paper certainly confirms: that "any ontologization of *phronesis* on the part of Heidegger would simply *destroy* this concept in its Aristotelian meaning" (*Heidegger and Aristotle: The Question of Being* [London: Athlone, 1996], 146;

see also 155). The third chapter (141-98) of Sadler's book argues against the prevalent thesis that Heidegger "appropriated" Aristotle's practical philosophy. I would certainly agree that what we have here is more destruction than appropriation. For a similar view, see Jacques Taminiaux, *Sillages Phénoménologiques* (Brussels: Editions OUSIA, 2002), 190, 198.

5. Heidegger appears to think that his focus on *techne* is supported by Aristotle's identification in chapter 2 of the method that pursues the human good with the *politike techne* (GA18, 68). But Aristotle does not speak of *techne* there, but only of episteme and *methodos;* furthermore, given the sharp distinction made in Book 6 between *techne* and *phronesis*, it is unlikely that Aristotle would characterize as *techne, politike* or not, "das Sichauskennen des Lebens hinsichtlich seiner selbst" (70), as Heidegger implies.

6. The result at which Heidegger is aiming here is stated with perfect clarity in the course given the following semester on Plato's *Sophist:* "Das *agathon* hat zunächst keine Bezug auf die *praxis*, sondern es ist eine Bestimmung des Seienden, sofern es *fertig, voll-ständig* ist," *Platon: Sophistes, Gesamtausgabe* 19 (Frankfurt am Main: Vittorio Klostermann, 1992), 123.

7. The following observation of Volpi, though written before the publication of the SS 1924 Aristotle course, is exactly on the mark: "With Aristotle, the practical issue represents a particular way of viewing human life, precisely in as much as the latter is capable of action and in as much as it is itself action. . . . With Heidegger, on the other hand, practical determinations are not determinations which exist alongside other possible determinations but represent the ontological constitution of Dasein itself. This means that as constitutive, their content is not something that Dasein can freely choose to have or not to have but is something from which it cannot be abstracted. Decision, for example, or *praxis* itself, are not conceived as possibilities which Dasein can realize or not, but become ontological predicates which characterize its being before, and therefore independent of, its will, its choice, its decision" ("Dasein as *Praxis*," 113). This is what Volpi calls "the 'ontologization' of *praxis*" (113). See also Berti, 97.

8. That Heidegger should show little interest here in the distinction between *praxis* and *poiesis* is due to the fact that he has no interest in the traits that for Aristotle would be most distinctive of the former, including *action itself.* For Heidegger, *praxis* is not "Handlung" but a determination of the being of man (GA18, 188-89); it is the "Wie des Seins-in-der-Welt" (176) and Dasein's "Sorge um sich selbst" (180). *Poiesis* of course is also all of this.

9. See my "Whose Metaphysics of Presence? Heidegger on *Energeia* and *Dunamis* in Aristotle," *The Southern Journal of Philosophy,* forthcoming.

10. Revealing in this context is Heidegger's reduction of Aristotle's suggestion that perhaps all living things pursue the same *hedone* because they all by nature possess something *theion* (1153b 31-32) to the claim that each being is concerned with its own being, its own *Fertigsein.* "Das Seiende als Lebendes ist ein solches Sein, dem es in seinem Sein aud Da-sein ankommt" (GA18, 243-44). Similarly, Heidegger interprets the claim that there is something in every living being that *ephiaite tou oikeiou agathou*" (1173a 5) as meaning that every living being "aus ist auf die eigentliche Daseinsfertigkeit" (243), even though Aristotle clearly states that the good that exists in living things is something *greater or better than they are* (*kreiton kath' auta,* 1173a 5).

11. ". . . daß *ergon* genommen wird in seiner eigensten Möglichkeit, nämlich *als*

sich vollziehend in der arete als wirklich da" (GA18, 100). Cf. the characterization of *arete* in the *Sophist* course (GA19, 53–54).

12. Dominique Janicaud, following Paul Ricœur and quoting his words, has argued that "le 'souci lancinant de la radicalité' empêche Heidegger de 'faire le trajet de retour'— non seulement de l'herméneutique générale aux herméneutiques régionales, mais des conditions de la praxis (et de la déconstruction de son concept même) vers ses mises en œuvre effectives (pratiques, éthiques et même politiques)," *Heidegger en France* I. Récit (Paris: Albin Michel, 2001), 465. He then later asks the important question: "mais cette remontée radicale au fondement ne déplace-t-elle pas l'attente vers un avenir toujours réservé, désertant la *praxis* effective? n'est-ce pas un aller sans retour? En tout cas, sans retour viable, non catastrophique?" (470).

13. Aristotle says here explicitly that *to echein legetai pollachos* (1023a 8), but Heidegger provides a lengthy and revealing paraphrase: "that is, different beings are addressed and are intended with different meanings through the expression at issue here, in such a way that this is not an arbitrary jumble, but has a relation to a fundamental meaning [*Grundbedeutung*] which through the demonstration of individual meanings can be brought to an intuition [*zum Sehen gebracht wird*]. We must see in what the diverse meanings of *echein* agree [*übereinkommt*], insofar as *echein* expresses being" (GA18, 172). Critique of this "paraphrase" itself merits another paper. Let it simply be said here that if Aristotle recognizes the existence of a *primary* meaning to which all the others bear some relation (the *pros hen* relation described in Book 4, chapter 2, of the *Metaphysics*), this is quite different from a fundamental meaning in which all the other meanings *agree* and which we could *see* within or behind their diversity.

14. Though even this narrowly philological cost is not negligible. As Victor Goldschmidt has rightly insisted, "La compréhension des œuvres échappe entièrement à l'alternative artificielle entre 'le dialogue pensant' et 'la philologie historique,' " *Platonisme et pensée contemporaine* (Paris: J. Vrin, 2000, 243). Goldschmidt sees philology as preserving the alterity of the text, where this alterity is essential to the experience of the text: "(Il est étonnant qu'à une époque qui se targue d'avoir découvert les problèmes d'autrui et de l'intersubjectivité, certains ressentent si peu l'*alterité* irréductible des textes, qui est pourtant l'objet d'une expérience aussi élémentaire que celle qui s'offre constamment à la sensibilité *extéro*ceptive)" (244). Heidegger's untenable philology is a failure to recognize the alterity of the text and thus a failure of philosophical dialogue.

15. It is significant, and striking, that in turning to Aristotle's discussion in *De part. an.* 1 of the *hexis theorias*, Heideger tells us that we will there "das Entsprechende kennenlernen, was wir bei der Diskussion der *arete* kennenlernen" (GA18, 209). But the *arete* discussed in Book 2 of the *Ethics* is radically distinct from any *hexis theorias*.

16. Jacques Taminiaux, writing on the SS 1924 course when only the transcript in the Marcuse Archive was available, saw this feature of the course clearly: "Tout se passe donc comme si, aux yeux de Heidegger, seul celui qui se consacre à la vie contemplative méritait pleinement le titre aristotélicien de *zôon logon echon*" (*Sillages Phénoménologiques*, 55). The course leads Taminiaux to think that in Heidegger's eyes "seule la recherche à laquelle se voue le *bios theorètikos* mérite vraiment le titre de *praxis*. De plus, lorsqu'il analyse les textes d'Aristote relatifs à la *phronèsis* et à la *mesotès* qui en est l'*ousia*, l'élucidation phénoménologique qu'il en donne néglige toute connotation de prudence, d'évitement de quelque excès" (62). See also *The Thracian Maid and the Pro-*

fessional Thinker: Arendt and Heidegger, trans. Michael Gendre (Albany: Suny Press, 1997), 41, 52. In contrast, Volpi wrongly claims that in Heidegger's reappropriation of Aristotle's concepts, *"theoria* is no longer viewed as the highest vocation that is to be preferred for a human being" ("A 'Translation' of the *Nicomachean Ethics?"* 202). Equally wrong is the following claim: "Certainly, as a rigorously ontological determination it [Heidegger's determination of understanding] precedes the distinction between theory and practice. But this by no means prevents Heidegger's characterization of it from being oriented to a specific frame of reference, and this is surely not that of *theoria,* but rather precisely that of *praxis.* So it is no wonder that practical elements nevertheless slip through Heidegger's ontological filter" (207). The same mistaken interpretation is to be found in Berti, 96.

17. Paul Ricœur's interpretation of *proairesis* moves in a direction completely opposed to Heidegger's by seeing in this Aristotelian notion a warning against the danger of translating knowledge from the theoretical domain to the practical: see *Du texte à l'action: Essais d'herméneutique II* (Paris: Éditions du Seuil, 1986), 267 ff., especially 277 and 285.

18. "Phänomenologische Interpretationen zu Aristoteles (Anzeige der hermeneutischen Situation)," *Dilthey-Jahrbuch für Philosophie und Geschichte der Geisteswissenschaften* 6 (1989): 255. Gadamer, who was clearly influenced by Heidegger's reading of Aristotle in the 1920s and had read at the time the 1922 Natorp-Bericht, was surprised to discover, with the publication almost half a century later of both the Natorp-Bericht and the *Sophist* lectures of WS 1924–25, the extent to which Heidegger reduced Aristotle's practical philosophy to theoretical philosophy and overlooked the determinate ethical content of the *Ethics:* on the Natorp-Bericht, see "Heideggers 'theologische' Jugendschrift," *Dilthey-Jahrbuch für Philosophie und Geschichte der Geisteswissenschaften* 6 (1989): 231; on the *Sophist* lectures, see *Aristoteles: Nikomachische Ethik VI* (Frankfurt am Main: Vittorio Klostermann, 1998), 67. We ourselves can now see the extent to which Gadamer's work on Aristotle was inspired by a very fruitful *misunderstanding* of Heidegger. As Taminiaux has remarked, "Si Heidegger lisait mal l'*Ethique à Nicomaque,* il n'a pu inspirer Gadamer que parce que celui-ci écoutait mal celui-là, et en tout cas entendait autre chose que ce que le maître voulait dire" (*Sillages Phénoménologiques,* 158).

19. In *Metaphysische Anfangsgründe der Logik im Ausgang von Leibniz,* a course delivered in the summer of 1928, Heidegger claims merely to postpone the question of ethics to what he calls *metontology,* the *Umschlag* of fundamental ontology, a turn (*Kehre*) to existentiell-ontic questioning (*Gesamtausgabe* 26 [Frankfurt am Main: Vittorio Klostermann, 1978], 199–202). That what we have in Heidegger is indeed only a *postponement* of ethics is a basic assumption of Lawrence J. Hatab's attempt to formulate a Heideggerian ethics: see *Ethics and Finitude: Heideggerian Contributions to Moral Philosophy* (Lanham, Md.: Rowman and Littlefield, 2000), e.g., pp. 1, 90, 103, 207.

20. I have argued elsewhere that Heidegger's "ontologization" of *phronesis* in the *Sophist* course of WS 1924–25 in the end assimilates it to *sophia:* see "On the Way to *Sophia:* Heidegger on Plato's Dialectic, Ethics, and *Sophist,"* *Research in Phenomenology* 27 (1997): 26–35. See also Jacques Taminiaux, "The Interpretation of Aristotle's Notion of *Aretê* in Heidegger's First Courses," in *Heidegger and Practical Philosophy,* ed. François Raffoul and David Pettigrew (Albany: State University of New York Press, 2002), 23–27;

The Thracian Maid and the Professional Thinker, 95, 187; and Sillages Phénoménologiques, 179–80, 195. In the latter text, Taminiaux expresses the point differently: neither phronesis nor sophia is privileged, but both are appropriated by, and amalgamated in, ontology. Sadler likewise sees that "Heidegger does not take offence at the higher authority of sophia" but rather considers that sophia "is still 'not high enough' for the Seinsfrage" (Heidegger and Aristotle, 147); "Heidegger wants to preserve the 'rank' of sophia in his own existential ontology" (157).

21. See, e.g., Sein und Zeit, 15th ed. (Tübingen: Niemeyer, 1984), 167, 286, 294. See also "Brief über den 'Humanismus'," in Wegmarken, 2nd ed. (Frankfurt am Main: Vittorio Klostermann, 1978), 329; Beiträge zur Philosophie, Gesamtausgabe 65, 2nd ed. (Frankfurt am Main: Vittorio Klostermann, 1994), 302. Referring to the ontological conceptions of guilt, conscience, and resoluteness in Being and Time, Hatab writes: "Nevertheless it would be a mistake to assume that these ontological notions have nothing whatsoever to do with ethical meanings" (79). Robert Bernasconi has argued that what Heidegger calls "metontology" is not an addition to ontology but a return to an ontic, or rather existentiell, ideal that already underlies and guides fundamental ontology (" 'The Double Concept of Philosophy' and the Place of Ethics," in Heidegger in Question: The Art of Existing [Amherst, N.J.: Humanities Press, 1993], 25–39). A crucial text Bernasconi cites is Heidegger's admission, which Heidegger asserts to be "a positive necessity," that "a definite ontic interpretation of authentic existence, a factical ideal of Dasein underlies his ontological interpretation of the existence of Dasein" (SZ, 310). As Bernasconi points out, in this case Heidegger "is not readily able to sustain the purity of the distinction between the ontic and the ontological" (33) by which he sought to exclude any ethical sense from the existentials of Being and Time, including Dasein's solipsism. I believe that the 1924 course both confirms that an "ontic interpretation of authentic existence" guides Heidegger's fundamental ontology and shows the ethical poverty and perversity of this "factical ideal" (and therefore of any "metontology" that would "return" to it). Bernasconi himself recognizes in Being and Time "the clear if unstated bias toward what in another context might be called the 'virtues of the philosopher' " (37).

22. Karl Löwith, who attended the 1924 Aristotle course, describes as follows the effect that Heidegger's teaching had on himself and others during this period: "Wodurch er zunächst auf uns wirkte, war nicht die Erwartung eines neues Systems, sondern gerade das inhaltlich Unbestimmte und bloß Appelierende seines philosophischen Wollens, seine geistige Intensität und Konzentration auf 'das Eine was Not tut'. Erst später wurde uns klar, daß dieses Eine eigentlich nichts war, eine pure Entschlossenheit, von der nicht festand, wozu? 'Ich bin entschlossen, nur weiß ich nicht wozu,' hieß der treffliche Witz, den ein Student eines Tages erfand," Mein Leben in Deutschland vor und nach 1933 (Stuttgart: J. B. Metzlersche Verlagsbuchhandlung, 1986), 29.

23. On Heidegger's strangely unpolitical politics, see my "Heidegger's 1933 Misappropriation of Plato's Republic," Problemata. Quaderni di Filosofia 3 (2003): 39–80. I believe that the Aristotle course of 1924 completely confirms Janicaud's suggestion: "on peut même soutenir que l'engagement de 1933—loin de témoigner d'une indifférence éthique—trahit plutôt les dangers d'une ethique héroïque de la 'décision résolue' insuffissament articulée aux exigences spécifiques de la rationalité éthico-politique" (Heidegger en France, 460).

24. I therefore believe that Heidegger's fundamental distortion of Aristotle's ethics in the SS 1924 course undermines Hatab's attempt "to open up an ethics with Heidegger's ontology that moves through, yet beyond, Aristotle's thought" (103). There is a fundamental incompatibility here that cannot be bridged simply "by highlighting elements in Aristotle that Heidegger did not explore" (103).

9 Back to the Cave: A Platonic Rejoinder to Heideggerian Postmodernism

Gregory Fried

It may seem odd to turn to Plato for a defense against Heidegger's critique of philosophy and against the versions of postmodernism that have proceeded from it. But the choice makes sense considering how Heidegger and much of the postmodern tradition that draws upon him (and Nietzsche) trace the purported nihilism of the West back to Plato and Plato's Socrates and his "doctrine" of the *ideas*.[1] Of course, Heidegger means by "doctrine" (*Lehre*) "that which, within what is said, remains unsaid,"[2] rather than a self-conscious teaching of the thinker; in Plato's case, this is the transition of truth as *aletheia* from unconcealment (*Unverborgenheit*) to the correctness of representation.[3] Nevertheless, I want to emphasize that while Heidegger and others impute to Plato a *doctrinal* way of thinking, this is not the only way to understand Plato. Indeed, Heidegger himself is far too imprisoned, even in his critique, by the Christian appropriation of Plato and Nietzsche's subsequent rejection of this Christianized Plato.[4] Furthermore, whatever their criticisms of him might be, many postmodernists who owe a debt of thinking to Heidegger have also accepted this reading of Plato as a decisive turn in the Western march toward nihilism (or logocentrism, or totalitarianism, or humanism; choose your poison). But such a Plato is not the only Plato.

A caveat: Heidegger at times insists, even in specific readings of Plato's texts, that he is confronting not Plato but Platonism;[5] I ask of the reader a similar latitude to address Heideggerianism if not Heidegger (and postmodernism if not postmodernists). I rely on a previous body of my own work, as well as that of others, so that we can engage a broad reading of Heidegger by way of a specific reading of Plato.[6] My goal here is to outline an alternative, one that would surely assume greater complexity if the full textual analysis, which here is impossible, of both the Plato and the relevant texts of Heidegger could take place. This, then, is a challenge and an invitation.

Freedom and Deconstruction

Both modernity and postmodernity have, at their core, a project of liberation. Of course, the postmodern departure from modernity entails a critique, if not a wholesale rejection, of the modern understanding of how this liberation is to be achieved. The thesis I want to defend here is that philosophy at its best, and in particular the philosophy of Plato as captured in the Platonic portrait of Socrates in the *Republic,* also has at its core a project of liberation, but not one that entails the incipient hubris that Heidegger and his postmodern followers ascribe to it. Part of the thesis is that the Platonic conception of philosophy anticipates (in principle if not in detail) the kind of criticisms deployed by Heidegger and the postmodernists. Since these critiques are well known, I will confine myself to a general overview.[7]

Elsewhere, I have tried to show how his appropriation of a single word from Heraclitus, *polemos,* sheds light on Heidegger's understanding of what it means to be human as well as his understanding of the meaning of Being itself. Heidegger translates the Greek *polemos* not as *Krieg* or *Kampf,* war or battle, but rather as *Auseinandersetzung,* that is, confrontation, or more literally, a setting-forth-and-apart-from-one-another. For Heidegger, both we and Being itself are essentially *polemical,* in an expanded sense of that word. As is well known, Heidegger rejects notions of Being as an ultimate ground, a supreme reality, a thing by reference to which we might know all other things. Being is what grants the world as we find it already given its pre-theoretical intelligibility, with beings set out (*gesetzt*) into delineated unities (*auseinander*) that we can make sense of and interact with. Being bestows meaning. But this meaning, this field of intelligibility that constitutes our world, is always on the move. To be human (or Dasein, to use Heidegger's term of art) is to find yourself always already confronted with a world of meaning that you have not made and that is constantly presenting you with interpretive decisions about how you are to go about being in it. While you cannot exist in a world without a given structure, since this is how meaning happens to us, you can either accept the structure of meaning *as* given and go with the flow, or you can confront that structure and beat a course within it. For Heidegger, I have tried to argue, the latter route is the proper burden of being human: to enter into a po-lemic with Being. This polemic is no cheap exchange of diatribes; it hap-pens whenever a human being genuinely analyzes, interprets, and reinter-prets the structures inherited from the past in order to rework them into a new constellation of meaning (but, importantly, never a completely new beginning, because every genuine inception relies on meaning already given). This polemical work can take place in something as seemingly or-dinary as preparing and serving a dinner (one need only consider the film *Babette's Feast*) or something as rarified as Heidegger's own reinterpreta-tion of the history of Western philosophy. Both are modes of what Heideg-ger called *Destruktion* or *Abbau*, dismantling or deconstruction. Crucial to Heidegger's idea of deconstruction is that all revolution is renovation; there is no creation ex nihilo. Every new departure is assembled from the dismantled elements of the old. Deconstruction does not annihilate the past; it breaks the past's hold on the present and frees up possibilities latent within the past that can be projected on the future.

For Heidegger and those postmodernists with a debt to him, *deconstruc-tion* must be the primary mode of liberation, because the given always threatens to become what is merely taken for granted. For Heidegger, of course, the notion of freedom is complex. The postmodern turn rejects the kind of freedom advocated by Descartes in *The Discourse on Method*—that if only we were to learn enough about the forces that rule physical reality, we might "render ourselves, as it were, masters and possessors of nature."[8] This conception of freedom takes Being (understood here as the totality or substance of beings as a whole) to be the realm of objective nature; such a nature is a potential and an actual threat in the face of which the absolute liberty of the subject would be consummated in the tools and method for bringing nature under its dominion. This modernist understanding of lib-eration then entails our progressive release from subservience to nature and our progressive subjugation of it, including—and perhaps above all— of *human* nature. A corollary to the modern program is that our liberation *from* nature to dominion *over* it demands that we also free ourselves from the dominion of tradition, for tradition as such involves the implicit as-sumption that the natural, given world must forever remain, in ways es-sentially hostile to our security, a mystery that cannot be grasped and mas-tered as a whole by unaided human reason. Because we cannot master nature, tradition demands that we maintain our humility and accept the accounts of our proper place in the whole as passed down to us by revela-tion or the ancestors. For the traditionalist, freedom means a paradoxical submission to the given. For the modernist, the given, as both nature and tradition, must be mastered whenever it inhibits our freedom.

This sketch may be broad, but let us work with it for a moment. For Heidegger, neither traditionalism nor modernism captures the essence of freedom—modernism because it presumes a hubristic opposition of humanity to Being, and traditionalism because it attempts to suppress the tragic necessity of the human confrontation with Being. For Heidegger, philosophy (or later, "thinking") is revolutionary—a tragic, polemical confrontation with Being understood as the given realm of intelligibility within which we always find ourselves already living. In this sense, he is no traditionalist: To take on the burden of being human, we must confront the given understanding of the world we inhabit. But nor is he a modernist: We never stand, as the Cartesian subject, against an objective reality that we may aspire to dominate wholly. We always exist within a world whose intelligibility—be this only a provisional and naïve intelligibility!—is already given to us. This *giving* is a historical-temporal phenomenon, the self-presenting of Being as an unfolding domain of meaning. This giving itself we can never master; we cannot make it our own in the sense of creation ex nihilo. And yet at the same time, as we inhabit the given world, we must confront that very givenness in facing the future; in this sense we can make the given our own by appropriating it. Capitulation to the given leads to vegetative traditionalism; wanton aggression against the given leads to an uprooted hubris. Freedom lies somewhere in between: in the recognition that our very ability to grasp and confront the given is dependent upon the prior givenness of meaning, a givenness we can never, as it were, get behind and master. Freedom is both ours to claim and Being's to grant; freedom resides in the polemical encounter between Being and ourselves.

For Heidegger, then, human freedom is first and foremost *deconstructive* because thinking must confront the given *structures* of intelligibility and dismantle them in order to unlock possibilities for a future implicit but unrealized in—and even *ob*structed by—the given state of affairs. He is no modernist, however, because he does not believe there is a transcendental position that we can occupy and from which we could oversee and master the flow of time and the flux of systems of intelligibility. We cannot take the seat of God and create ex nihilo a world whose unshakable foundations are constituted by our own absolute will, knowledge, and power. All *revolutionary* thinking is precisely a re-turn, a revolving to elements of the deconstructed past that are given a new constellation of meaning. Our confrontations with the given are *necessarily* tragic: they may result in epochal shifts in meaning, but these revolutions must always in turn succumb to the flux of Being. At our creative best, we are at most, for Heidegger, the sacrificial bearers of history, not its masters.

The core to Heidegger's charge against Plato is that the "doctrine" of the ideas falsifies Being by obscuring truth as a temporal and polemical unveiling. By locating Being in an eternal and otherworldly domain of suprasensuous forms, and by making truth the conformity of our assertions with these forms, Plato has succeeded in transforming Being from the unfolding of the field of meaning as it is given temporally into a transtemporal domain of eternally static absolutes (PDT, 180–82). Truth as *aletheia* is no longer the free opening of a world of meaning to us; truth is now the marker of our correct apprehension of a permanent, if transcendent, reality. According to Heidegger, with Plato philosophy begins its confusion of Being and beings and therefore its nihilistic decline into a forgetting of Being as the unfolding bestowal of meaning; philosophy degenerates into a search for the key for the humanistic mastery of Being itself: "The beginning of metaphysics in the thought of Plato is at the same time the beginning of 'humanism'" (PDT, 181). Truth, as the criterion of philosophical and later scientific rigor, now becomes located in statements, or assertions, that correspond to a fixed reality. It is only a matter time (that is, until Descartes) before the connection is made between *assertions about* reality and assertions that both reflect reality *and* permit us to *assert ourselves upon* reality as our dominion and so as the fullest expression of our freedom.

Plato contra Heidegger

Socrates identifies himself in Book 1 of the *Republic* as one *who does not know.* He ends his long struggle with Thrasymachus about the nature of justice by saying that "as a result of the discussion I know nothing [*meden eidenai*]" (354b–c), and he begins it in the same way: by protesting that he is one who "does not know and does not profess to know" (337e). This looks like a version of the proverbial expression of Socratic ignorance: that human wisdom consists in grasping that one "is worth nothing with respect to wisdom."[9] Of course, Socratic irony is as famous as this quip about wisdom, and Thrasymachus is astute enough to call Socrates on his "habitual irony" (337a). We must give Thrasymachus his due: If ironizing is a kind of lying, then Socrates does indeed seem to know more than he says. This is unmistakable to even the casual reader of the dialogues, and even more so in a dialogue as long and complex as the *Republic:* Socrates has thought through the issues and arguments before, and he often sets up his opponents many moves ahead. But this is not, as Thrasymachus maliciously insinuates, due to some crafty strategy to win prestige in the arena of elenchus—and thereby fees for teaching. If Socrates dissembles about the nature of his wisdom, it is because that wisdom is complex and potentially disconcerting to precisely those about whom he is most concerned in his conversation with Thrasymachus: the young men gathered at the home of Cephalus who are themselves on the cusp of making life-defining decisions about the nature of justice.

Thrasymachus does have a point, however: Socrates does seem to know (I use the word advisedly) more than he lets on. In Book 6, Socrates says, while discussing "what the good itself is," that "it looks to me as though it's out of the range of our present thrust to attain the opinions I now hold about it" (506e). Socrates clearly has an agenda—not the vulgar one that Thrasymachus imputes, but rather the nobler one of turning a group of promising young men away from the allures of a life of injustice. Thrasymachus has made a compelling case for the natural goodness of a life of tyranny. So although Socrates knows "nothing," he knows enough to know that it would be "impious" (*me . . . hosion*, 368b–c) to cede the field to injustice. How can this be, if he means what he says about his "human wisdom"? Even in Book 6, when Glaucon presses him in the name of justice to give his views of the good, Socrates asks if "it's just to speak about what one doesn't know as though one knew?" (506c).

But these Socratic denials of wisdom do not amount to a nihilistic skepticism. The nihilistically skeptical Socrates is the portrait one often gets from enthusiastic but hasty first readers of the dialogues, usually when they are young and just entering into philosophy: It's the wise-guy Socrates who wants to deflate anyone and everyone, who is so brilliant in the game of elenchus that he *can* beat anyone out of their opinions. But Socrates does not beat just anyone and everyone out of any and every opinion—and not because he is at a loss for arguments. The young Glaucon and Adeimantus *say* they want to believe in justice, yet confess that they are almost won over by Thrasymachus; they would like to have their wavering faith in justice restored by Socrates (358c–d). Does he give that faith its final push? He does quite the opposite. Why?

Because he is a *zetetic* skeptic. The term derives from the Greek *zetein,* meaning to search, to seek.[10] Philosophy for Socrates is a searching, a seeking, a yearning—an *eros*—for wisdom. Every hunt, as Socrates famously suggests (at *Meno*, 80d–e), must begin with the scent of the quarry; we must have some intimation of what we are seeking, or else the search quickly becomes meaningless and philosophy gives way to nihilistic destruction of any and all belief.[11] Surely this is why he says that failing to defend justice would be impious. Socrates is not lying about the kind of wisdom he possesses, but he *is* dissembling. This is because an *intimation* of the good—or of any anything decisive to the way we should live—is by its nature elusive and hard to communicate. Socrates is willing to attest to his pious *conviction* that justice, virtue, wisdom, and the like all exist. What he hesitates to do is to state his opinion—or even that he has an opinion—as to what these *are*, because to describe and defend an intimation concerning the most decisive guides in life is to risk dispersing it altogether and thereby losing those listeners whose own convictions are at their most delicate: the young. He says this explicitly: "[T]o present arguments [*logous poiesthai*] at a time when one is in doubt and seeking [*apsistounta de kai zetounta*]—which is just what I am doing—is a thing both frightening and slippery. . . . I'm afraid that in slipping from the truth where one least ought to slip, I'll not only fall myself but also drag my friends down with me" (450d–451a). Socrates is no absolute seer; *logos* does not lead invariably to insight, and he fears that conversation now may unhinge vital ethical beliefs.

Nevertheless, Socrates understands that there are times when one must run this risk; one cannot leave the young in the hands of a teacher like Thrasymachus. This is why zetetic philosophy is not mysticism; while it adheres to a certain kind of faith in the meaningfulness of phenomena, it remains open to questioning and to reappraising all articulated intuitions about that meaning and the theoretical elaborations of these intimations. Socrates does, in the end, offer *arguments—logous*. Philosophy must remain open to rational debate precisely because the souls of the young are at stake. Mystical claims to gnostic insight will not win over a Glaucon or an Adeimantus; Socrates is prepared *rationally* to defend and criticize his own intimations, as need be, which distinguishes his reliance on them from rank intuitionism.[12]

Now, this portrait of a zetetic Socrates is admittedly at utter odds with the portrait that Socrates himself draws of the philosopher-kings—and queens!—of Kallipolis, the ideal city, built in speech.[13] Socrates and his interlocutors give these people the right and the duty to rule because they are *knowers*: "Since philosophers are those who are able to grasp [*echontos dunamenoi ephaptesthai*] what is always the same in all respects, while those who are not able to do so but wander among what is manifold and multiple in all ways are not philosophers, which should be the leaders of a city?" (484b). We know the answer: The philosophers should rule! These are *echonic* philosophers (from the Greek *echein*, to have, to hold). They *possess* the truth; they *grasp* what is "always the same" and, presumably, can wield it. Theirs are not mere intimations. They "come to the end" of their study (504c–d). They *know* the forms of justice and virtue; they have *seen* the good in its full glory and can understand and apply it without mediating metaphors such as Socrates' sun or divided line. To know such things is to understand fully what is best for human beings, just as to know how the body works is to understand when an operation should be performed. Just as we want doctors who are knowers to tend the body, we need philosophers who are knowers to tend the city. They *have* what it takes.[14] This version of the philosopher approximates the humanistic model that Heidegger takes to task.

The remarkable thing is that Socrates does *not* present *himself* as an echonic philosopher, which is to say that *Plato* does not represent him as the type of philosopher that the internal argument of the *Republic* establishes as paradigmatic. This is no small irony: In the most famous philosophical work that makes the most famously exalted claims about philosophers, the famous philosopher making such claims does not pretend to be such a philosopher himself!

What are we to make of this? Is it just Plato's little joke? But if *Socrates* is not a philosopher, who can hope to be? Is Socrates *in fact* an echonic philosopher whose dissembling irony is so profound that we cannot see that he has just stepped into the cave after a long sojourn in the light of the Good that is even beyond being (509b: *epekeina tes ousias*)? No. Plato is not playing the buffoon, and although Socrates knows more than we may think (if there is a zetetic way of knowing), he is not a philosopher-king.

This distinction at work in the *Republic* between zetetic and echonic philosophy affects the whole metaphysical-ontological-political-ethical-pedagogical teaching of Books 6 and 7, comprising the sun as an image of the good, the divided line as an image for the articulation of Being, and the parable of the cave: it takes on a different meaning depending on which account of the nature of philosophy you think is the right one. Heidegger and his descendants have accepted the traditional view that Socrates and Plato cleave to the echonic model of philosophy: Platonism is a *theory*, or more to the point, a *doctrine*, and a decisive one for the West, of how philosophy may come into possession of the truth. After all, "everyone" from St. Augustine to Nietzsche says this is what Plato is about, so it must be so.[15] The divided line shows how reality, or Being, is divided into separate realms, one worldly and corrupt, one supersensible and pure. The cave parable then describes how one may ascend the divided line by correct representations of reality; this then is Plato's conception of the truth. Finally, the philosopher's vision of the good, the sun that sheds light on all reality and serves as the foundation of Being, renders all knowledge cohesive and secure. According to Heidegger, the good in Plato is the idea of the *enabling* (PDT, 174–75/133–34); it is what makes possible the essence of everything in terms of each thing's specific *idea,* and thereby enables "all forms of prudential insight that inform practical activity" (PDT, 176/135). Through the idea of the good, "*Aletheia* comes under the yoke of the *idea*" (PDT, 176/136). To *know* the good, to possess the ideas, is to understand how to make *use* of everything that is. Heidegger locates in Plato the onset of nihilism: the will to subject Being to a representable system of truth that can be placed at the service of the subjugation of nature, a project which forgets that truth is an unconcealment not subject to the will. The conception of philosophy as possession is not far removed from the Cartesian vision of mastery over nature; it lacks only the Cartesian notion of a method to yield the data and the technology needed to bring the world to heel.

But the story of the cave reads differently depending on whether one accepts the echonic or the zetetic model of philosophy. The immediate context of the dialogue itself, of course, would lead one to apply the echonic model. After all, the parable arises in a discussion of how to educate those worthy of rule, the philosopher kings and queens. Whatever we may say about their process of education, its result is a vision of the final and absolute source of all being, all reality; and more than this, it lends an understanding of how reality is articulated, and in such a way that the seeker now becomes a possessor of an inerrant truth. He or she can see the reality present in all phenomena, even in the shadows of the cave. This ability to grasp the real in all its articulations is what both enables and entitles the echonic philosopher to rule.

How would the zetetic model map onto the parable? The beginning of the story might be the same: The person enchained by the dominant opinions of his or her circumstances may, under the influence of some accidental experience or the deliberate questioning of the right kind of teacher, break the bonds of the given. This person might then ascend a difficult path of education—but toward what? Perhaps toward the light at the end of the tunnel, but if being zetetic means seeking, this can last only as long as the tunnel. To emerge into the light means to reach the absolute truth, to have and to hold it, and to return with it into the cave as the power and the authority to rule.

It seems that someone like Socrates is condemned always to ascend the tunnel, never to emerge into the light. And yet he clearly *does* see light at the end of the tunnel in two senses. First, he has his intimations of the truth. While these are not yet the full possession of the truth, they are hopeful glimmerings that lead him onward and give the search meaning. Furthermore, he can *imagine* what the echonic experience of emerging into the full light of the sun *might* be like. In fact, this is precisely what Socrates is doing in recounting the parable of the cave, for he himself does not claim to have made it out.

To merge Heideggerian and Platonic idioms: The world is the realm of the cave—its beliefs, its customs, its social and political arrangements. To stand up, to throw off the chains, is to deconstruct: to take notice of the unnoticed structures that bind our thinking and to break their hold. Many postmodernists remain fixated at this level: They become intoxicated with the initial thrill of liberation from the bonds of traditional structures, convinced that any new imposition of structure is simply a new style of ideological enchainment. Yet they secretly long for the would-be tyrant to make his attempt at subjugation because they are addicted to fighting all positing of structure, without realizing that there can be no intelligibility without some structure. To the postmodern anarchist, this is freedom—a purely negative dialectic, and it ever *requires* that unjust authorities arise so that freedom can manifest itself again through the deconstruction of their doctrines and regimes. Liberation becomes a perpetual adolescence.

Heidegger was not the anarchist that some of his postmodernist readers have become. He did believe, at least in his middle period, that great creators could serve as a conduit for a new dispensation of Being, a new arrangement of the intelligible world, after the past had been deconstructed. Construction might follow deconstruction, but because Heidegger did not believe in the notion of a final vision of Being, there could be no standard for what new construction would be best. I suspect that this faith in unhinged creativity is one reason for Heidegger's complete lack of practical wisdom in siding with the National Socialists.[16]

The Socratic or zetetic model of philosophy, by contrast, does allow for guidance to action. The *intimation* of a transcendent truth gives us something to go on, but it demands precisely the modesty that would counter the hubris that Heidegger at his best detects in the modern project. For it is not yet possession of the absolute; it is not yet a *doctrine,* if by doctrine we mean a *theory* that an author is determined to defend in the form of an orthodox *system.* Indeed, Plato nowhere presents a theory of forms or ideas, only various hypotheses offered by Socrates that serve as tentative responses to an array of inescapable problems.[17] To coin a term, in zetetic philosophy, deconstruction is followed by *preconstruction,* the provisional construction of the outlines of an integrated account of something in the light of a truth only partially glimpsed. Such preconstruction must leave itself open to revision or even to complete rejection, but in the realm of praxis, it can provide principled standards of action that are precisely *not* doctrinaire.

Zetetic philosophy is bold enough to depart from the given but modest enough to return to it without laying claim to the final story. That is why it can also be *reconstructive* as well as preconstructive. It does not remain fixated on casting off the chains of the given past; it understands that attempts at an integrated understanding of the world, whether philosophical or traditional, must fail to attain the absolute. Therefore, even in preconstructing a better arrangement in the light of the best account we can give so far, we must always make what use we can of the intimations of that truth that are latent in the tradition to which we belong. This is reconstruction; it is also clearly what Socrates is attending to in the new departure he describes in the *Phaedo:* namely, to listen to what people say about what matters (*Phaedo,* 99d–100a). Surely this is what is going on in Socrates' enthusiasm for Cephalus's belief that justice exists, even as Socrates demolishes Cephalus's specific account of justice. And surely reconstruction is at work in Socrates' pious defense of the young against Thrasymachus's incitement to tyranny. So we have three moments to the zetetic journey: the liberation from the bonds (deconstruction), the ascent upward (preconstruction), and the return to the cave (reconstruction). All three moments are necessary for the full expression of human freedom.

But then why does *Plato* give us this double model of Socrates as a zetetic philosopher and of the echonic philosopher as the ideal Socrates proposes? Precisely because of the need for preconstruction. Another word for it would be *hypothesis* (cf. 533b–d). Without setting up (*-thesis*) something beneath (*hypo-*) the unsatisfactory given as its support, however temporary a scaffold this may be, the search will lapse into despondency, hopelessness, and nihilism. If the given is unsatisfactory, and we seek to make it better, then some intimation of the good is needed as an indication that our striving is not meaningless. But this intimation need not be, indeed should not be, final and absolute. This, again, is what distinguishes zeteticism from intuitionism or doctrinaire absolutism. Plato deliberately establishes a tension between the echonic and zetetic models of philosophy because philosophy, especially for the young, might never get started without the echonic promise, but it will also be stillborn as philosophy if it believes that it has already arrived at its destination. Plato presents this tension and does not resolve it for us, because mature philosophizing requires that we resolve it for ourselves—in a resolution that is precisely *not* completed but always under way.[18]

So Plato has even Kallipolis, the best city, decompose. Absolute possession of the truth cannot be maintained absolutely, if at all. And in the cosmic parable of the Myth of Er, Socrates leaves the young men with a vision of the whole that is a *mythos,* not a full and thorough rational account, a *logos.* As a myth, it is a substitute for the complete, echonic logos of the truth that he cannot provide. As *mythos* it serves positively the goals of *logos:* as a modest confidence in reason; it reinforces the intimation that the world does make sense, as a whole, and therefore that rational inquiry also makes sense—not by *making sense* of the whole as such, completely and absolutely, but precisely as inquiry guided by the glimmering light at the end of the tunnel.

So, finally, Plato presents the two models of philosophy, the echonic and the zetetic, simultaneously, because the zetetic "journey" (621d) needs, as its fuel, the echonic preconstructions of the truth about the whole. But Plato presents these preconstruction as myths (the Er story) or as unrealized ideals (Kallipolis and the philosopher-rulers)—and what is an unrealized ideal but a myth?—precisely because they are *only* intimations, and as such, they must be deconstructed to serve as the very fuel for which they are intended in spurring on zetetic philosophy's search. Philosophy, then, is a journey of reconstructions that ends only with death, as Plato and Socrates tell us in so many ways. Far from setting up the goal of an absolute knowledge to which we may aspire as the tool of our domination over the whole, Plato's reconstructive vision of philosophy establishes a reason for being modest even as we dare to recollect the pieces of the whole. Platonic freedom is to be found neither in anarchistic deconstruction nor in the systematic imposition of a final theory, but rather in the outrageously everyday dance between myth and reason.

Conclusion: Back to the Cave

This brief sketch has attempted only the beginning of a defense against a Heideggerian reading of Plato. Certainly a fuller treatment is needed, but perhaps we can anticipate some objections.

One would be that this analysis is too narrow: "Plato's Doctrine of Truth," one might say, is not Heidegger's best effort—indeed, other treatments are far more subtle. For example, in *The Essence of Truth,* in a specific discussion of the escape and subsequent *return* to the cave, Heidegger writes that "Truth . . . is not something that one abidingly possesses, and whose enjoyment we put aside at some point in order to instruct or lecture other people, but unhiddenness *occurs* only in the *history* of permanent freeing" (ET, 66/91). Here, Heidegger's analysis seems compatible with the zetetic interpretation. Several things about this: one is that Heidegger's writings are equivocal as to whether nihilism begins with Plato or with Platonism. Another is that, even assuming the latter, Heidegger fails adequately to rescue Plato, in the kind of sustained recuperation he bestows upon a Heraclitus, from the nihilism he ascribes to Platonism. Finally, to make sense of what we don't *possess,* much depends here on what Heidegger means by the historicality of the liberator's return to the cave and the "unhiddenness" achieved there.

In the passage noted above, Heidegger goes on to describe the escaped prisoner who returns to the cave as confronting a *history* that "is always a matter of the unique task posed by fate [*Schicksal*] in a determinate practical situation, not of free-floating discussion. The liberated one will go into the cave and give his view on what, down there, is taken as beings and the unhidden" (ET, 66/91). We know from *Being and Time* that fate as *Schicksal* is no crude, mystical predetermination of events but rather the ontological given that one's own possibilities of meaning are bound up in the structures of meaning carried forward by one's community in its history. Here, we can agree with Heidegger: We cannot fail to address our most pressing concerns in terms that make sense to the finite world in which we find ourselves. But Heidegger goes on to argue that the truth to be won here, in going back to the cave, is the truth of *aletheia* as the alpha-privative, as *Auseinander-setzung,* that is, as confrontation, as a setting-apart. This is Heidegger's ontology of the *polemos,* which I have detailed in *Heidegger's Polemos,* and according to which here, unhiddenness is torn from concealment by a "*primordial* struggle (not mere polemics) . . . the kind of struggle which first *creates* its enemy and assists its enemy to the *most incisive antagonism*" (ET, 67/92; translation modified). Because for Heidegger this *polemos* at the heart of truth is always historical and only historical, "we come to suspect that Plato does not yet grasp it, or no longer grasps it, in a *primordial* manner"; and: "in Plato the fundamental experience from which the word *a-letheia* arose is already disappearing" (ET, 67–68/93). For Heidegger, then, Plato's truth as genuine transcendence is a falling away from the conflictual heart of truth as unconcealment. We cannot *possess* the latter truth because we do not own or master history or fate. And yet, without the touchstone of truth in Plato's sense, as an ideal to strive for, can there really be an escape, a return, and a redemption (however partial) for the prisoner or the cave? Heidegger's polemical truth binds us just as fast to the cave wall as the shadows, for historicality has no exit, but Plato's zetetic truth has a trajectory and destination, even as it strives and struggles with the given.

Another objection (one connected to the first) is that the zetetic model of philosophy, while not absolutist in its own particular claims, still makes the absolute, or the transcendent, its ideal, even if that ideal is merely approximated and never attained. As such, it is really only a debased version of the same old otherworldly Platonism that Nietzsche derided and that Heidegger deconstructed. There is some truth to this charge, but much of the weight of the charge itself depends on how much of a threat one takes transcendent ideals to be. But without any *intimation* of such ideals, ethical and political standards become indefensible as matters of rational discourse, together with all criteria for action, and surely this is also a serious threat. Heidegger and the postmodernists may be right to emphasize our finitude and our temporality, but the result of their deconstruction of the Western tradition is a lapse into an extreme relativism and historicism from which no appeal to transcendent principles is possible without hypocrisy. Although I cannot defend the point in detail here, I would submit that zetetic philosophy begins with and returns to our finitude, just as the prisoner begins in and returns to the cave, and thereby allows finitude and transcendence to enter into a dialectic. Plato's lesson is that this dialectic can never be resolved, and that any attempt to resolve it will result in philosophical and political disaster. Plato's bold modesty is what saves him from the worst excesses of modernism: We may seek the transcendent, but we ought not to assume that we can occupy a position of absolute knowledge because we cannot finally and completely transcend our finitude.

This leads to a third objection:[19] The passage upwards from the fire in the cave to the sun outside it, Plato says, is a "rough, steep, upward way" (516e); would not many give it up in despair, if it never reaches an end? If we postulate a transcendent truth, but never reach it, won't those who follow this path finally become disillusioned and turn to either nihilism or dogmatism for comfort? This is indeed a danger, but it is one that freedom must risk.[20] Surely it is the existential epistemology that any democracy must embrace, at some level, or else the deliberative electoral process must be seen as a sham, to be replaced by a leadership that either claims total knowledge or prohibits the search for wisdom altogether in favor of dogmatic traditionalism. And recall that zetetic philosophy is not nihilistic skepticism, debunking just any claim to wisdom. Robust liberal education and strong civic institutions must be the preparers and preservers of a prudent freedom. There is no formula for this.

Everything hinges, then, on the *intimations* of transcendence, for these are what provide hope on the upward path; education and institutions nurture and sustain these. An intimation, I would hazard, arises when, through rational reflection or discussion, we recognize the limitation of an accepted opinion, grasp a new, potential truth, and return to our old opinion to find it and all its filiations more fully illuminated in their historical context; an intimation, then, gathers to it all three moments of the zetetic journey. I would submit that nearly anyone who has thought critically about a matter of practical importance has had such an experience. Granted, I have not yet defended this adequately here, but Heidegger himself argues that intelligibility is not possible without some fore-structures of meaning that we posit, or, more properly, within which we find ourselves always already *positioned*. These intimations of meaning allow us to make a fuller sense of our circumstances whenever we engage in an act of interpretation—which is always, since we *are* hermeneutical beings; it is our calling to enter into a polemical encounter with the structures of meaning within which we find ourselves.

To be sure, for Heidegger, the fore-structure is always the finite product of specific historical Dasein, not an intimation of the transcendent, but I would argue with Plato that without intimations in his sense, the experience that nearly all of us have, of engaging in philosophy, of entering into a discussion of a topic across the boundaries of culture and history, would be impossible. Our intimations of justice or virtue or wisdom may all begin within the finite bounds of our own historical locations, but they point to a realm that transcends them without utterly obliterating our finite habitations.[21] We are contingently, not absolutely, free, but this contingency intimates the absolute. Hence the necessity of reconstruction after the liberation of deconstruction: Because total transcendence is beyond us, we should not despise, forget, or annihilate the cave within which all meaningful inquiry begins and to which it must go back, if we follow the allegory—and we must, for human existence begins and ends enclosed by finitude, although it is punctuated by transcendence. To accept the burden of philosophy as zetetic and polemical (in the full rather than narrow sense) is to recognize it as a lifelong, ongoing task, one that when properly understood, far from causing us despair, opens us up to the richness of the human condition—suspended, as it is, between finitude and transcendence.

Notes

Acknowledgment: I am grateful to the remarks of participants at the Heidegger Conference in Norfolk, Va., where an earlier version of this paper was delivered in 2003. I also wish to express thanks to several friends and colleagues who generously read and commented upon this paper: Steven Crowell, Marina McCoy, Richard Polt, David Roochnik, and Bob Scharff. Its faults, however, are all mine.

1. I consider reasonably uncontroversial the assertion that many postmodernists share some version of Heidegger's interpretation of Plato. A few examples of the best and most influential postmodernist readers of Heidegger must suffice. Consider this *celebration* of the "an-archic" deconstruction of standards and ideals by Heidegger in Reiner Schürmann, *Heidegger on Being and Acting: From Principles to Anarchy,* trans. Christine-Marie Gros (Bloomington: Indiana University Press, 1987), 6–7: "Anarchy expresses a destiny of decline, the decay of the standards to which Westerners since Plato have related their acts and deeds in order to anchor them there and to withdraw them from change and doubt. It is *the rational production of that anchorage*—the most serious task traditionally assigned to philosophers—that becomes impossible with Heidegger" (see also 17, 40, 44, 86, 174, 180, 215, 287–88, 295). Or consider John Caputo's heroic, but I think flawed, attempts to disentangle (and so salvage) Heidegger's (and Nietzsche's) critiques of Plato's disdain for finitude and flux from what Caputo ultimately takes to be Heidegger's (and Nietzsche's) unwitting reiterations of Plato's essentialism and elitism; see John D. Caputo, *Against Ethics* (Bloomington: Indiana University Press, 1993), 2, 12, 90, and *Demythologizing Heidegger* (Bloomington: Indiana University Press, 1993), 164 and generally throughout. Derrida constitutes a particularly difficult case, since he endeavors to show that multiple readings of Plato are possible; yet he does this to overturn the traditional Plato as totalizing idealist and thereby honors Heidegger by trying to go on beyond him in the critique of metaphysics; see Jacques Derrida, *Dissemination,* trans. Barbara Johnson (Chicago: University of Chicago Press, 1981), 98–99. Lacoue-Labarthe also tries to out-Heidegger Heidegger by suggesting that in siding with the Nazi aestheticization of politics, Heidegger had simply replicated Plato's "fiction" of politics as a work of art imitative of the *ideas;* see Philippe Lacoue-

Labarthe, *Heidegger, Art and Politics,* trans. Chris Turner (Oxford: Blackwell, 1990), ch. 7. For a treatment of this topic, see Catherine Zuckert, *Postmodern Platos* (Chicago: University of Chicago Press, 1996), especially ch. 8 for a discussion of Plato and Derrida; see also Gregory Fried, *Heidegger's Polemos: From Being to Politics* (New Haven: Yale University Press, 2000), ch. 5.

2. Martin Heidegger, "Plato's Doctrine of Truth," trans. Thomas Sheehan, in *Pathmarks,* ed. William McNeil (Cambridge University Press, 1999), 155/109; also 176/135–36. This essay (henceforth cited as PDT, with English followed by German pagination) is probably the best known of Heidegger's treatments of Plato and especially the cave analogy in the *Republic.* There are, however, other important readings of this text and Platonism in general by Heidegger. These deserve a fuller analysis, prevented here for reasons of space. See Martin Heidegger, *The Basic Problems of Philosophy,* trans. Albert Hofstadter (Bloomington: Indiana University Press, 1982), 283–86/400–405; *Phenomenological Interpretation of Kant's Critique of Pure Reason,* trans. Pavis Emad and Terrence Maly (Bloomington: Indiana University Press, 1997), 269–70/398; *Nietzsche,* vol. 1: *The Will to Power as Art,* trans. David Farrell Krell (San Francisco: Harper and Row, 1979), chs. 20–25; and *The Essence of Truth: On Plato's Cave Allegory and Theaetetus,* trans. Ted Sadler (London: Continuum, 2002), Part 1; cited henceforth as ET. There is also the thinly veiled reference to the three classes of Kallipolis in Heidegger's discussion of knowledge, military, and labor service in his Rectoral Address; see "The Self-Assertion of the German University," in *The Heidegger Controversy: A Critical Reader,* ed. Richard Wolin (New York: Columbia University Press, 1991), 35–36.

3. This point is complicated by the fact that in 1969 Heidegger seems to retract his claim that this transition takes place *in* and *because of* Plato. I cannot address this in detail here, but the key issue is not whether Plato is the *source* of the transition, but rather whether Plato can be taken as the decisive *expression* of it, and in a manner that determined the subsequent history of Western thought. See Martin Heidegger, *On Time and Being,* trans. Joan Stambaugh (New York: Harper and Row, 1972), 70/78.

4. I do not wish to conflate Heidegger's and Nietzsche's readings of Plato. Nietzsche's emphasis lies in the suprasensory aspect of the "theory" of ideas and the nihilism implied by this; Heidegger's emphasis lies in the contention that the meaning of truth itself takes on an epochal shift in Plato. Nevertheless, Heidegger accepts (with his own qualifications, of course) Nietzsche's contention that nihilism has a decisive onset in Plato, and that Plato's otherworldliness and moralism get subsumed by Christian theology and ethics (and many of his postmodern readers follow Heidegger in this). Heidegger's treatment of Nietzsche as the last metaphysician in an ontotheological tradition beginning with Plato is well known, so let this one passage suffice: "[Nietzsche's] pronouncement 'God is dead' means: The suprasensory world is without effective power. It bestows no life. Metaphysics, i.e., for Nietzsche Western philosophy understood as Platonism, is at an end. . . . [N]othing more remains to which man can cling and by which he can orient himself." Martin Heidegger, "The Word of Nietzsche: 'God is Dead,'" in *The Question Concerning Technology and Other Essays,* trans. William Lovitt (New York: Harper Torchbooks, 1977), 61/212–13. Heidegger fundamentally agrees with Nietzsche's diagnosis that modernity is in crisis thanks in part to Plato, but he disagrees about the precise nature of the illness and its cure. For perhaps the most famous brief exposition of Nietzsche's view of Plato's place in the history of philoso-

phy, see "How the 'True World' Finally Became a Fiction," in Friedrich Nietzsche, *Twilight of the Idols*, trans. Richard Polt (Indianapolis: Hackett, 1997), 23–24. Another crucial text for Heidegger's reading of Nietzsche on Plato is in *Nietzsche: The Will to Power as Art*, chs. 20–24.

5. See, for example, *Nietzsche: The Will to Power as Art*, 151: "We say 'Platonism' and not Plato, because here we are dealing with the conception of knowledge that corresponds to that term, not by way of an original and detailed examination of Plato's works, but only by setting in rough relief one particular aspect of his work." Also, 204: "Plato's work is not yet Platonism. The 'true world' is not yet the object of a doctrine."

6. Some of the best critiques of Heidegger on Plato, to which I am very much indebted here, are by Francisco J. Gonzalez: "Dialectic as 'Philosophical Embarrassment': Heidegger's Critique of Plato's Method," *Journal of the History of Philosophy* 40, no. 3 (2002): 361–89, and "Confronting Heidegger on Logos and Being in Plato's *Sophist*," in *Platon und Aristoteles—sub ratione veritatis: Festschrift für Wolfgang Wieland zum 70. Geburtstag*, ed. Gregor Damschen, Rainer Enskat, and Alejandro G. Vigo (Göttingen: Vandenhoeck and Ruprecht, 2003).

7. For the outline of Heidegger's thought in this section, see Fried, *Heidegger's Polemos*, especially chs. 2–5, where I substantiate these themes textually in Heidegger and in postmodernists indebted to him; space prevents me from doing so here.

8. René Descartes, *Discourse on Method*, 4th ed., trans. Donald Cress (Indianapolis: Hackett, 1999), 35 (Adam and Tannery, 62).

9. *Apology*, 23b. All translations from the *Republic* are from Plato, *The Republic of Plato*, trans. Allan Bloom, 2nd ed. (New York: Basic Books, 1991); for the *Apology*, I rely on *Four Texts on Socrates*, trans. T. G. West and G. S. West, rev. ed. (Ithaca: Cornell University Press, 1998).

10. The Pyrrhonist skeptics were the first to describe themselves explicitly as "zetetic," but Socrates was not a skeptic in their sense, and so my use of this term should not be construed as an attempt to conflate his thought with theirs. Socrates expresses to Meno his wish *skepsasthai kai suzetesai* (to examine and to seek together) what virtue is (80d). See the rest of this passage for further uses of *zetein*. For zetetic Pyrrhonism, see Sextus Empiricus, *Outlines of Pyrrhonism*, vol. 1, trans. R. G. Bury (Cambridge: Harvard University Press, 1933), 2–3, 156–88, 162–63 (I.1.2, I.2.11, I.2.19). At issue between Pyrrhonist and Socratic zeteticism is whether the search alone has merit or if it requires, in order to avoid nihilism, what I call below a preconstruction of the aim of the search. Zeteticism calls for the latter; Pyrrhonism abstains from such suppositions.

In his debate with Kojève about whether philosophy must always be sectarian because of its putative "subjective certainty," Leo Strauss has also characterized Socrates as a zetetic. Strauss sees an alternative if we recall that "philosophy in the original meaning of the term is nothing but knowledge of one's ignorance," that "philosophy is not wisdom but quest for wisdom" and "as such is neither dogmatic nor skeptic, and still less 'decisionist,' but zetetic (or skeptic in the original sense of the term)." See Leo Strauss, *On Tyranny*, rev. ed. (Ithaca: Cornell University Press, 1968), 208–10. Strauss recognizes that zetetic skepticism differs from nihilistic skepticism, because its very search presumes a meaning, or a goal, or what I am calling a preconstruction; nihilistic skepticism attacks both dogmatism and the very meaningfulness of the search for truth. Once again: What is at issue then is the status of the preconstruction, and Strauss is oddly silent on this topic. Perhaps, for him, the politically relevant point is that meaningfulness of the search *be posited*, not that it be detailed in any way, let alone defended as such. One must ask if this is sufficient to hold off nihilism.

11. Of course, the famous term that Socrates employs in this context is *anamnesis* (see *Meno*, 81c–82a), usually translated as *recollection*. I cannot fully defend my use of *intimation* here, but I will say this: Socrates explicitly presents the notion of *anamnesis* as a matter of religious piety, a kind of myth, that he must "trust" as true in his zetetic pursuit of truth (81e: *hoi ego pisteuon alethei einai ethelo meta sou zetein arete hoti estin*); he does not claim to know it, and certainly not as a *doctrine*. Rather, it is a *heuristic* device, a hypothesis, that he offers to make sense of a phenomenological datum: that we must have *some* pre-theoretical understanding of what it is we are seeking in any inquiry, or else the search could not even begin. That we already have some access to what we do not yet know is a genuinely and profoundly puzzling matter, but without his version of philosophical piety, Socrates warns, we would fall prey to a sophist's trick, and "it would make us idle, and fainthearted men like to hear it, whereas my argument makes them energetic and keen on the search [*ergatikous te kai zetetikous*]" (81d–e). This is the zetetic philosopher's manifesto against nihilism, and my point is that the *prior* phenomenological given is that we indeed *do* have such pre-reflective understandings of what we seek. It is the status and the meaning of these *intimations* that is philosophically problematic, and it is only as a heuristic and stopgap solution that Socrates offers up *anamnesis* as a resolution in order to proceed in his conversation with Meno. So I would say that the problem of *intimation* is phenomenologically prior to the Socratic *hypothesis* (not theory!) of recollection, and Socrates himself understands this. To put it another way, *intimation* describes the phenomenon as a problem, and *recollection* offers a provisional explanation of how intimation is possible so that all other philosophical inquiry does not become pointless. Otherwise, Meno would lose faith in learning about virtue and become "idle." In this sense, the "doctrine" of recollection is a pedagogical and ethical second-best, made necessary by an ethical urgency in the absence of absolute knowledge. I rely here on Grube's translation of the *Meno* in Plato, *Complete Works*, ed. John M. Cooper (Indianapolis: Hackett, 1997). Cf. Jacob Klein, *A Commentary on Plato's Meno* (Chicago: University of Chicago, 1965), 94–99 and ch. 5.

12. Compare the discussion of "reflective equilibrium" in John Rawls, *A Theory of Justice* (Cambridge: Harvard University Press, 1971), 20–22, 48–51.

13. Here I follow David Roochnik in employing the name that Socrates himself gives to the city constructed in speech: Kallipolis, "the beautiful city" (572c2). See David Roochnik, *Beautiful City: The Dialectical Character of Plato's Republic* (Ithaca: Cornell University Press, 2003), 8.

14. Indeed, they seem to have much of what Descartes is seeking, minus the technological mastery—which is, I think, the meaning of Plato's very serious joke about the failed technocratics of the infamous nuptial number, a formula designed to produce ideal matings among the citizens of Kallipolis (546a–547a). If the rulers' wisdom could hold, then such a dominion over nature would be possible; but it cannot hold, since the absolute echonic vision is impossible for us, and such attempts at mastery must end monstrously.

15. Perhaps the most conventional and paradigmatic modern exposition of Plato

as echonic philosopher adhering to a *doctrine* of the forms can be found in Russell's essay "Plato's Theory of Ideas." See Bertrand Russell, *A History of Philosophy* (New York: Simon and Schuster, 1945), ch. 15. It never even crosses Russell's mind that Plato may not identify totally with Socrates, much less that Socrates himself is at all tentative about his *hypothesis* concerning the ideas. For a postmodernist version of the echonic Plato, see Schürmann, *Heidegger on Being and Acting*, 215, where he asks, "Quite as happiness for Plato is the *possession* of the subsisting Good, [so does not nihilism] consist in the full *possession* of presencing, in a total presence that stills all desire and all absence?"

16. See Fried, *Heidegger's Polemos*, 251–55.

17. On this point, I am indebted to the work of Drew Hyland and Stanley Rosen and to conversations with David Roochnik. See Drew Hyland, *Finitude and Transcendence in the Platonic Dialogues* (Albany: SUNY, 1995), especially ch. 7; Stanley Rosen, *Nihilism: A Philosophical Essay* (New Haven: Yale University Press, 1969); and Roochnik, *Beautiful City.*

18. As Francisco Gonzales points out, it is puzzling that Heidegger, who insists that Dasein is *unterwegs,* cannot see this very *unterwegs* at the heart of Plato's dialectic, a dialectic essentially different from the Hegelian. See Gonzales, "Dialectic as 'Philosophical Embarrassment,'" 374. My own sense is that this myopia in Heidegger is because he cannot imagine a thinking that is both *under way* and not also utterly bounded by historical finitude. Apart from rare moments, Heidegger seems unable to read Plato as anything but the writer of treatises. The Platonic *dialogue,* as such, as an instantiation of the *dialectic* between finitude and transcendence, is quite simply invisible to him.

19. I am grateful to Alan Rosenberg for suggesting this line of critique.

20. Here I agree with Stanley Rosen that nihilism is endemic to the human condition; any attempt to eradicate it will only aggravate the problem. Freedom must always include the freedom to deny meaning and standards, and the defense of these against nihilism must remain alive to there being no final solution to the predicament. See Rosen, *Nihilism,* especially ch. 6. Again, this means that we must in every generation do what Socrates does in the *Republic:* defend the rational faith in justice for the young.

21. Consider the example, in the American context, of Frederick Douglass, who deconstructed the racist opinions of his day, but who in doing so also *reconstructed* a politics grounded in the founding principles of the polity. Hence, his intimations of justice animated and made possible his *deconstructions* of injustice, his *preconstructions* of a model of justice freed from the injustices of history, and his *reconstructions* of actual political life as he found it. See, for example, "What to the Slave Is the Fourth of July?" in *The Oxford Frederick Douglass Reader,* ed. William L. Andrews (New York: Oxford University Press, 1996). Much the same point could be made about Martin Luther King Jr.

10 Plato's Other Beginning

John Sallis

Beginning is what is most formidable.

Think of the beginning of a sentence or of an essay or of an entire book. The beginning, the very first word, must anticipate, before anything has been said, all that will be said. With the first word, the whole of what one would say must already be in play, even if one's intention never simply precedes its realization in speech, even if one genuinely knows what one wants to say only when one has succeeded in saying it. Or think of the beginning of an intricate geometrical proof, of how the first equation or construction must anticipate, before it has been traversed, the entire course of the proof. In order to begin, one must somehow know what, on the other hand, one cannot, as one begins, yet know. Or imagine a painter at the moment when he first puts brush to canvas. At that moment when he begins to paint, the entire picture must somehow be in view, even though as such it cannot be in view, not even, as we say, in the mind's eye. Imagine—or, though the prospect is daunting, at least *try* to imagine—a composer as he sets down the very first note or chord, hearing somehow at that moment the entire, still unsounded composition, the composition that even when sounded will necessarily be sounded and heard, not in a moment, but across an expanse of time. Could one ever hope to imagine how Beethoven, almost totally deaf, could have sensed where to begin so as to arrive, with artistic necessity, at the choral setting of *An die Freude*?

And yet—if bordering on the unimaginable—beginnings are made. Sometimes their character as beginnings is emphasized, as when one begins with a discourse about beginning. Or as in the final movement of the Ninth Symphony, which begins by quoting, in order, the themes of the preceding movements, interrupting each, in turn, before then letting the final theme begin to sound very softly in the double basses, as if emerging from silent depths.

Even as a beginning is made—and one hardly knows how—it remains formidable. For one cannot but be keenly aware from the beginning, in the very moment when one begins, that the stakes are very high indeed. If the beginning is faulty or limited, everything will be compromised. Eventually one will be compelled to return to the beginning, to make another beginning that compensates for what was lacking in the first beginning. Or rather, to make another beginning that *attempts insofar as possible* to compensate: for one cannot always simply undo having already begun.

In the Platonic dialogues, too, beginning is nothing less than formidable. As interrogated and as enacted, beginnings are pervasive in the dialogues. For instance, the ascent represented and enacted at the center of the *Republic* is described as an ascent to the beginning of the whole (*ten tou pantos archen*).[1] It is also, at once, an ascent from the cave-like condition in which humans find themselves in the beginning, hence an ascent from one beginning to another, from—as Aristotle will put it—what is first for us to what is first in itself. Furthermore, one could think of the question of the polis, the question that overarches the entire dialogue, as a question of beginning, as a question of how to begin anew with a polis as secure as possible from the corruption to which political life is otherwise exposed. This aspect of the political question reaches its comedic climax when it turns out that the founding of such a city will require the expulsion of all who are more than ten years old. In order to begin anew, it must become a city of children (see *Rep.* 541a).

The *Timaeus* is even more permeated with the enactment and interrogation of beginnings. Indeed an injunction as to how to begin is set forth in the dialogue: "With regard to everything it is most important to begin at the natural beginning" (*Tim.* 29b). And yet—most remarkably—the *Timaeus* itself violates the very injunction it sets forth. Not only does it defer the beginning of Timaeus's speech, inserting prior to it speeches by Socrates and Critias that are quite different in character; but also, even once Timaeus begins to speak, it turns out that he has not begun at the natural beginning and so is eventually compelled by the very drift of the discourse to interrupt his discourse and set out on another, to make another beginning.

Even if this other beginning in the *Timaeus* has a certain distinctiveness, even if its sense is incomparable, it is not as such unique. Indeed the dialogues abound with various kinds of fresh starts and new beginnings. One of the most decisive occurs in the dialogue in which all the discursive and dramatic elements are brought to utmost concentration on the end, on death; precisely here, in the *Phaedo,* as the centralmost discourse of this dialogue, there is an account of Socrates' beginning, of his venturing another beginning. As he prepares to die, Socrates turns to the past, to his own beginning; he tells his friends the story of how he first began with a kind of direct investigation of nature and of how, after such investigations failed, he came to set out on a second sailing by turning from things to *logoi*, making thus another beginning. But among all the polyphonic discourses of the Platonic dialogues, there are none in which this turn to *logoi* has not already been taken. It is always the second sailing that bears Platonic thought along. It is as though Platonic thought makes its first beginning only in launching another beginning, as if, in first beginning, it already sets out on another beginning.

It cannot but appear remarkable, then, that Heidegger writes of the first beginning in terms that, though generalized, more or less identify this beginning with Plato. At the very least it will be necessary to say, in response, that if indeed Plato's thought constitutes a first beginning, it will prove to be a far more complex beginning than the expression *first beginning* might at first suggest. For within this alleged first beginning there are, as the examples just cited show, multiple instances of another beginning.

Yet a great deal more specificity is required in order, first of all, to determine the precise sense in which Heidegger takes Platonic thought to be the first beginning and then, secondly, to hear the resonance evoked in the Platonic texts themselves by this characterization. In listening to this resonance, it will be a matter of determining whether these texts accord with and confirm the characterization of Plato's thought as first beginning or whether within these texts there are retreats that go unsounded and that can effectively recoil on that characterization.

What, then, does Heidegger mean by first beginning? In *Contributions to Philosophy* this expression designates the beginning of philosophy, of what later comes to be called metaphysics. The first beginning occurs in and through the Platonic determination of being as *idea*. This determination establishes the distinction between intelligible *idea* and sensible thing as the fundamental—that is, the founding—distinction of philosophy or metaphysics. This distinction provides then the fundamental framework for all subsequent philosophy or metaphysics. The sequence of determinations of and within this framework constitutes the history of metaphysics, which reaches its end when, in Nietzsche's thought, the distinction between intelligible and sensible is completely inverted and thus its possibilities finally exhausted.

In designating this beginning as the *first* beginning, Heidegger does not intend to suggest that it is a *simple* beginning. It is not a matter of a beginning made for the first time, preceded by nothing else of its kind. Indeed it turns out that what Heidegger takes to occur in Plato's thought is a beginning *in the form* of a transformation, a redetermination, a change. As founding metaphysics, this beginning is *first* only in distinction from the other beginning that would be ventured beyond the end of metaphysics. This other beginning is what *Contributions to Philosophy* would prepare—that is, this text is engaged in crossing over to the other beginning.

How are the two beginnings related? There are expressions in other texts, if not in *Contributions* itself, that suggest a certain mutual externality, such expressions as *Überwindung*—or even *Verwindung*—*der Metaphysik*. The relation would, then, be such that what was begun in the first beginning would have run its course, have come to its end, so that now this first beginning could be left behind—as something overcome, gotten over—as one ventures another beginning. And yet, there is no such externality: in venturing another beginning, one does not simply leave the first beginning behind; one does not simply abandon the metaphysics to which the first beginning gave rise. In *Contributions to Philosophy* Heidegger writes: "The other beginning is the more originary taking-over of the concealed essence of philosophy."[2] Thus, in the other beginning something essential to philosophy that, on the other hand, remained concealed from philosophy is to be taken over in a way that is more originary than was the case in philosophy. It is to be taken over in such a way that it does not remain, as in philosophy, simply concealed.

Thus the other beginning, beginning beyond the end of metaphysics, is at the same time a return to the first beginning, a return that enters into the first beginning so as to grasp it more originarily than in the first beginning, so as to grasp somehow that which, though essential to the first beginning, remained—in the first beginning—concealed. The double character of this move, that it is a move beyond metaphysics that, at once, goes back into the beginning, is perhaps most succinctly expressed in the following passage from *Contributions to Philosophy:*

> The leap into the other beginning is a return into the first beginning, and vice versa. . . . The return into the first beginning is . . . precisely a distancing from it, a taking up of that distance-positioning [*Fernstellung*] that is necessary in order to experience what began in and as that beginning. For *without* this distance-positioning—and only a positioning in the other beginning is a sufficient one—we remain always, in

an entangling way, too close to the beginning, insofar as we are roofed over and covered [*überdacht und zugedeckt*] by what issues from the beginning.[3]

One could say: what is decisive is to move through the first beginning, to move disclosively from the first beginning back to that which, though essential to it, remained, in the first beginning, concealed. What is decisive is the move from the intelligible-sensible framework that governed metaphysics back to what within that framework remained concealed. What is decisive is the move from the Platonic determination of being as *idea* back to that which, precisely through this determination, came to be concealed.

Heidegger insists on the distance required in order to carry out this move. He insists that sufficient distance is provided only by being positioned in the other beginning, that is, only from a stance beyond metaphysics, only from the position that results from twisting free of the Platonic-metaphysical distinction between intelligible and sensible. Only if one gets out from under the roof of metaphysics can one—according to Heidegger—find one's way back from the determination of being as *idea*, back to that which came to be concealed precisely through this determination. Heidegger is insistent: only from the distance of the other beginning can one carry out this regress within—this regress back through—the first beginning.

It is this insistence that I want to put in question. My intent, however, is not to show that such a regress is broached at certain critical junctures in the history of metaphysics, though there are indeed crucial indications of this in, for instance, Plotinus, Schelling, and Nietzsche. Leaving open in the present context the question whether such a regress remains closed to those who remain under the roof of metaphysics, the question I want to raise concerns Plato himself. Can one mark in the Platonic texts themselves a regress from the determination of being as *idea* to that which subsequently in the history of metaphysics remains essentially concealed? Does Plato in founding metaphysics also destabilize it through a regression to that which escapes metaphysics? Does there belong to the first beginning a countermovement toward another beginning, Plato's other beginning?

In order to develop this question, it is necessary to focus on the interpretation of Plato that is at work in Heidegger's determination of Platonic thought as constituting the first beginning. This interpretation is primarily that expressed in *Plato's Doctrine of Truth,* the redaction of which belongs to the very years in which Heidegger composed *Contributions to Philosophy* and the other manuscripts closely linked to it. If one takes *Contributions to Philosophy* as carrying out primarily the leap into another beginning, one can regard *Plato's Doctrine of Truth* as carrying out the complementary return into the first beginning.

Since *Plato's Doctrine of Truth* seems to go furthest in this complementary direction, I shall limit my discussion to it.[4] Although this text is well known—perhaps all too well known—I will need to crystallize the parameters and the determining schema of the interpretation developed in this text. In this way it will be possible to mark with some precision the limit of Heidegger's interpretation of Plato's thought as first beginning and also to draw from Heidegger's texts certain resources for rethinking what Heidegger puts in question, for rethinking this questionable moment beyond the debate with this text. Yet even as we retrace the configuration of Heidegger's text, some features may begin to strike us as strange, if not as outright provocative.

Radicalizing and ironizing an ancient distinction, Heidegger casts his interpretation as one directed to Plato's teaching (*Lehre*) regarding truth, as aiming to say what remains unsaid in the Platonic text. At the very outset—most remarkably—he says this unsaid, exposes in writing the unwritten teaching, thus already in the beginning circling back from the interpretation, still to come, that will uncover the hidden teaching. It is as if the text—this text on beginnings—began by transposing the end, the outcome of the interpretation, to the beginning. Even before the text to be interpreted is cited, Heidegger says what only the interpretation of that text can reveal, says the unsaid, writes the unwritten: "What remains unsaid there [that is, in the text still to be cited, translated, and interpreted] is a change [*eine Wendung*] in the determination of the essence of truth."[5] From this beginning one can read off, in advance, most of the parameters as well as the determining schema of the ensuing interpretation. Two determinations of truth will be exhibited: first, the pre-Platonic determination and, then, the determination that is effected in the Platonic text and that comes to prevail in the history of metaphysics. It is to be shown that in the Platonic text—specifically in the passage with which Book 7 of the *Republic* begins—a change is effected from the earlier determination to what will become the metaphysical determination. It will turn out that what effects this change, what drives the transition from one determination of truth to the other, is the Platonic determination of being as *idea*.

The schema can also be construed from the perspective of *Contributions to Philosophy*. Then, over against the exhibiting of the constitution of the first beginning, there would take shape a double gesture with respect to the older determination of truth: on the one hand, the regression that recovers it by moving through the first beginning; on the other hand, a demonstration of how in Plato's text a repression of this other determination is already operative.

Book 7 of the *Republic* begins with Socrates enjoining Glaucon to "make an image of our nature in its education and lack of education." Heidegger's interpretation of the passage that ensues is discreetly guided by the most telling words in Plato's text. One such word is *paideia*, rendered as *Bildung* or, even less adequately, as education. The image that Socrates makes for Glaucon, that he describes and asks Glaucon to envision, has to do with education. By casting what he says in relation to the image of a cave, Socrates makes an image of our nature in its education and lack of education. Thus the image that Socrates actually makes and Glaucon envisions is not just that of a cave, but rather of the movement through which the soul undergoes education. The expression by which Socrates describes this movement is *periagoge oles tes psyches,* a revolution or turning-around of the entire soul. Heidegger emphasizes this turning-around; and in order to designate that to which this turning-around is oriented, he brings into play another of the telling words used by Socrates in the passage. It is for Heidegger the most telling word: *to alethes,* which Heidegger translates not as *the true (das Wahre)*, but as *the unconcealed (das Unverborgene)*. In this translation, in the shift that it effects, Heidegger's entire interpretation is broached.

The image of our nature that Socrates makes is thus an image of the way of education as a way on which the soul turns around toward the unconcealed. What the image actually lays out, according to Heidegger, are the four stages belonging to this way. Turning away from the captivating images within the cave, the soul comes to see more unconcealedly the things of which it had previously seen only images. Proceeding still further, emerging from the cave into the open space above, the soul comes to behold the very look of things, that is, the *eide* that shine through things and make them look as they do. It comes to behold the *eide* themselves and no longer merely the *eide* shining from afar through things. Here there is genuine liberation as the soul comes before the most unconcealed (*to alethestaton*). And yet, the progression through these three stages, this progression toward the ever more unconcealed, requires still another, a fourth, stage. Only if the image is extended to include finally a return to the cave does it genuinely image our nature in its education *and lack* of education. It is the privation that prescribes the final stage: because lack of education (*apaideusia*), that is, ignorance, is never simply left behind, education requires continual engagement with and overcoming of this condition. For Heidegger this stage, too, is determined by orientation to unconcealment. The unconcealed must, he says, always be wrested from concealment, and so to unconcealment as such there belongs a continual overcoming of concealment. *Paideia* reaches its fulfillment only in a modality of unconcealment in which this essential connection to concealment is appropriated. In returning to the cave, the escaped prisoner enacts such an appropriation.

These brief indications suffice to show how Heidegger's interpretation begins. His first move is to show how the originary Greek determination of truth as unconcealment remains operative in this Socratic discourse on education. Not only are the stages of education determined by orientation to unconcealment, but also in the very image of a cave there is imaged the character of unconcealment: a cave is an open space in which things can appear in a certain light, an open space that is yet enclosed, just as unconcealment—which in other contexts Heidegger calls the open space of a clearing—is, as it were, enclosed by the concealment from which it must be wrested. Thus, Heidegger's first move is to recover the older determination of truth as it is still operative in the Platonic text. Even before laying out the first beginning, Heidegger has already carried out the regression through it to the originary determination of truth as unconcealment.

Heidegger's second move goes against the first. What he proceeds to show is that in the passage on education there is also another determination of truth at work and that this determination, which will become the metaphysical determination, is already dominant. It seems—remarkably—that what most testifies to this dominance is the shape of the story, the way the story is shaped around the various sites and moments that belong to it. In a decisive passage he writes: "The illustrative power [*Veranschaulichung*] of the 'allegory of the cave' does not come from the image of the closedness of the subterranean vault and the imprisonment of people within its confines, nor does it come from the sight of the open space outside the cave. For Plato, rather, the expository power behind the images of the 'allegory' is concentrated on the role played by the fire, the fire's glow and the shadows it casts, the brightness of day, the sunlight and the sun. Everything depends on the shining forth of whatever appears and on making its visibility possible. Certainly unhiddenness is mentioned in its various stages, but it is considered simply in terms of how it makes whatever appears be accessible in its look (*eidos*)" (GA9, 225). Everything seems to depend on the story's being drawn more toward one side than the other, more to the side of appearances and of what makes them possible, the glow of the fire inside the cave and the sunlight that brightens the day outside. To be sure, truth as unconcealment is also portrayed, especially in the image of the enclosed openness of the cave. But in the way the story is told—or at least as Heidegger takes it to be told—this side is dominated by the emphasis accorded to the look (*eidos, idea*) and to the lighting that enables the look to shine forth.

The outcome that Heidegger takes the story to have is well known and requires only the briefest reminder. Heidegger indicates that what has come into force in the Platonic text is a shift, which, displacing *aletheia* as unconcealment, sets the *idea*, as it were, at the center. Thus, unconcealment comes to be assimilated to the *idea*, comes to be regarded as made possible by the *idea*. Coming thus under the yoke of the *idea*, truth comes to be redetermined in reference to the *idea*, as the correctness (*orthotes*) of vision of the *idea*, as agreement (*homoiosis*) with it. And whereas truth as unconcealment counted as a trait of beings themselves, truth as correctness belongs to human comportment toward beings.

This, then, according to Heidegger, is the unsaid of the Platonic texts, Plato's unwritten teaching: the change from the determination of truth as unconcealment of beings to truth as the correctness of human knowledge. This is what, though happening in the text, goes unremarked, remains unsaid.

If one agreed that this is indeed Plato's teaching regarding truth, then there would be little hope of discerning in the first beginning a countermovement that might constitute another beginning. For Heidegger's conclusions do not allow even a genuine ambiguity to remain, much less a countermovement. Rather, there remains only a trace of the originary determination of truth, a trace that, because of the dominance of the *idea*, is already destined to disappear entirely.

This is how things would stand if one agreed that what Heidegger identifies as Plato's teaching is in fact such. And yet, not all have agreed. One who did not agree is Paul Friedländer. His criticism of *Plato's Doctrine of Truth* and his extended exchange with Heidegger is well known and need not be retraced here through its various phases.[6] Suffice it to say that even when Friedländer withdrew one of his principal criticisms and granted that the sense of *aletheia* as unconcealment was in play very early among the Greeks, he still continued to insist on his other principal criticism, his rejection of what he calls Heidegger's "historical construction," namely, the thesis that in Plato there occurred a change from truth as unconcealment to truth as correctness.

Another who, after the debate with Friedländer, no longer agreed with this thesis was Heidegger himself. When I spoke with him about Plato in 1975, I was surprised at the candidness with which he voiced his dissatisfaction with his book *Plato's Doctrine of Truth*. The book was, he said, no longer tenable (*nicht mehr haltbar*). Yet this only reiterated what Heidegger had written in a text composed in 1964. In the text "The End of Philosophy and the Task of Thinking" he writes: "But then the assertion about an essential transformation of truth, that is, from unconcealment to correctness, is also untenable [*nicht haltbar*]."[7]

What are the consequences of this very remarkable retraction? Can the determination of Platonic thought as the first beginning remain intact, that is, somehow be reconstituted? Can the historical framework of *Contributions to Philosophy*, the opposition between the first beginning and another beginning, remain in force, or is it, on the contrary, thoroughly destabilized? More specifically, how is the relation between the two determinations of truth to be reconfigured in the Platonic text once Heidegger's thesis of a change from one to the other has been set aside? Can it be simply a matter of now granting that the Platonic text is ambiguous or two-sided, that both senses of truth are operative there? Even then, it would still be imperative to determine just how these two senses belong together in the Platonic text.

How might one today venture such a reconfiguration—beyond the debate over Heidegger's interpretation and even in a certain countermovement to that interpretation? One possibility can be opened perhaps by something that can be gleaned from Heidegger's specific statement regarding the alleged outcome of the change in the determination of truth. In this statement Heidegger says that after the change "The *idea* is not a presenting foreground [*ein darstellender Vordergrund*] of *aletheia* but rather the ground that makes it possible" (GA9, 234). The formulation suggests—or in any case can be taken to suggest—that *prior* to the change the *idea is* a presenting foreground of *aletheia*. But then if there is no change, if the alleged change did not occur, one might well suppose, without limitation or qualification, that the *idea* simply—or not so simply—is a presenting foreground of *aletheia*.

The *idea* would be the look by which things come to be present, the look that, shining through them, presents them as the things they are, that is, *in their unconcealment.* Yet as such the *idea* would be only foreground, would be set against the background of concealment from which the look of things would have to be wrested and to which these looks, the things themselves, would always remain attached. Thus the *idea* would be nothing other than the moment of unconcealment belonging to *aletheia.* But then, there would be no more demanding imperative than that the *idea* always be thought *in relation to concealment,* that it always be thought as bound back to concealment.

Thus one would say: the look of things stands out from and remains bound to concealment, that is, is limited by concealment. Yet the difference thus installed in the first beginning is so enormous—not to say monstrous— that its consequences are virtually unlimited. Still, it can be expressed by the slightest modification: in place of saying, "Being is determined as *idea,*" one would now say "Being as determined is *idea*"—or perhaps a bit more clearly: "Being as determinate, but not Being as such, is *idea.*"

The reconfiguration of the two determinations of truth can now be very simply sketched. Truth as *aletheia* would make possible truth as correctness by setting forth a look, a presenting foreground, to which apprehension could correspond and so be correct. Yet the look would be bound to concealment, and consequently the apprehension would be bound always to take account of the bond to concealment. Taking account of concealment could not, however, consist in apprehending it as though it were just another look. Taking account of the bond to concealment would rather consist in setting all apprehension of looks *within its limits.* In Socratic terms, it would consist in installing all learning within the horizon of a certain awareness of ignorance. But then, the very sense of truth as correctness would—as often in the dialogues—be exposed to slippage, would begin to mutate into something that would look other than the concept of truth that can, all too easily, be traced in the history of metaphysics. And yet, this mutant truth is perhaps not entirely missing from this history, if it is thought otherwise than simply as the history of metaphysics.

But what about the beginning? Or the beginnings?

If the moment of unconcealment is thought as *idea* and if it is this determination that constitutes the first beginning and founds the history of metaphysics, then in thinking the bond of the *idea* to concealment Plato would have installed an irreducible countermovement toward *another beginning.* This other beginning, Plato's other beginning, would occur as a turn back into concealment.

Let me mention, then, in conclusion and all too briefly, two passages from the *Republic* that broach this turn back into concealment.

The first passage has to do with the highest *idea, tou agathou idea*. What is meant in saying that this is the highest idea? This idea is such that its shining, its luminosity, provides the light in which all other ideas shine; it makes possible the shining of all other ideas. Thus, whenever any idea becomes manifest and is apprehended, this highest idea must have shown itself and, it seems, have been apprehended. And yet, in a passage (517b) immediately following the one employing the cave image, Socrates says of the idea of the good that it is *mogis horasthai*, scarcely to be seen. Indeed, in *Plato's Doctrine of Truth* Heidegger cites and translates this passage, and then in a marginal note written in his own copy of this text he says: "*Agathon* of course *idea*, but no longer coming to presence [*nicht mehr anwesend*], therefore scarcely visible" (GA9, 227). Yet how can there be an idea that does not come to be present—and hence visible—considering that the very sense of idea is to be a look presentable to a vision? How can it be that precisely the highest idea, the one whose luminosity all others presuppose, is itself less than fully luminous, scarcely to be seen? Is it not a matter here of installing, at what would be the very pinnacle of unconcealment, an integral bond to concealment—indeed concealment, not just as something to be appropriated *after* the highest vision (as in the return to the cave), but as something integral to the highest vision, a refusal that would haunt it as such?

The second passage occurs in the discussion of that figure of a line cut in two unequal segments, each of which is then also cut in two in the same proportion. In Book 6 Socrates draws a contrast between the penultimate segment, corresponding to *dianoia*, and the highest segment, corresponding to *episteme* or dialectic. At the penultimate stage, the progression of vision is, as at the lower stages, by way of images, "using as images the things that were previously imitated" (*Rep.* 510b). In this dianoetic eikasia one takes as images those things previously taken as originals, and one's vision proceeds through these images to their originals. It is precisely this dyadic image-original structure that, it seems, would finally be left behind at the highest level, that of dialectic. At this level all images would, it seems, be left behind for the sake of a vision of the *arche*, the beginning, which is not itself an image of something else.

This discussion is resumed in Book 7 following the passage on education. Once Socrates has gone through a detailed articulation of the penultimate stage, Glaucon is eager to proceed to dialectic and to go through it in the same way so as to arrive at "that place which is for one who reaches it a haven from the road, as it were, and an end of his journey" (*Rep.* 532e). To Glaucon's request, Socrates answers: "You will no longer be able to follow, my dear Glaucon, although there wouldn't be any lack of eagerness on my part. But you would no longer be seeing an image of what we are saying, but rather the truth itself, at least as it looks to me" (*Rep.* 533a). Here *the truth itself* (*auto to alethes*) means the unconcealed; it has nothing to do with correctness. Here, at the end of the journey—figured on the line, imaged by the movement up out of the cave—one would see the original truth, the true (that is, unconcealed) original, which presumably in its pure luminosity would no longer be an image of some further original. *Or rather,* it would be a matter of seeing the truth—Socrates says—*as it looks to me* (*moi phainetai*), that is, in the appearance that it offers to me, the *image* that it offers, casts, in my direction, *and so,* in distinction from the *look itself.* Indeed Socrates continues: "Whether it is really so or not can no longer be properly insisted on." Thus, with subtlety and irony, Socrates is saying that even at the end of the road one will see only an image of the true, *not* the true in its undivided, full luminosity. Or, to speak more directly, there is no end of the road, no haven where one would finally have the highest idea present without reserve before one's vision. Always there would remain images, difference—that is, the bond to concealment.

Once Plato's other beginning is allowed to come into play, one might again—though differently—radicalize and ironize the ancient tradition about Plato's unwritten teachings, about the unsaid of Plato's text. Now one might well take *lethe,* concealment, to be this unsaid. This would not be an unsaid that could just as easily—or at least without too much difficulty—have been said. It is not that Plato somehow just neglected to say it. Rather, it remains unsaid because it resists saying, because it borders on the unsayable, because it withdraws from *logos,* refuses to submit to the question: *ti esti?,* "What is . . . ?" And yet, it is not simply unsayable but is somehow inscribed, is the unsaid *of* Plato's text.

In what one might be tempted to take as Heidegger's last word on Plato, he tells of one of the ways in which this unsaid, *lethe,* came to be inscribed by the Greeks. In his lecture course *Parmenides,* Heidegger says: "The last word of the Greeks that names *lethe* in its essence is the *mythos* concluding Plato's dialogue on the essence of the polis."[8]

And yet, we know that this *mythos* is not merely a story told at the end of the dialogue, that it does not merely conclude the *Republic* as something added on at the end. Rather, this *mythos* is in play throughout the dialogue, in virtually all that is said and done in the course of the dialogue. It will, then, have installed *lethe* everywhere, not only in the central images and figures of the dialogue, but from the very moment Socrates, beginning his narration—beginning thus again—says: "I went down yesterday to Piraeus."

Notes

1. *Rep.* 511b–c. Further references to Platonic dialogues are given in the text. Translations are my own.

2. Martin Heidegger, *Beiträge zur Philosophie (Vom Ereignis), Gesamtausgabe* 65 (Frankfurt am Main: Vittorio Klostermann, 1989), 436. Translations are my own.

3. Ibid., 185–86.

4. There are two lecture-courses that cover much the same material as *Plato's Doctrine of Truth* and that clearly provided the basis for Heidegger's redaction of the essay. The first constitutes the initial half of the course *Vom Wesen der Wahrheit* presented in the Winter Semester 1931–32 (published *Gesamtausgabe* 34 [Frankfurt am Main: Vittorio Klostermann, 1988]). The second constitutes the initial half of the course of the same title presented in the Winter Semester 1933–34 (published in *Sein und Wahrheit, Gesamtausgabe* 36–37 [Frankfurt am Main: Vittorio Klostermann, 2001]). In both cases the second half of the course consisted in interpretation of selected passages from the *Theaetetus*.

5. Heidegger, *Platons Lehre von der Wahrheit*, in *Wegmarken, Gesamtausgabe* 9 (Frankfurt am Main: Vittorio Klostermann, 1976), 203. Further references are given in the text as GA9 followed by page numbers.

6. See my discussion in *Delimitations: Phenomenology and the End of Metaphysics*, 2nd ed. (Bloomington: Indiana University Press, 1995), 176–80.

7. Heidegger, *Zur Sache des Denkens* (Tübingen: Max Niemeyer Verlag, 1969), 78.

8. Heidegger, *Parmenides, Gesamtausgabe* 54 (Frankfurt am Main: Vittorio Klostermann, 1982), 140.

Contributors

Claudia Baracchi is Associate Professor of Philosophy at The New School in New York City.

Walter A. Brogan is Professor of Philosophy and Director of Graduate Studies in Philosophy at Villanova University.

Günter Figal is Professor of Philosophy at University of Freiburg.

Gregory Fried is Associate Professor of Philosophy and Department Chair at Suffolk University.

Francisco J. Gonzalez is Associate Professor of Philosophy at Skidmore College.

Drew A. Hyland is the Charles A. Dana Professor of Philosophy at Trinity College in Hartford, Connecticut.

John Panteleimon Manoussakis is Visiting Assistant Professor of Philosophy at Boston College and the American College of Greece.

William J. Richardson is Professor of Philosophy at Boston College.

John Sallis holds the Frederick J. Adelmann, SJ, Chair in Philosophy at Boston College.

Dennis J. Schmidt is Professor of Philosophy, Comparative Literature, and German; and co-director, Institute for the Arts and Humanities at Pennsylvania State University.

Peter Warnek is Associate Professor of Philosophy at the University of Oregon.

Index

(The names of Plato, Aristotle, and M. Heidegger have been excluded from this index as they occur with great frequency.)